Countering Insurgencies in India

An Insider's View

Countering Insurgencies in India

An Insider's View

EN Rammohan, IPS (Retd)

(Established 1870)

United Service Institution of India
New Delhi

Vij Books India Pvt Ltd
New Delhi, India

Published   by

Vij Books India Pvt Ltd
(Publishers, Distributors & Importers)
2/19, Ansari Road, Darya Ganj
New Delhi - 110002
Phones: 91-11-43596460, 91-11- 65449971
Fax: 91-11-47340674
e-mail : vijbooks@rediffmail.com
web: www.vijbooks.com

ISBN: 978-93-80177-97-7

CONTENTS

Foreword   vii

1.   Introduction   1

2.   Insurgent Frontiers of Northeast India   5

3.   The Naga Insurgency   94

4.   Manipur's Multifaceted Insurgencies   117

5.   The Insurgent Groups of Tripura   139

6.   The Kashmir Insurgency   147

7.   Rise of Naxalism and its Implications for National Security -

      A Political, Security and Socio-Economic Campaign   199

Introduction

Independent India's first insurgency was announced in embryo on 14 August 1947, when Angami Zapu Phizo held an independence ceremony on 14 August 1947, a day before India's independence. It took some time for the insurgency to mature and it exploded in 1955, after Phizo slipped into East Pakistan through the North Cachar and Jaintia hills, met the Pakistan Army, who agreed to equip and train his guerrillas. The Government's reaction was to send in State, Armed Police battalions' and later the Army to tackle the insurgency. At that time the State Armed Police battalions only had some experience of hunting dacoit gangs in Madhya Pradesh. Regrettably the Army and the Police battalions had no experience of guerrilla warfare. The State also made fundamental mistakes. The judiciary made very little effort to see that the counterinsurgency was fought legally. When ambushed by the Naga Underground, the Army and the Police battalions suffered casualties and reacted by taking it out on the hapless people of the nearest villages where the ambush had been laid. Regrettably the Judiciary did not step in to control excesses by the Armed Forces. The result was further alienation of the Naga people. This was a failure of both the civilian administration and the judiciary.

It was around this time that two books on how to fight insurgencies were published. The first was by Col. David Galula who had fought in Algeria and the second was by Sir Robert Thompson, who fought in Malaya. Both these truly professional soldiers laid down a classic principle of Counterinsurgency. They postulated that in any insurgency the first objective was to protect the people. Hunting for the guerrilla was a secondary task. The cause of why the people had taken to arms was to be understood. Then the people were to be taken into confidence and explained that the force deployed was primarily for their protection. The action was to be taken to see that their way of life was not to be disturbed by deployment of forces. For this it was necessary for the civilian administration to be closely associated. For example if a Company was to be deployed near a village in the Naga Hills, they should have adopted a Naga village. The civil administration should then have moved in and improved existing infrastructure, like improving the water supply, building and improving roads, improving the agriculture, horticulture and animal husbandry of the village, so that the villagers would find themselves better than before the force was deployed near them. In this process the insurgents would lose any chance of getting food supplies from that village. In short the village and its people should be convinced that life was much better after the force had moved near their village.

Robert Thompson's book Defeating Communist Insurgency is the Bible of Counterinsurgency. He enunciated that any counterinsurgency campaign must be scrupulously legal. Operating in Malaya where the insurgency was started by Chinese infiltrators from Communist China, who tried to win over the Chinese settlers in Malaya working as poor rubber tappers in the rubber plantations. They lived in shanty towns situated in different vacant places and on the edge of the rubber plantations and the thick jungles of eastern Malaya. In the counterinsurgency module the Chinese settlers were resettled in newly built villages, where there were ration shops, water supply and good sanitation. Also each settlement had a platoon guarding it. This also prevented the communist terrorists (CTs) from getting food supplies. Overall, the administration was improved in all departments giving good governance to the people. The architect of all this was Sir Gerald Templar who was the Governor and turned Malaya around from a near takeover by the CTs.

The objective of compiling these essays of six insurgencies in India was to examine whether, having the sterling example of two Counterinsurgency specialists, who laid down a doctrine of how to fight a successful counterinsurgency before us, did we apply the lessons learnt by them and apply the methods they adopted? Regrettably, we did not learn any lessons from these two specialists.

Our oldest insurgency of the Nagas in Nagaland and the Manipur Hills is still festering though ten years of a ceasefire has led to no conclusions. The insurgent groups of Manipur are nowhere near winning nor is the State anywhere near solving the issues in that miserable state. The administration of Nagaland and Manipur is ridden with corruption. The Central Government and the parties in power there have through the agencies of a band of unholy contractors bled both these states white. In all these sixty odd years 70 to 80 percent of development money sent to the Northeastern states has been brought back to Delhi by this unholy band of contractors. In Assam as explained in detail, the Centre was responsible for illegally changing the cutoff date for detection of foreign nationals from Bangladesh which triggered off the insurgency in Assam. The insurgents of the ULFA who had sought shelter in Bangladesh were all returned to India after the change of Government in Bangladesh in 2008. One group led by its self styled commander is still hiding in Burma. As far as the administration of Assam is considered it is only slightly better than Nagaland or Manipur.

In Kashmir it is the Centre that triggered off the insurgency that Pakistan had failed to initiate on several occasions from 1947 to 1989. During this long period, instead of encouraging the Sufi culture of Kashmir, we have allowed fundamental sects like the Jamaat-e-Islami and the Ahle Hadith to spread. Regrettably we have never ensured a corruption free government in Jammu and Kashmir. Good governance has never been achieved in any of these insurgent states with the sole exception of Tripura. It is only in this state has the Government given clean administration to its people. Two totally honest Chief Ministers ably supported by an equally honest Chief Secretary R.Shankaran gave Tripura state the cleanest administration of any state in India. One of the major reasons for the successful counterinsurgency was that the people felt that their government was clean and development reached them at the grassroots.

We are in the throes of a Maoist Communist led insurgency in Andhra Pradesh, Chhattisgarh, Jharkhand, Bihar and part of Maharashtra. There are also clear indications of this insurgency spreading to large urban cities.

The causes of this insurgency have been clearly informed to the Governments of the States concerned and the Centre. It is because of caste discrimination of the Scheduled castes and the Scheduled Tribes. Through hundreds of years of caste discrimination, the scheduled castes and tribes were denied ownership of agricultural land. After independence, when Land Ceiling laws were legislated, except for three states, none of the other states have implemented the Land Ceiling laws. In the Forests where the Scheduled tribes, the Adivasis, were pushed into the forests, today, they are being evicted from forests when minerals are discovered there, so that the State or private agencies can establish mines for extracting the minerals. The fifth schedule of the Constitution directs that it is the Governor of the State who has to administer the Forests through a Tribal Advisory Council. This schedule of the Constitution has been thrown into the dustbin. The Government of the country is directly confronting its poorest and most backward citizens like some medieval baron who ruled with the might of his sword!

The question before the Nation is whether we are going to administer this country as per the Constitution and the laws of the land or are we going to use our armed forces to crush the genuine demands of its poorest citizens"?

Insurgent Frontiers of Northeast India

Preface

The Insurgencies that has plagued the Northeast is rooted in the unwritten history of that beautiful land. Recorded history of the Northeast is available from the *Cheitharol Kumbaba* of the Meitei people of Manipur, but it is restricted to the Meiteis people only. Recorded history of Assam is available from plates left behind by the *Kshatriya* kings of Kamrup of the 4th century AD. The most important factor to be understood of the Northeast is that it is anthropologically Mongoloid people who migrated to the area from Northwest China many thousands of years ago in waves and settled in the hills and valleys of this beautiful land. There is no record of this and one can only get some rare glimpses of this migration from the folklore of the different tribes that settled in the Northeast. All these groups had only dialects and no written language. Many years after they settled, there was a migration of Aryans, Dravidians and Austrics from the Gangetic valley. These people had a written language and the Hindu religion with a caste structure. There is no record of this migration and whether there was opposition from the local Mongoloid people. Caste was an unknown factor to the Mongoloid people of the Northeast. The clash of the Caste Hindus and the Mongoloid people is the root cause of most of the insurgencies in the Northeast. The social structure of the Caste Hindus and the Mongoloid people are diametrically opposite. In the caste hierarchy of the Caste Hindu, the Mongoloid people came at the bottom. The separation of the Naga Hills, Mizo Hills and Meghalaya, the Khasi, Jaintia and Garo Hills, the insurgencies in the North Cachar Hills and Karbi Anglong Hills, the Boro insurgencies in Udalguri are all because of this root factor. There have been further factors like religion that has contributed to organic differences between the caste Hindus and the Mongoloid people, many of whom converted to Christianity.

In the conflict that developed in the Naga Hills and the Mizo Hills it is this feeling of caste superiority that led to a parting of ways. Regrettably mainland India was also steeped in the same caste interlock and there was lack of understanding by the Indians from the mainland who handled the Northeast. It was only western anthropologists like Verrier Elwin and Haimendorf who understood this crucial factor. There have been many Indians from the mainland who have worked in the Northeast who have also submerged their caste in handling the people whom they administered. They were easily accepted by Mongoloid society, but they were few and far between and there were no such people among the senior politicians and bureaucrats who administered the country from the mainland.

The insurgency in Assam of the United Liberation Front of Assam does not fit into this mould. Here, it was an issue between the Assamese caste Hindu people and the Politicians in the Centre who looked the other way at the unhindered migration of Bengali Muslims and Hindus into Assam that constituted their vote bank that led to the insurgency. This can be clearly understood when the Foreigners Movement is dispassionately examined. Strangely in this case, it was the caste Hindu people of India who did not side with the Caste Hindus and Muslims of Assam. The Mongoloid people were not directly concerned in this dispute, though they were the main losers in the primordial issue of this agitation. This was land and not religion as we will see in this chapter that talks of Assam, the Foreigners Movement, and the United Liberation Front of Assam.

ASSAM, THE FOREIGNER'S MOVEMENT AND THE UNITED LIBERATION FRONT OF ASSAM

Geography and History

The Assam valley and the hills of the Northeast came into being in a cataclysmic event many eons ago when a part of the continent of Antarctica,

Gondwana land, separated and moved northeast and collided against the Asian land mass. At that time the Tethys Sea extended right up to the area where the Himalayan range stands today. The impact of Gondwana land colliding with the Asian land mass resulted in a giant buckling of the Asian land mass, throwing up several ranges of mountains, the Hindu Kush, Karakoram and the Himalayas. It is this last range, the mighty Himalayas, which inspired Kalidasa to call it the massed laughter of the Gods, which now forms India's northern borders. When these mountains were thrown up, the Tethys Sea drained westwards and its remnant is the Mediterranean Sea. The Dead Sea, Caspian Sea and the Aral Sea are the trailing remnants of the once mighty Tethys Sea. North of the Himalayas a lake was formed, the Mansarovar. From its eastern side a river called the Tsang Po flowed east till it reached a small gap in the Himalayan range at Gayling. Here the Tsang Po turned south and flowing through deep gorges poured into a verdant valley as the Brahmaputra. Flowing south west it gouged out a valley south of the Himalayas. Its southern border was a range of low hills. These hills starting from the western end of the Brahmaputra valley have been named after the Mongoloid people who settled there. These are today the Garo, Khasi, Jaintia, Mikir, North Cachar and Naga Hills. At the eastern end a north south range was formed called the Patkai range. Today this marks the eastern border of India with Burma. The Brahmaputra is watered by a string of tributaries coming from the Himalayas, the Subnansiri, Siang, Manas, Aye, Beki and by an equal number of rivers flowing north from the Garo, Khasi, Jaintia, Mikir, North Cachar and Naga Hills, the Umtru, Dhansiri, Dayang, Dekhow and Dissang. The Brahmaputra was therefore a very fertile valley. After crossing the Garo Hills, the Brahmaputra turns south and flows into the Bay of Bengal as the Jamuna and later as the Meghna. South of the range of hills the Barak River takes its source from the Manipur Hills and finding a gap between the North Cachar Hills and the Mizo Hills, flows into the Surma valley and thence into the East Bengal plains to finally join the Jamuna.

The Indian subcontinent is visited by a yearly rainfall, the South West Monsoon that sweeps in from the Arabian Sea in end May, waters the subcontinent and finally peters out against the Himalayas by September.

The Brahmaputra by its peculiar North East- South West configuration forms a kind of funnel. The moisture generated by the myriad rivers flowing from the south and north into the wide Brahmaputra triggers pre-monsoon showers right from March in this verdant valley. Thus this beautiful valley gets the highest rainfall in the country.

It is generally accepted that the first inhabitants of the Brahmaputra valley and the hills to the north and south were Mongoloid people who came from Northwest China in several waves. Some migrated south and east and populated what are today Burma, Vietnam, Cambodia, Laos, Thailand and the other countries of Southeast Asia. Some settled in the Brahmaputra and Surma valleys and the hills around, while yet others moved further west to populate what is today Bhutan, Sikkim, Nepal and Tibet. There is no historical record of these migrations, but there is evidence that a great migration took place in the form of stories and folk tales carried from father to son by several tribes of the Northeast. Some of these are now being researched and published. All the Mongoloid people who migrated and settled in the Northeast of India had only a spoken language or dialect, except for one group the Meiteis of Manipur valley. In the Brahmaputra valley, the Mongoloid people who settled constitute the following tribes-Boro Cacharis, Thengal Cacharis, Sonowal Cacharis. Dimasa Cacharis, Chutiyas, Rabhas, Morans, Borahis, Mech and Rajbongshis. At different periods many of these groups established kingdoms with a king ruling them. The Chutiyas had their capital at Sadiya, the Dimasa Cacharis at Dimapur and the Rajbongshi Koch kingdom in the west of the Brahmaputra valley. The Koch kingdom extended to what is now North Bengal. Archaeological remains of the Capital of the Dimasa Cacharis at Dimapur are quite impressive. The Meitei people of Manipur who settled in the fertile Imphal valley also developed a script for their language and ruled their kingdom that included the Imphal valley, the hills surrounding the valley and the Kebaw valley which is now in Burma. The other major groups who established a kingdom were the Khasi and Jaintia people who settled in the Khasi and Jaintia Hills. Their capital, Jaintiapur is now in Bangladesh. The only other group that established a kingdom was the Tripuris who had settled in the low hills and plains of Tripura.

Anthropologically three specific strains of people migrated into the Northeast of India. These are the Tibeto-Burman, the Mon-Khmer and the Tai Chinese. All the groups who migrated into the Northeast are Tibeto-Burmans, except for the Khasis and Jaintias who are Mon-Khmer and the Ahoms, who are Tai Chinese. The Ahoms were a breakaway Shan group from Burma who migrated and settled in Upper Assam in the thirteenth century.

It is not known when the Caste Hindu people of the Gangetic valley migrated and settled in the Brahmaputra valley. It is also not known how the Mongoloid people of the Northeast adjusted with them. But it is a fact that this happened. The present caste Hindu people of Assam have Mongoloid features in their physiognomy. The language of the Assamese is based on Sanskrit with a liberal mixture of words from the dialect of the Boros, and other groups in the Valley. The first historical evidence of the people of the Brahmaputra valley are from copper plates left behind by a Kshatriya king, Pushyavarman, ruling in Kamarupa, that has been dated to the 4th century AD.[1] Anthropologically three groups have migrated to the Brahmaputra valley-the Aryans, Dravidians and Austrics.

In the 12th century two groups of people entered the Brahmaputra valley. The Slave Kings had established their capital in Delhi in the 12th century AD. In their expansion eastwards, their army led by Muhammad Ibn Bhaktiyar crossed the Karatoya river which was the first of the great rivers flowing south from the Himalayas as you cross the Bihar plains and march towards the Brahmaputra valley. They entered Kamrup and were challenged by the Kshatriya king Prithu who defeated the invading Muslim army. This battle was in 1206 AD. The Muslim army retreated but recouped and attacked the Hindu army. In one battle Prithu, the raja was killed, but ultimately the Muslim army retreated from the Brahmaputra valley. During their sojourn in Kamrup, the Muslim invaders converted some of the Assamese caste Hindus to Islam. A number of Boros apparently served as mercenaries in the Muslim army. However none of them were converted to Islam. The Assamese Muslims who owe their Muslim origin to the Slave

---

[1] *The History of Assam*, Edward Gait, page 22.

King armies are a very small minority among the caste Hindus of Assam today. They are distinguished from the Bengali Muslims from East Bengal by several features. Their women are not in *purdah* and the Assamese Muslim generally does not marry more than one wife. In fact many of the Hindu well to do leaders marries more than once. None of the Mongoloid people of the Brahmaputra valley were converted by the invading Mulsim armies. The retreating Slave King's army left behind a Mosque which they constructed in Hajo which has become something like a *Dargah*. It is called *Pua Mecca*.

It was during this period that a Shan Prince from Burma fell out with his king and decided to migrate west into the Brahmaputra valley. Sukapha, the Shan Prince in question crossed the Patkai range and entered the Brahmaputra valley. He easily defeated the Chutiyas and Morans who were controlling the area and established himself near present day Nazira a town in Sibsagar district. The Shans were Buddhists, while the Chutiyas, Morans, Borahis and Dimasa Cacharis were animists, who were on the edges of Hinduism. The Ahoms established their kingdom and gradually expanded till the whole of Assam came under their sovereignty. When the Mughals were ruling in Delhi an army was sent to subjugate the Eastern areas of the country. After Bengal was subjugated, their army entered Assam and there ensued several battles with the Ahom army. The Ahoms also had a navy in the Brahmaputra. After several encounters, the Mughal army was finally defeated by a redoubtable general of the Ahom army, Lachit Barphukan. During the sojourn of the Mughal army in Assam, some of the Assam people were converted to Islam. This second wave of conversion was also minor and like in the previous instance of the Slave king Army, the converted Assamese Muslim women did not go into purdah, nor did the Muslim men marry more than one wife.

The Ahom dynasty ruled for 600 years, the second longest surviving dynasty of any kingdom that was established in India since the beginning of recorded history. In the early part of the 18th century, the British East India Company which had established control over Bengal, moved into Lower Assam, where the Ahoms had become weak. It was at this time that the

King of Ava (Burma) decided to conquer the region to the west of their country-Assam and Manipur. The kingdom of Manipur had a running fight with the Burmese kings. Depending on their strength, the Manipur kings would move into Kebaw valley and further into Burma. Similarly when finding themselves strong the Burmese army would fight their Manipuri counterpart and occupy part of their area. Between 1822 and 1823, the Burmese king invaded Manipur and Assam simultaneously, one army marched north through the Kebaw valley and laid waste the countryside of southern Manipur, while another army marched across the Patkai Range, following the route taken by Sukapha four centuries earlier and entering upper Assam, laid waste to the area. The Burmese were particularly cruel and killed thousands of people both in Manipur and in Assam. The Ahom princes fled to Cachar where there was a British garrison and appealed to the East India Company's army for help. The British sent troops to both Manipur and Upper Assam and defeated the Burmese armies. In Manipur a brave general of the Manipur army, Ghambir Singh led the combined forces of the East India Company and the Manipur army and chased the Burmese army beyond the Kebaw valley. The British East India Company signed a treaty with the Burmese at Yandaboo in 1826. In Manipur the British kept a garrison and allowed the king to rule. In Assam, they removed the Ahom king and annexed Upper Assam.

The British East India Company in Assam

The British soon found that tea grows well in Assam. The British East India Company formed a Tea committee and set up an experimental tea garden in 1836. Rules were framed to make available waste lands for the Tea planters to open up Tea gardens. By 1870, 0.7 million acres of land had come under tea cultivation. The history of Assam changed with the advent of the British. The Burmese army had lain waste the whole of Upper Assam. Thousands of people were killed and dozens of villages completely destroyed. Between 1837 and 1851, Major John Butler of the 55th regiment of the Bengal Native Infantry travelled widely through Assam. His, is one of the early European accounts of Assam. He wrote-"In the thirty miles from

Mohandijua and Deemapore, not a vestige of any habitation or a human being could be found."[2] After the dark spell of the Burmese invasion, the Ahoms and the common people looked up to the British rule to bring stability and peace to their lives.[3] Maniram Dewan, who later revolted against the British and was hanged in 1858, had initially wished the British-"uninterrupted and undiminished sovereignty for thousands of years."[4] The British had however come for commerce and things soon changed. The whole history of Assam was to be drastically changed for the worse.

A number of factors combined to start a wave of migration into Assam. The first was the requirement of labour to work in the tea gardens as the Assamese were not willing to work there. The reason was not that they were lazy but that they had plenty of land for cultivation and they wanted to have homesteads on their own land. They also grew more than sufficient for their consumption. The British needed labour to work in the tea gardens. Not finding the labour in Assam, they scouted far and wide and found surplus labour in Bihar, Chota Nagpur, Orissa and even faraway Madras. These Adivasis did not own land and were surplus in their regions to work in the lands of the upper castes that controlled the administration in those states. They were brought by train and steamer to Assam, kept in transit sheds in Paltan Bazaar in Guwahati and then taken to the different tea gardens. The Adivasi people were given a subtitle of "Tea Garden Labour." They were strikingly different from the Assamese caste Hindus and very different from the Tribal population of Assam. Like the Mongoloid Tribals of Assam, they were Animists and they only had a dialect but anthropologically they were Dravidian. The British now faced a different problem. After the devastation of the Burmese army, they found that the rice production was not enough to feed the population of the state. The British had come to Assam mainly from the swampy plains of East Bengal, where the Bengali Muslims were extremely hardy peasants and devils for cultivation of paddy, jute and vegetables. Since there were thousands of acres of vacant cultivable land,

---

[2] *Travels and adventures in the province of Assam*, John Butler.

[3] *Anglo-Assamese Relations*, 1711, 1826. Chapters 8,9 and 10. S.K. Bhuyan.

[4] Ibid.

they decided to encourage the East Bengali Muslims to migrate to Assam. At first the Bengali Muslim peasants were slow to take up the offer of settlement in Assam. The East Bengal plains were already crowded and soon the land hungry peasants began to migrate. The first Bengali Muslims settled in the plains of Goalpara district in the year 1902/03. They soon spread out into Kamrup and Nowgong districts.

The third group of people that the British brought into Assam was the Marwari trader. The East India Company officials had come across this middleman in Fort William, Calcutta and found his smooth and obsequious way of operating very useful. The Mongoloid people who had settled in the Brahmaputra valley lived by barter. Very few Vaisya traders migrated into the Brahmaputra valley along with the Brahmins, Kshatriya and Sudras. In fact many caste Hindus took to trading by barter in Assam. The Tea Garden Managers wanted to have a Vaisya trader in each garden to cater to the needs of the labour, to open shops for groceries and to cater to his needs. The British therefore called the Marwari traders to come to Assam and take over the Middleman's role. And they promptly came. To this day each Tea Garden has a Marwari shop that caters to the needs of the labour and even advances the wages of the labour to the Manager on Bank Holidays. The Marwari then finding a vacuum spread to all the villages and towns in Assam. Today he is the main wholesaler for virtually all commodities. Guwahati's Fancy Bazaar is today a Marwari enclave. There are similar Marwari localities in all the towns of Assam.

The British then discovered oil and coal in Upper Assam. While the Marwari again captured the main commodities market, Labour and Technical personnel had to be brought from outside the State. The fourth group of people that the British brought was the Bengali babu to do the clerical work in the Tea Gardens, in the oil and Coal industry and in the Government offices of the East India Company. There were very few Assamese who had studied English to take all the jobs available and the Bengalis filled up the vacuum. This became the main cause for the bitterness between the two communities later. In a few years as the administration settled, the British officer lobby preferred to get the Bengali *babu* to do his clerical work. This patronising of the Bengali did not go down well with the Assamese lobby. Besides by the year 1901, according to Amalendu Guha, non indigenous elements came to constitute more than a quarter of the population of Assam.[5] However by now there were a sizeable number of students from Assam in Calcutta. They founded an *Assamiya Basha Unnati Sadhani Sabha* in 1988. They brought out a journal *Jonaki*. They also wrote a number of articles bemoaning the state of affairs in Assam. In a paper reflecting the state of the economy in Assam, Kamalakanta Bhattacharya wrote that the Assamese should constitute an independent self reliant nation.[6] He warned that with the development of communications foreigners would pour in to occupy the fertile soil of Assam and its identity would be jeopardised. This was the first expression of the idea of a *Swadhin* Assam by its intelligentsia.

Meanwhile the migration of the Bengali Muslims from East Bengal continued apace. Within thirty years they had made a dent in the demography of Assam. In the census report of 1931, the Census Commissioner of Assam, C.S.Mullen wrote-"Probably the most important event in the province during the last 25 years, an event moreover which seems likely to alter permanently the whole future and to destroy more surely than did the Burmese invasion of 1825, the whole structure of Assamese culture and civilization-has been the invasion of a vast horde of land hungry Bengali immigrants, mostly Muslims from the districts of East Bengal....Whither there is waste land thither flock the Mymensinghias....Without fuss, without tumult, without undue trouble to the district revenue staff, a population which amounts to about half a million has transplanted itself from Bengal into the Assam Valley during the last 25 years...It is sad but by no means improbable that in another 30 years Sibsagar district will be the only part of Assam in which an Assamese will find himself at home."

It is in this context that the writings of a leading Assamese intellectual are of interest. Ambikagiri Roychoudhury, though a leading Congressman gradually grew disillusioned and through the Assamiya Samrakhini Sabha,

---

[5] *Planter Raj to Swaraj*, Amalendu Guha, chapter 2, page 39.

[6] *Literature and Society in Assam*, Tillotama Misra.

he wrote to Nehru in 1937, that if the Central Congress leadership did not view their fears regarding the Bengali Muslim influx seriously, then Assam should secede from India. After 1947, when the Congress government in Assam failed to stop infiltration from East Pakistan, Roychoudhury started espousing the cause of an independent Assam through his *Jatya Mahasabha*. At a meeting held on 1st January 1948, the Jatiyo Mahasabha declared-"Assam should come out of the Indian Union and become an independent country like Burma.[7] Yet another intellectual who spoke of an independent Assam was Jnananath Bora. He spoke of the historical background of Assam and pointed out that the ancient kingdom of Kamarupa from the 4th to the 7th century remained a Hindu kingdom without being part of any empire at Delhi. But for the British incorporating Assam as part of their empire there was no basis for Assam being part of India.[8] In this context there are two points of considerable interest. The first is that the kingdoms of Assam and the remaining states of the Northeast were never part of any Hindu or Muslim ruler of mainland India. This is true of the southernmost kingdoms in Tamilnadu and Kerala also. Secondly, the Ahom kingdom lasted 600 years till the British took it over. No kingdom, except the kingdom of Tripuri Rajas in India has ever lasted so long. A feeling of separateness gradually grew in Assam among the intellectuals in the 1930s and 1940s.

Alienation

Two factors led to a feeling that Assam was getting step brotherly treatment. These were the way the Central Congress leadership treated the Assam Congress leaders in the run up to partition and the authoritarian attitude of India's first Prime Minister and Home Minister immediately after partition on the issue of refugees from East Pakistan. Notwithstanding the fervour with which the Assamese took part in the quit India movement in 1842, when scores of people were killed in police firing, they felt very badly let down when they found the central leadership of both Nehru and Patel

---

[7] *Assam's Attitude to Federalism*, Girin Phukan, New Delhi 1984.

[8] *Kamrup aru Bharatvarsha*, Jnanath Bora, Awahon. (Assamese) Vol. 8. No. 3. Calcutta 1936.

expressing unhappiness at Assam's refusal to accept the grouping plan of the Cabinet Mission placing Assam along with Bengal. Initially, Nehru and Patel had advised Assam to oppose the grouping. Later Nehru expressed his unhappiness at the wording of the Assam Assembly's resolution opposing the grouping. The feeling that the Assamese leadership got was that for the good of India, Assam could be sacrificed. In fact, Nehru and Patel said as much.

The fact was that Nehru and Patel was keen to clinch the issue quickly and felt that Assam opposing the deal might delay the grant of independence. Naturally the Assam leaders felt that Nehru wanted independence soon but was not bothered about seeing that Assam was in India and could allow it to go to Pakistan. Ultimately it was Assam's opposition that led to dropping of the Cabinet Missions' proposal. Jinnah and the leaders of the Muslim League were keen that the whole of the Northeast should go to Pakistan. In the Commission that was set up for the east, it was the casting vote of Cyril Radcliff that gave the Northeast to India. In the process, The Chakmas suffered a virtual death sentence, when their district of the Chittagong Hill Tracts, 98 per cent Buddhist was given to Pakistan by the casting vote of Cyril Radcliff. If only Nehru and Patel had explained the situation to Mountbatten the genocide of the Chakmas could have been avoided.

After partition there was continual migration of Bengali Hindu refugees from East Pakistan into Assam. When Gopinath Bordoloi, the Chief Minister objected to settling more refugees after three lakhs were settled in Assam, Nehru expressed his unhappiness and even threatened to reduce financial aid to Assam. The seeds of distrust sown during this period between Assam and the Centre were to grow further in the sixties and the seventies. By 1961, the flow of Bengali Hindu refugees from East Pakistan to Assam had reached a figure of 6 lakhs and 28 thousand.[9]

In 1957, the Centre decided to construct a 3.3 million ton oil refinery in Bihar to refine the crude oil that was being produced in the oil wells in Upper Assam. The crude oil was to be taken by a 700 kilometer long

---

[9] Census of India. 1961

pipeline to Barauni. The indignation of the Assamese people boiled up into an agitation that was the first of its kind after the civil disobedience movement of 1942. All the political parties participated in the agitation organised by a Sangram Parishad. The obviously lame excuse that was given by the centre that the Refinery was located in Barauni because of security reasons, was like salt in Assam's wound. The Sangram Parishad and the Assamese people asked –"If the refinery cannot be protected in Upper Assam, how could the oil fields in Upper Assam and the pipeline 700 kilometres long be protected." The ultimate concession of a 0.65 million ton refinery at Noonmati, near Guwahati only confirmed the fact that Assam was getting step-brotherly treatment from Delhi. It was getting clear that Assam would not get justice from Delhi. Then came the debacle of the Chinese invasion, with the rout of the Indian Army at Tawang and the virtual decimation of a full division. The district head quarter of Tezpur was ordered to be evacuated, when Nehru made a "farewell" speech on All India Radio that his heart went out to the Assamese people. This deeply hurt their sentiments. Working as a Police officer in Upper Assam, I heard this being discussed by many cultured Assamese families.

The years following the Sino-Indian war were difficult for Assam. There was shortage of rice that led to agitations throughout the valley. Assam was not a deficit state for rice and the only reason for the shortages was because of hoarding by Marwari's that controlled the trade in essential commodities, and extensive smuggling of rice to East Pakistan. Posted in Hojai in 1967, I found that though this was the rice bowl of Assam, collection of levy rice in Hojai was nil, while far away North Lakhimpur, constantly under floods, which had the lowest production of paddy had a 100 per cent collection of rice. The reason for this was that the rice from Hojai was being smuggled to East Pakistan, via train to Karimganj and then to East Pakistan through the porous border, while since North Lakhimpur was in the far Northeast of Assam, there was no scope to smuggle out rice. The complete domination of all commercial activities by the Marwari's finally burst out into a violent conflagration at Guwahati on the 26th of January 1968. It is interesting to analyse this sudden explosion of violence. This I did, when I was posted in Guwahati as Additional Superintendent of Police under the redoubtable K.P.S.Gill in 1969. The trouble started in the Judges Field where the Republic day parade is held every year. Even as the function was underway the crowd was restive, with anti national slogans being shouted. The function was hastily concluded and then the crowd, pulled down the national flag, burnt it and then moved towards the Fancy Bazaar, the business centre, where all the Marwari wholesalers had their godowns. The crowd consisted of students of the Cotton College one of the oldest colleges of Assam located across the Judges field and also students of the Guwahati University, organsied into a loose band called the *Lachit Sena*, named after Lachit Barphukan a renowned General of the Ahom Kings who had defeated the Mughal army. The Police simply disappeared from the scene as the crowd looted all the Marwari godowns and shops and set fire to most of them. While the damages resulted in losses worth crores of rupees, not a single person was injured. This is an interesting point. It was as if the mob wanted to tell the Government in Assam and Delhi that they were giving a warning to set things right. This time no one was being touched. Next time blood will be shed. It simply could not happen that in rioting that lasted several hours, not a single person was injured, but property worth crores was burnt. The Police looking the other way was obviously part of the plan! Incidentally the *Lachit Sena* was never heard of again. The agitation was taken over by more sinister forces. Regrettably the warning signs of this incident were not heeded by Delhi and they continued their policies of treating Assam like a colony like the East India Company did.

That the Centre had not heeded the warning call was amply demonstrated in 1969, by the Centre as it planned to set up another oil refinery outside Assam. Hearing of this plan, the Leftist parties and the student unions organised a massive agitation. In a rehearsal of the Foreigners agitation that was to come in 1979, students boycotted schools and came to Guwahati in buses and courted arrest in thousands. I was Additional Superintendent of Police in Guwahati and handled this agitation under K.P.S.Gill. We could do nothing but arrest the students, remove them in buses to temporary jails in the stadium and release them at the end of the day. The daily figures of such arrests were in lakhs. The Guwahati Police, the Magistracy and the Jails were stretched to their limits. The slogan of the students was –"*Tez deem, Tel ne diun*". We will give blood but not oil. Luckily the ten odd days of the agitation did not degenrate to violent incidents. The Government capitulated before that and announced that the refinery would be set up in Bongaigaon. This was the second warning cry from Assam. Though Delhi capitulated this time they had not learnt their lessons as will be seen in the sequence of events that led to the next agitation.

Meanwhile, the leftist movement in West Bengal had seen a spurt after the Cultural Revolution in China and the Naxalbari uprising, leading to the creation of a more extreme- Communist Party of India Marxist-Leninist (CPI ML). A scouting team of this group was sent to Assam and they set up cells in Kamrup and Darrang districts. In both districts, land holdings were small and getting smaller. Farmers found that their annual crop was not enough to feed their families for the whole year. These were ideal conditions for the CPI ML to exploit. There was a brilliant officer in Assam Police, Priya Kumar Goswami who was the Additional Superintendent of Police Special Branch Kamrup. He first unearthed the establishment of the CPI ML cells in the district. With his sustained intelligence network he was able to detect an attempt by them to place some explosives on the railway track. He had penetrated the group and a well timed raid in a house of the railway colony at Maligaon led to the recovery of traces of gun powder in the house and torn strips of a white dhoti that was used to wrap up the improvised bombs. An alert police party who were patrolling the railway track from Guwahati to Maligaon surprised a group that was trying to place the bombs that they had prepared. One of the parties was arrested and the improvised bombs recovered. Later the torn dhoti was matched with the strips used to wrap up the bombs and the whole plot unearthed.

This foray of the CPI ML group into Assam extended to Darrang district. A cell was established by a school teacher of Bihaguri School near Tezpur. A number of his students were his followers. However, the group turned chauvinist and formed a body called the Assam Peoples Liberation Army and managed to get an AK 47 rifle. It was this group who first used this weapon against the police during the run up to the 1983 election that was forced on Assam. However, more of this later.

Two issues had by now crystallised in Assam, the continually deteriorating economic situation and the continuing illegal migration of Bengali Muslims from Bangladesh. The annual economic growth rate of Assam for the period 1970-80 was a mere 0.4 per cent compared to the all India average of 1.43 per cent for the same period. The number of the unemployed during this period increased by 270 per cent, while that of the uneducated unemployed was 343 per cent. The job sector in the State Government was stagnant. It was well known that the Central Government and its public sector were unsympathetic to local recruits. The Employment Review Committee of the Assam Legislative Assembly said as much in its report.[10] There was a reason for this. During the British rule virtually all Central Government departments had their eastern region H.Q.s located at Calcutta. This continued well after independence. Recruitment for subordinate posts was all made from there and the local applicants from the Northeastern region were seldom successful in the interviews. The percentage of Assamese employees in the Central Government offices and Public Sector Undertakings never exceeded 30 per cent, while in other states local employees had more than 90 per cent representation.

In the 1970s it also began to dawn on the Assamese people that the three main industries of the State-Tea, Oil and Coal were not having any impact on the economy of the State. 756 Tea Gardens of Assam produced 55 per cent of the country's Tea and earned foreign exchange of Rs. 500 crores. Assam however got only Rs. 22 crores as Sales Tax., while West Bengal got Rs. 42 crores for the year 1980. This was because many of the Tea Companies had their HQs in Calcutta. In the case of plywood the State got just Rs. 35 lakhs, while the Centre got Rs. 80 crores for the same year.[11] The production of crude from the Oil fields of Upper Assam had gone up from 0.1 million in 1962 to 3.5 million tons per year in the 1970s due to the discovery of new oil fields. The royalty paid to Assam in 1979 was a

---

[10] *The Periphery Strikes Back*, Udayan Misra, chapter 5, page 123. Institute of Advanced Study Simla.

[11] Assam a Colonial Heartland. Tilottama Misra. *Economic and Political Weekly*, Bombay. Vol. 15. No. 39.

mere Rs. 42 per tonne. The Centre refused to raise the State's share of royalty, despite pleas from the State. The feeling that the Centre was only exploiting the State's Natural Resources began to gain increasing credence among the Assamese people as the 1970s progressed.

The second issue of illegal migration from East Pakistan and then Bangladesh was an even more important problem and regrettably the Centre did not deal with it, or if they showed they did, it was most perfunctory in its approach. This was because by the 1970s the Party in power at the Centre realised that the immigrant Muslim labourer was a solid vote bank.

The British had originally encouraged the immigration of Bengali Muslim peasants from East Bengal to help increase the production of paddy. However, the result of this policy was that from a trickle the migration of Bengali Muslim peasants from the East Bengal districts became a flood and then became an inundation. By 1920 itself, the Assamese leadership represented to the British to restrict further occupation of vacant lands by Bengali Muslims from the districts of East Bengal. The British, realising the gravity of the situation introduced the Line System that designated the area in each district that could be settled by the immigrant Muslim from East Bengal. This did not deter the flow of Bengali Muslim immigrants from East Bengal. Taking recourse to bribing the local Government officials both civil and police, immigrant Muslims coming from East Bengal managed to settle in the demarcated line system land designated for the Assamese farmers. In this kind of transaction it was the backward tribal, mainly the Boros in Darrang, Goalpara and Kokrajhar and the Lalungs in Nowgong, who suffered as it was in the designated Tribal blocks that the maximum resettlement of immigrant Muslims from East Bengal took place, where even the caste Hindu Assamese peasant could not be settled. Dalgaon is a designated Tribal block between Karupettia and Rowtha on the Guwahati Mangaldoi road. When I was posted in Tezpur as the Deputy Inspector General of Police Northern Range in 1982, and travelled in this area, I knew at once that there would be communal trouble along the fault lines between the Boro Tribal land and the area where the immigrant Bengali Muslims had settled. As predicted there was trouble in this area between the Caste Hindu Assamese and the Bengali Muslim immigrants during the infamous elections of February 1983. There were no clashes between the Bengali Muslims and the Boros, because the Boros and the Bengali Muslims were for the elections at that time. The fourth Saadullah Ministry from 1942 to March 1945 dereserved grazing reserves in Kamrup, Nowgong and Darrang districts for settling East Bengali Muslim peasants. When invited by the Assam Government to witness their efforts in the Grow More Food Campaign, Lord Wavell wryly remarked that their efforts was more in the way of "Grow more Muslims"!

By the end of the 1950s, most of the vacant cadastral land had been occupied by the hordes from East Bengal. The immigration however continued. The Brahmaputra and its tributaries have land on either bank that is low lying called *dao matti* in Assamese. These lands are inundated during the rainy season, but become sand banks in the dry season.

The configuration of the sand banks varies each year. In mid stream, these islands are called *chapories* or *chars*. On either bank the *dao matti* that emerges is used for *pam khethi (*cultivation of sesame, mustard etc) by the Assamese villagers who live on the high ground on either bank. The Chars, or Chapories, shifting sand banks in mid stream and the *dao matti* for the pam khethi on either bank constitute non cadastral land as their configuration varies from year to year and so no *pattas* or land documents are made for such land. The *dao matti* exposed on the banks of rivers are traditionally allotted by the headmen (*Gaonburas*) to people of the adjacent villages. The immigrant Bengali Muslim immigrants still flowing from the East Bengal districts now began to settle on the Chars and Chapories and also on the *dao matti* on the banks of the rivers. The soil of the *dao matti* and the chapories is extremely fertile and paddy, sesame and mustard are grown with very little effort. The Assamese peasants never cultivated the *Chars* and *chapories,* but they used to cultivate the Dao matti along the river banks, planting sesame and mustard as *pam khethi*. When the immigrant Muslims settled on the *dao matti* along the river banks, the *pam khethi* of the Assamese villagers living along the river banks was disturbed. These were pressure points and in the brutal elections of 1983, there was massive rioting on such disputed low lying areas.

Life on the *chars* and *chapories* was extremely difficult. When the rains came they would be flooded. The immigrant Muslims had learnt to survive on such chars and chapories in the rivers of East Bengal. They lived in temporary huts on the *chars* and *chapories*. When the floods, came they would take their cattle, goats, and chickens into their boats and float out of the high flood. When the flood receded and the *chars* and *chapories* resurfaced in a new configuration they would reconstruct their temporary huts and settle on the new *char* or *chapories*. Incidentally throughout Assam none but the immigrant Bengali Muslim dared to live on the *chars* and *chapories*.

During the British period the Congress politicians did not interfere in land allotments to the immigrant Bengali Muslim peasants except for the Sir Sadullah Ministry. After independence the politicians did not interfere in such allotments till the 1970's. During this period it was the corrupt bureaucrats at the lowest levels and sometimes at the higher levels who for a bribe got the illegal Bengali Muslim immigrant settled on even tribal belts. The Bengali Muslim community had a system of local governance that worked well in this respect. A group of Bengali Muslim peasants of a village or a group of villages were controlled by a more educated person who was called the *Diwani*. The *Diwani* was the person who remained in touch with the local Officer in Charge of the Police Station, the Revenue *Shirastadar,* the Sub Deputy Collector and even the Sub Divisional Officer or Deputy Commissioner. It was he who managed to settle illegal immigrant Bengali Muslims on vacant lands by suitably bribing the officials mentioned above. Illegal Bengali Hindu immigrants also came into Assam and managed to get citizenship certificates issued for a consideration. They however did not settle very much on land. They went into the towns as petty traders and lower level employees in private business or the government. In any case Bengali Hindu immigrants as refugees from East Pakistan were officially settled in Assam for years after independence as part of the Central Government's policy.

The continual illegal migration of Bengali Muslim peasants into Assam continued unabated throughout the 1950s. In the early 1960s it was the Director of the Intelligence Bureau who alerted the Central Government to this continued immigration and settlement in the districts of Assam. By now some of the districts of Assam had recorded nearly 50 per cent Bengali Muslims. These were Goalpara, Kamrup, and Nowgong districts. I was posted in Hojai Sub Division in 1967, after initial training in Jorhat and was amazed to see that beyond Doboka south of Nowgong the majority of the peasants were immigrant Bengali Muslims. In fact Morajhar Police Station had a 98 per cent Bengali Muslim population. The remaining 2 per cent were Bengali Hindus! There were no Assamese farmers at all in this district. Mr. B.N.Mallick's alert to the Central Government led to the creation of a Pakistan Infiltration Branch being created in Assam Police. These posts were set up in areas of heavy concentration of immigrant Bengali Muslims. All the districts were given copies of the National Register of Citizens based upon Section 6 of the Indian Citizenship Act of 1955 which prescribed the cut off year for Indian Citizenship as January 26 1950. All investigations under the Foreigners Act in detection of illegal immigrants of both Hindus and Muslims from East Pakistan were based on the National Register of Citizens of that district. If the suspects name figured in that Register, he was a bonafide citizen of India who had migrated into India before that date and had been conferred citizenship. Till the 1950s and 1960s, detections and deportations were quite strictly done. I had myself supervised several cases under the Foreigners Act in Nowgong and Kamrup districts. There was no interference from politicians whatsoever. It was later in the seventies that the politicians discovered that the immigrant Bengali Muslim was a crucial factor in the polling and the Congress party began to use this community as a vote bank. Henceforth the National Register of Citizens was thrown into the waste paper basket in the investigation of cases under the Foreigners Act. This also coincided with the development of committed bureaucracy, a dubious gift of Indira Gandhi, the Congress Prime Minister to Indian Bureaucracy after she imposed the emergency on the country in 1975. I was posted to Tezpur in Assam from Shillong in 1982 and was travelling to Tezpur via Guwahati to take over charge. It was the peak of the Foreigners agitation and I halted for a few hours in Guwahati to meet the senior officers to be briefed. I was taken aback by the reply from the Inspector General Special Branch, when I asked that we should pay special interest to the detection and deportation of foreigners from Bangladesh.

His reply was that there were no foreigners in Assam! In other words the Bengali Muslim illegal immigrants were the vote bank of the party in power and the unwritten orders were that they should not be detected!

The Foreigners Agitation

The 1970s saw a distinct downturn in the political system of the country. This was the development of the detestable system of committed bureaucracy, where by the bureaucrat was given unwritten instructions by his political masters and he had to obey these orders. If he did not, he was transferred and a more willing bureaucrat was posted in his place, who would carry out the illegal orders of his political masters. This led to a steep rise in the corruption levels in Government. In Assam it was this committed bureaucracy that led to the biggest mass agitation that took place in India after the civil disobedience movement of 1942. In fact the Foreigners agitation as it was called took its inspiration from this movement. The roots of the Foreigners agitation started with the liberation of Bangladesh in December 1971, after the Pakistan Government clamped down on East Pakistan and an insurrection for liberation and creation of Bangladesh broke out in March 1971. When General Yahya Khan ordered the clampdown in East Pakistan, a battalion of the east Bengal regiment, then based in Chittagong revolted killed their Pakistani officers and crossed the border into Tripura under Major Ziaur Rehman who was commanding the battalion. There was large scale migration of both Bengali Hindus and Muslims into India to escape the brutal atrocities unleashed on the citizens of East Pakistan. This was because the *Jammat-e-Islami* and other Muslim fundamentalist groups sided with the Pakistan army against the Bengali people, both Muslims and Hindus. Hundreds of intellectuals and college students were killed, women and girls brutally raped before being killed. There were mass graves in which the bodies of this holocaust were buried. The Government of India quickly organised the refugees who poured into India in camps and assisted in raising and training the *Mukti Bahini*, a guerrilla force to combat the Pakistan army. The Government of Bangladesh in exile was established in India on 25 March 1971. Sectors were created on the borders of West

Bengal, Assam and Tripura to base the *Mukti Bahini*. In November the Indian Army moved in and in a quick operation encircled the Pakistan army divisions that led to a surrender of more than 90,000 troops in December 1971 and the liberation of Bangladesh.

Mujibur Rehman the leader of the party that had won the majority of seats in the elections and who was not allowed to become the Prime Minister of Pakistan was released and came back to an emotional and rousing welcome. Very soon he met Indira Gandhi, the Prime Minister of India and in their meeting an agreement called the Indira-Mujib pact was signed. One item was not recorded in the minutes of the meeting and this was the root of the problem for the Northeast. Mujib told Mrs. Gandhi that he could not take the thousands of people, both Hindus and Muslims who had illegally migrated to India before 25th March 1971. Mrs. Gandhi agreed. This was an illegal act as there was no legal basis for changing the date, January 26, 1950, enshrined in the Citizenship Act of India 1955. Lakhs of Hindus and Muslims from East Pakistan had migrated to India between 1950 the date given for permitting citizenship of India after the division of India and Pakistan as per section 6 of the Citizenship Act of India legislated in 1955. The migration of Hindus from East Pakistan had taken place because of religious persecution. This was understandable. For example when the hair of the Prophet Muhammad was reportedly missing from the Hazratbal Shrine in Srinagar, more than a lakh of Hindus from East Pakistan were forced to flee into India after communal riots broke out there in 1963. The migration of Muslims from East Pakistan from 1947 onwards had no basis. It was therefore totally illegal for Mrs. Gandhi to agree to the request of Mujibur Rehman that Muslims of East Pakistan who had migrated, obviously illegally between 1950 and 25th March 1971 could be permitted to stay in India. Soon after this meeting, directions were given to the states bordering Bangladesh, - West Bengal, Tripura and Assam that the cutoff date for Bangladeshi migrants would be 25th March 1971. This was plainly an illegal direction as the cutoff date was 26 January, 1950 as per section 6 of the Citizenship Act of 1955.

This was the time when committed bureaucracy had become the norm in the country. Committed bureaucracy was not the preserve of the Congress party only. The Communists practiced it in West Bengal and Kerala, the DMK in Tamil Nadu and the Congress where ever they ruled. In Assam, the illegal immigrant Bengali Muslim was already a vote bank of the Congress party. Verbal orders went out that Foreigners Act cases should not be registered against Bengali Muslims who had come before 25th March 1971. The National Register of Citizens was thrown into the waste paper basket as it was no longer relevant! There was only one problem. There was no legal validity for this new date 25th March 1971. And it was on this date that the Foreigners agitation was to focus.

For some years, the issue of the illegal migration of Bengali Muslims and Hindus from East Pakistan was agitating the minds of the Assamese people. The All Assam Students Union (AASU), The Assam Sahitya Sabha, a regional party called the Purbanchal Lokha Parishad (PLP) and a social group called the Ahom Jatiyathibadi Yuba Chatra Parishad (AJYCP) were discussing this issue and representing the Government to take some action. With the discussions of the AASU, and other social bodies, the people of Assam were beginning to be aware of the problem of illegal migration from Bangladesh. It was in 1979, that the issue was precipitated. In that year, the sitting MLA from Mangaldoi, a Sub-Division of Darrang district, Tezpur, died in office. A bye-election was to be conducted. Before that a large number of petitions were submitted to the Chief Election Commissioner at Delhi, stating that there were a large number of illegal Bengali Muslims from Bangladesh who had managed to also get their names included in the electoral rolls of the Mangaldoi constituency. When the Chief Election Commissioner received these complaints, he asked his officers to go to Mangaldoi and enquire into the matter and advise him. The officers, who went to Mangaldoi, after enquiry, reported that a large number of illegal Bengali Muslims immigrants had managed to get their names included in the electoral rolls. The Chief Election Commissioner then held a conference and spoke that he would not conduct the by-election unless this matter was enquired. It was at this time that the government of Morarji Desai was destabilised by the Congress and Charan Singh was made a defacto Prime Minister. The Muslim lobby then pressurised the Congress leadership to have the polling conducted in this constituency. The Chief Election

Commissioner was called and told to conduct the polls without revising the electoral rolls. Humbly acquiescing to this direction, the Chief Election Commissioner called a fresh press conference and announced that he would conduct the by polls on the basis of the 1976 electoral rolls. Hearing this announcement, the AASU, the AJYCP, the PLP and the Assam Sahitya Sabha met on the date after the announcement of the Chief Election Commissioner, formed the Gana Sangram Parishad and announced the commencement of the Foreigners agitation in Assam. On 6th November 1979 a mass rally of students was organised at Guwahati by the AASU. Four days later the first phase of the agitation was started with thousands of people courting arrest in offices throughout the State in Assamese majority areas. The jails naturally could not accommodate such large numbers of people. The Government then reached an understanding with the people courting arrest. They were formally arrested, kept for the day in some temporary jail, which could also be an open ground and released at the end of the day.

The agitation quickly picked up momentum. Schools and Colleges were closed and soon offices also were closed as office staff also courted arrest. Soon the Oil Refinery at Noonmati was also affected as volunteers blocked the supply of oil. The organisers also adopted various methods like asking all the people to switch off all lights between 6 PM to 7 PM or come out on the streets at a specified time and sound cymbals and similar instruments. Frequent shutdowns of all shops in the state were also called for. As the movement gained momentum, the Gana Sangram Parishad the coordinating body of the Assamese people asked all political parties to boycott the elections.

There is no doubt whatsoever that the movement had the complete backing of the Assamese people. As a direct witness to the agitation I can vouchsafe that such a movement had not taken place after the civil disobedience movement of 1942. From children of ten years to elder citizens of 70 to 80 years, both rural and urban, everyone participated in the agitation. They were asking for the detection and deportation of all immigrants from East Pakistan and now Bangladesh on the basis of the Indian Citizenship

Act of 1955 and the National Register of Citizens prepared on the basis of this act. For them it was a last ditch fight to ensure the survival of their identity and culture.[12]

The Gana Sangram Parishad projected the movement as a national cause, but there was a veiled secessionist undercurrent to it. Two of the constituents of the movement, the *Ahom Jatiyatibadi Yuba Chatra Parishad (AJYCP)* and the regional party, the *Purbanchal Loka Parishad (PLP)* nurtured secessionist feelings. The AJYCP was raised in 1978 and it was to be the main feeder organization for the future insurgent group, the United Liberation Front of Assam (ULFA). The AJYCP shunned politics, but had excellent organising capacity. One organisation formed by one of its leaders, Joynath Sharma, was an example of the inner discipline of the movement. This was the *Swecha Sevak Bahini* or youth volunteer corps. This had representatives in every Assamese village and in every locality of its towns. News of an impending *bandh (*forced closure of work*)* was disseminated throughout the state by this organisation before the Police or the Special Branch got wind of it. Different departments of Government were captive to the movement.

The Assamese have a unique institution, the *Naam Ghar* (Prayer House), a place of worship without idols, gifted by her great religious reformer, Shanker Dev. Every village and locality has its Naam Ghar. Here the local people gather, after the day's work is done, to sing hymns and discuss the affairs of the State. I was posted in Tezpur in 1982-83, when the Foreigner's agitation was at its peak. One evening, I was at a friend's place sitting on his verandah. Opposite was a Naam Ghar. Suddenly we saw that a number of housewives of the locality were gathering. It was rather early in the day for such a gathering. The ladies who had assembled sat down had a brief discussion and then quietly dispersed. My friend then asked me if there was a bandh the next day. I was surprised and said that I had not heard of any bandh. My friend said- "Then what was this meeting of housewives about?" I went back to the office and rang up the Inspector General Special

---

[12] *The Periphery Strikes Back*, Udayan Misra, chapter 5, page 132.

Branch and asked him whether there was a bandh the next day. He replied that he did not know of any bandh. I told him that I was sure there would be a bandh the next day and told him to check up from his sources again. An hour later, he rang me up and told me that AASU had called for a bandh the next day. He also asked me how I had come to know about this. How could I tell him that a chance sighting of a group of ladies collecting in a Naam Ghar at an odd time had given me the clue?

As the movement progressed a group slowly started taking to violence. There were cases of intimidation and violence and finally bomb blasts on the pipeline. India's Intelligence Agency contacted the leaders of the Foreigners Movement and was in touch with them. The contentious issue was the new cutoff date that had been decided by the Government after the meeting of Mujibur Rehman with India's Prime Minister. The AASU leaders were called to Delhi and the ruling party tried every blandishment to make them accept the new cutoff date. The students stood steadfast. All that the students were asking was for the Government to function in accordance with the constitution and the law of the land, in this case the Indian Citizenship Act that stated that the cutoff date for getting citizenship in India after 15th August 1947 was 26 January 1950. And they could not change this date on the basis of a verbal agreement with the President of Bangladesh!

The students were asking the Government to identify illegal immigrants who had come across the border of East Pakistan illegally and had settled down in Assam, very often after bribing the Assamese petty bureaucracy, but who were now being protected by political parties who had made them a vote bank. The bankrupt political leadership in Delhi was now only thinking of the next day of the next election. There was no one to think of the next generation, of the nation's tomorrow. There were no Statesmen in Delhi, only petty politicians. A national tragedy was looming and the crescendo was rising.

Despite several meetings and holding out of carrots, the AASU refused to accept 25 March 1971 as the cutoff date, insisting for 1950 as prescribed in the Citizenship Act of 1955. Meanwhile preparations for holding the elections in Assam were going ahead taking into account that the AASU and the other bodies would boycott them. In January 1982, in a meeting with the AASU leaders, they were again asked to agree to the 25th March 1971 date. They refused. It was decided that they would be arrested and the elections forced on the people of Assam. Accordingly, the student leaders were arrested at Borjhar airport Guwahati on their return and detained. Very soon it was clear that the people of Assam would boycott the elections; that the State Government servants would refuse to serve as polling personnel. Incredibly the election was to be based on the 1976 electoral rolls ignoring the report of the Chief Election Commissioner, in 1979, when the by polls were to be held in Mangaldoi Parliamentary constituency, that there were foreigners enrolled in the electoral rolls and the by polls would not be held until the electoral rolls were revised! Obviously, this would be the case in all the constituencies where there were sizeable Bengali Muslim settlers. With the announcement of the polls in three phases in February 1982, began the movement of the largest contingents of paramilitary force ever sent to any State till then.

The first signs of trouble began with the burning of small bridges. In Assam the Brahmaputra flowing northeast to southwest divides the valley into two. On the North and South bank a large number of rivers and streams flow into the Brahmaputra from the foot hills of the Himalayas and the Garo, Khasi, Jaintia, Mikir, North Cachar and the Naga Hills. These in turn have a large number of tributaries. Thus besides a number of large bridges there were hundreds of small bridges and culverts in both the North and South banks. It was these small bridges and culverts that were being burned. It was impossible to guard all these small bridges and culverts. Burning them meant that the small streams were not crossable for any four wheeled transport. Obviously this was done to ensure that the polling parties could not reach their designated polling booths! Very obviously this was the work of the *Swecha Sewak Bahini*, the youth volunteer corps of the AASU.

I was posted in Tezpur as the Deputy Inspector General Northern Range and I wrote to the Director General that all intelligence sources had dried up. Our regular sources disappeared and refused to meet the officers running them. The odd sources that still worked were those run at the level of the Superintendent of Police or the DIG. I informed my HQs about the burning of bridges and the disappearance of sources, quoting from Sir Robert Thompson's Defeating Communist Insurgency,- "One of the first signs of a growing insurgency is the drying up of information." But there was nobody to listen.

There were typical incidents that blared out a message that an insurgency was looming over the State. Patherighat was a small bazaar in the interior of Mangaldoi Subdivision. A small patrol post of Sipajhar Police Station was located in one room of a two roomed Primary School. A section of the Assam Police Battalion was sent to this school. One day the Assistant Sub Inspector, the in charge of this post was returning on his cycle after visiting his parent Police Station, Sipajhar, when he noticed smoke spiraling up from the direction of his post. He speeded up and when he reached the Post found the building in flames. The six constables and the section of Assam Police battalion were sitting under a tree with their weapons, bedding, furniture and the CGI sheets of the roof of the post beside them. According to the Head Constable of the AP battalion, who was in charge, a crowd of about one thousand people, old and young had assembled near the post armed with tins of kerosene and asked them to vacate. They said that they did not want to commit any offence, but as the Government was not listening, to their request to delete the names of foreigners from the voting list, they could not allow any voting to take place in the school. They had therefore no choice but to burn down the school building.

They asked the Head Constable to remove their belongings, weapons and even the CGI sheets of the post. Meanwhile the Head Constable and his men had all taken position with their rifles. Then an old man in front of the crowd told the Police that they could fire if they wanted, but they were more than a thousand and how many could the Police kill before they were overpowered? The Head Constable said that he chose discretion before valour and vacated the post. There were many incidents like this. In some the Police fired killing dozens of people leading to unpleasant situations.

By now the Intelligence agencies of the country had long since ceased to give independent professional intelligence to the Government and had committed to the Party in power. It is to the everlasting shame of the Intelligence Agencies of the Government of India that they did not give a true assessment of the ground situation to their political masters, but with servile sycophancy toed the line of the political leaders. A senior Intelligence officer had been posted to the Northeast a few weeks before the elections. He was one of the few professional officers in the agency. He had not handled the Northeast earlier and he was horrified by what he saw and heard. A report was put up to him by his subordinate for being sent to the HQs in Delhi. The report was false and did not reflect the real situation on the ground. It was obviously a doctored report to suit the political masters in Delhi. He refused to sign it and went on tour to assess the real state of affairs on the ground. He was horrified at what he saw and heard at first hand, came back and wrote a factual report that if the elections were held, there would be a blood bath! When he saw the report, his Intelligence Chief came to Guwahati the next day, meanwhile summoning the senior officer from Shillong to Guwahati. When this officer received him at the airport, he was rudely chastised for sending his report and told peremptorily on the tarmac itself that he was reverted to his parent cadre and he should immediately hand over. He had spent twenty years in the Intelligence Agency and paid the price for his honesty. As for the Intelligence Chief he was later rewarded for his "loyalty" as Governor of several states, where he continued in his sycophantic career for many years.

The extraordinary election of February 1983 was not an election in any sense of the term. It was a battle between the Assamese people and the Central Government. As for the actual election it was a farce. In the Assamese constituencies, out of more than 100 odd polling booths only 20 odd could be set up and these too with a platoon of CRPF personnel for each booth! In the rest of the booths, they could not be set up because the small bridges enroute had been burnt. Also the polling parties could not be sent on foot as the distances were too long and mobs of hundreds were waiting enroute to attack the force enroute. In two cases at least when Paramilitary forces tried to brave the mobs and proceed to the polling booths, they were forced to retreat and in the process of retrieving themselves had to open fire with Light Machine Guns on the mobs who were armed with bows and arrows, spears, and some twelve bore guns, making it the first time that Light Machine Guns were used against civil mobs in this country. In most of the cases, the mobs collected the dead and injured when retreating and the Police could not get the actual figures of the dead and injured in each incident.

All the departments of the State went on strike from the 2nd February 1982, except for the Health Department. The roads towns and bazaars were deserted. When driving by one had the eerie feeling of being watched, but not a single person was to be seen. More than 6000 people were killed in the ethnic clashes and police firing. The party in power had split the population in two groups, the Assamese on one side and the Bengali Muslims and the Boros on two other sides. The Boros were also further divided. The Saraniya Boros, who had taken *sharan* with the Hindus, were with the Assamese, while the main Boros who remained as tribals were for the elections and so against the Assamese. The Central Intelligence Agencies were responsible for building up this divide during the run up to the elections. Political leaders also played a role in this game touring the Tribal and Immigrant Muslim areas instigating both these groups against the Assamese.

The Horrifying Elections of 1983—Mangaldoi

The 2nd of February had probably been fixed for the public revolt to start. Significantly neither the Central, nor the State Intelligence had any clue of this, nor sitting in Tezpur, did we get any clue to this and we were overtaken by surprise when the mayhem started. The National Highway coming from Guwahati to Tezpur on the north bank had two wooden bridges with several spans between Baihata Char Ali, Sipajhar and Mangaldoi. There was also a small concrete bridge between Sipajhar and Mangaldoi. The two wooden bridges were guarded by a section of Armed Branch constables armed with 0.303 rifles. They were poorly trained and were no match for the situation developing. The district however could not deploy the Central Reserve Police (CRPF) for this task. On the morning the villages adjacent to these three bridges came out to attack and burn them. The objective was to cut off Mangaldoi and Tezpur from Guwahati so that elections could not be held. I am sure that the Police Stations at Mangaldoi and Sipajhar had got wind of this but did not tell the Superintendent of Police in Tezpur. Simultaneously mobs attacked government offices that were earmarked for polling booths in the same area. On hearing of this the SP Tezpur left for Mangaldoi and with the SDO Civil there deployed CRPF and managed to save the two wooden bridges after opening fire in several places. The SP himself opened fire on the Bor Nadi Bridge killing and wounding some of the attackers. I followed a little later with a company of CRPF and reached there in the afternoon. The SDO and the SP were still in Sipajhar in the field clearing the road and placing picquets so that road movement could not be disrupted. I deployed force all over Mangaldoi town after declaring curfew and was moving round the town, when the SP and the SDO returned and informed us of the developments between Mangaldoi and Sipajhar. Inspector Handique who was with the SDO had been sent back to Mangaldoi escorting a marriage party that was coming from Guwahati and was held up at Sipajhar. Neither the marriage party nor the Inspector had arrived. A force was sent towards Sipajhar but could not find any trace of the Inspector. The whole night was spent in patrolling Mangaldoi town and the axis from Mangaldoi to Sipajhar in the west and to Kalaigaon in the North. A patrol sent at first light went up to the concrete culvert between Mangaldoi and Sipajhar and found that a mob had tried to burn the concrete bridge! The brutalized body of Inspector Handique was found thrown in the *nullah* over which the culvert was built. The marriage party that was being escorted meanwhile had been brought and told us the gruesome story of the previous day. Inspector Handique escorting the marriage party found a huge mob of about 500 odd people stacking bundles of grass and wood on the concrete culvert to try and burn it. Inspector Handique challenged the mob and when they refused to leave, opened fire from his pistol the only weapon he had. The crowd took the bullets, several people falling after bullets hit them, and then fell upon the brave but hapless Inspector and brutally beat him to death.

Back in Mangaldoi, we got information the same night that a Police post at Burha, about 45 kilometres to the northwest was under attack. The information was given over VHF from the post. A Platoon of CRPF had already been positioned there. The Post Commander was on the VHF and since it was too far off I gave directions on VHF to the Post Commander. I could hear the shouting of the mob on the VHF. I directed the Post Commander to carefully control his fire and pick off the leaders of the mob, instead of firing in panic. I could hear the stones falling on the CGI sheets of the post and then the sound of measured firing by the CRPF Post Commander and his men. The situation was controlled within half an hour and the mob retreated with five of their number killed and several injured.

There were two cases of communal clashes in Mangaldoi Sub Division during this period of which we came to know later as the communication to these areas were disrupted. The first was in *Chawalkhoa Chapori* and the second in Khoirabari a Bengali Hindu settlement about 25 kilometres north of Mangaldoi. *Chawalkhoa Chapori* was an extended area of low level land on the right bank of the Brahmaputra River near two big Assamese villages *Bor Thekrabari* and *Horu Thekrabari*. This low land on the bank of the river was the *dao matti* of the two villages mentioned above. The villagers of these two villages used to cultivate mustard and sesame on these two islands separated by a channel or *huti*. Some years earlier a number of Illegal Bengali Muslims settled on this island and managed to prevent eviction. The settlement had grown quite big and more than a thousand Bengali Muslims were living on this low land at the time of the elections. All these people were obviously illegal immigrants and should have been struck off the electoral rolls, but for the inaction on this by the Chief Election Commissioner as noted earlier. When the election was declared, the volunteers from the two villages *Bor Thekrabari* and *Horu Thekrabari* went to *Chawalkhoa Chapori* and told the inhabitants that they should not vote in the election. They refused to agree to this. They were then threatened by the volunteers that if they tried to vote they would be attacked. Both sides then prepared by collecting *daos, lathis* and other weapons and on the night preceding the election date the villagers from *Bor Thekrabari* and *Horu Thekrabari* attacked the villagers of Chawalkhoa Chapori. The battle was one sided and more than a hundred Bengali Muslims were killed and several injured, before the Assamese villagers retreated. Since *Chawalkhoa Chapori* was cut off from the main road, the injured were taken by boat to Kharupettia a market town upstream, which had further repercussions on the polling day as will be seen later.

Next to *Chawalkhoa Chapori* downstream was another long island called *Kirakara Chapori*. Adjacent to this island on the mainland was a village called Sanua inhabited by Assamese Muslims. These were Assamese Hindus who were converted during the invasion of the Slave Kings or the Mughals. These villagers had received a grant from the Government and had purchased more than hundred buffalos and kept them on the *Kirakara Chapori*, which was notified as a grazing reserve by the SDO Mangaldoi. Shortly before the elections, the villagers of Sanua noticed that a number of Bengali Muslim immigrants had landed on Kirakara Chapori built shelters and were tilling the land. A number of Assamese Muslim villagers from Sanua went across to *Kirakara Chapori* and told the Bengali Muslim trespassers to stop tilling and vacate the island. The trespassers refused to vacate and said they would continue to till the land. The Sanua Villagers then went to Mangaldoi and complained to the SDO about the trespassers. The SDO Mangaldoi then sent an officer to enquire and report after verification on the ground. His officer visited the island and reported about the trespass. The SDO then ordered eviction of the trespassers and sent a Magistrate with armed force from the district Armed Reserve. The Muslim lobby was equally fast and took it up in Delhi, who probably informed the Principal Advisor to stop the eviction! It was President's Rule in Assam. The SDO Mangaldoi was called on telephone and told to hold the eviction. This was an illegal order as the SDO had ordered the eviction in his capacity as a Magistrate. The SDO replied that the eviction had already been done and the huts of the trespassers had been demolished. He had kept a section of the District Armed Reserve on *Kirakara Chapori*. This force was however withdrawn as the election drew near. When the Armed force withdrew, the infiltrators came back and resettled on *Kirakara Chapori*. When the villagers of *Bor Thekrabari* went to *Chawalkhoa Chapori* to warn the Bengali Muslim inhabitants, the Assamese Muslims of Sanua accompanied them and told the infiltrators who had come back after the armed force had withdrawn to leave the island. They refused to do so and they were warned by the Assamese villagers that they would attack them if they stayed. Accordingly when the Assamese Hindu villagers of Bor Thekrabari went to attack the Bengali Muslim settlers of *Chawalkhoa Chapori*, the Assamese Muslim villagers of Sanua went to attack the Bengali Muslim infiltrators on *Kirakara Chapori*. When I visited the *Chapories* after the elections to enquire into the various incidents, the Bengali Muslim settlers of *Chawalkhoa Chapori* told me that on the night of the attack, they were surprised to hear cries of *Allah-Hoo Akbar*, coming from the attackers of Sanua villagers! One of the Assamese Muslim boys of Sanua village was killed in this attack. The monument erected for him by the AASU, stands to this day in Sanua village, testimony to the fact that the Foreigners Agitation was not communal. The issue was land and not religion.

The date of the first election came. All the constituencies of Mangaldoi Subdivision were to go to the polls. The polls were countermanded in the Assamese majority constituencies because of the serious law and order situation and the inability to reach the polling stations. Polling was held only in the non Assamese majority areas of Udalguri, Mazbat and Dalgaon. The first was a Boro area, the second a Tea Garden Labour area and the third a Bengali Muslim majority area. I was moving round in the three aforesaid constituencies, when I received a message from Mangaldoi control that a Bengali Muslim mob had attacked the majority Hindu Assamese village of Dhola. We rushed to Dhola and found that the CRPF deployed there had opened fire on the Bengali Muslim mob that attacked the Dhola village and driven them back to their area. A number of Assamese people of Dhola were killed and some injured and a part of Dhola village was set on fire. A number of Bengali Muslims were killed and some injured. After sorting out the area and leaving CRPF picquets, we moved on and surprised an Assamese mob setting fire to a Bengali Muslim village. We opened fire, dispersed the mob, but could not save the village. Luckily all the Bengali Muslims had fled before the attack. That night was spent in patrolling the faultiness between the Assamese and Bengali Muslim areas. Luckily there were no further incidents. It was as if the cumulative energy that led to the horrifying attacks and arson of the last ten days had spent itself after the polling.

As I drove back to Tezpur, my HQs, before going to North Lakhimpur for more arson, rioting and killing I had only one thought in my mind-"Did the powers that be in Delhi, the Political leaders, the fawning bureaucrats and the groveling sleuths of the Intelligence Agencies realise what forces they had let loose by their idiotic policies. How many lives had gone in that one week of rioting, police firing and would these passions ever cool down? All this only to get a vote bank for the party in power! I concluded that we did not have any Statesmen who could see fifty years into the future in our country, only politicians who thought till just the next election!

North Lakhimpur

The road from Tezpur to North Lakhimpur is 120 kilometres long and passes through enchanting country. Since the District administration was busy with all forces concentrated in Mangaldoi, the volunteers of the AASU had a free hand on this axis and they did a thorough job, by felling huge trees across the road and cutting wide ditches on the highway. Beyond the concrete bridge on the Zia Bharali River just fifteen kilometres from Tezpur, the road to North Lakhimpur was effectively blocked. Luckily all the forces required for the elections were air lifted from Tezpur by the Air Force. The Commissioner and I went by helicopter to North Lakhimpur on the 10th of February 1983. The situation in North Lakhimpur was chaotic with almost all connecting roads from the national Highway to the Arunachal foothills on one side and the Brahmaputra River on the other completely blocked. All that we could do between firing on mobs trying to block polling parties from reaching the polling booths, and mobs trying to set on fire buildings earmarked for polling booths, was to set up all the polling booths meant for the interiors on the national Highway.

In the midst of running round firefighting, on the morning of the 11th of February I had gone to the room of my batch mate, the Commissioner to brief him of the developments. I was on the telephone in his room when he beckoned me and asked me to talk to a person who was in conversation with him. I recognized him as a leading Congress politician from Arunachal Pradesh. He asked me how things were and I told him that things could not be worse. He agreed and told me that something was going to happen in Gohpur in the next two days that would take away some of the pressure from the Police. I did not understand what exactly he meant and asked him to clarify what he meant. He repeated what he had said, that in the next two days, something was going to happen in Gohpur that would take away the pressure from the Police. I then asked him what was going to happen in Gohpur that was worse than what had already happened. To this he simply said- "Wait and see". I was called again to the telephone and I left. It was some hours later after some more firefighting that I recollected this conversation. For the rest of the day, I kept recollecting this uneasily. The next morning at about 1100 hours, a crash signal from Gohpur informed me that a big mob of Boros living in the Gohpur Reserve Forest, that they had trespassed and cleared some years ago, had attacked the large Assamese village of Gohpur and also several adjacent villages, killing several persons, and setting fire to dozens of houses. As I reacted by organizing a company of Para Military Force and was setting out for Gohpur, I suddenly remembered what the leading politician from Arunachal had told me the day before in the Circuit House. He had told me that something would happen in Gohpur that would take away the pressure from the Police. How did he know of this beforehand?

We could only reach halfway to Gohpur. The road had been dug up and we would have to walk thirty kilometres to reach Gohpur. We therefore had to return. There was a company of CRPF in Gohpur and the Inspector posted there had to manage with this force. We returned and continued the firefighting. The polling in North Lakhimpur was as big a farce as the polling in Mangaldoi. In most of the polling booths only a few hundred ballots were polled against an electorate of one lakh or more. It was only in the predominantly immigrant Bengali Muslim constituency that polling was normal. When I returned to Tezpur on 15 February it was again by helicopter. As we flew over Gohpur I could see fires burning in Gohpur Reserve forest area, several houses of Gohpur village had been broken. It was only after the polling in Tezpur that I could piece together what had happened in Gohpur and solve the mystery of what the politician from Arunachal had told me in the Lakhimpur Circuit house.

Tezpur

The elections in Tezpur Sub Division were on the 21st of February 1983. Two incidents happened before the polling day. The first incident was a firing on a bus carrying CRPF personnel on night patrol. On the outskirts of Tezpur on the road coming in from Guwahati there was a large village called Dipota. This village was a little notorious. A posse of two sections of CRPF and a Police Sub Inspector had left on a patrol well after night had fallen. There was a small nullah that crossed the highway at the end of Dipota village. As the bus went up the concrete bridge, a shot rang out from the left. There was a sound of the bullet hitting the metal body of the bus. The bullet after deflection hit the Sub Inspector who was sitting on the left front seat directly over the heart and he died instantly. The CRPF personnel immediately jumped out of the bus and ran down to the nullah. No one could be found. The ambush party had probably retreated immediately after firing one shot. The CRPF radioed the information to the Police Station and I was informed at about midnight. Since the Superintendent of Police was on tour, I went to the spot immediately along with the SHO of the Police Station. We stopped our vehicles well behind the bridge on the Dipota nullah and taking cover of the shadows on either side of the road moved cautiously towards the nullah. A platoon of the CRPF had come with me. I talked on the VHF set to the Platoon Commander of the CRPF Platoon that was in the bus and learnt that the single round fired was from the left side of the nullah. Near the bridge I divided our party into two and sent one to the left and another to the right of the bridge. After clearing both sides, I climbed up to the bus and saw that the bullet had hit the steel handle of the door of the bus deflected and then hit the Sub Inspector. Looking back from the door of the bus to the nullah on the left I roughly calculated the trajectory of the bullet and then climbed down to the nullah on the left and simulated firing a shot at the door of the bus and then asked the CRPF boys to search to my right for the empty case of the round that was fired. A short search and an empty case was recovered. I could see that the empty case was not from a round of a 0.303 rifle. The CRPF Sub Inspector looked at it and said that it was an empty case of an AK-47 round. I had a sudden chill as I heard this. No AK 47 rifles had been used till then in Assam. The group that operated that night in the Dipota Nullah had an AK-47! My mind immediately went to the Naxalite cell that had been established some years earlier in Bihaguri by the Headmaster of the Bihaguri School. One of his protégés was a boy called Arpan Bezbaruah, who lived in Dipota. We had been looking for him for some time. He had started what he called the Assam Peoples Liberation Army (APLA). I knew his house and on an impulse decided to search the place. After sending the body of the unfortunate Sub Inspector to Tezpur I led the CRPF group to the house of the suspect. We surrounded it and asked the inmates to open the house. After some time the door was opened by a girl who when asked said whether Arpan Bezbaruah was in the house replied in the negative besides abusing the CRPF for disturbing the peace at such an unearthly hour. We found no one in the house and no ammunition or a rifle. Then we searched the compound and found a cloth bundle hidden between bunches of banana plants. When we opened the cloth bundle we found several live rounds of 0.303 and AK 47 and also several fired empties of both the bores. We left after seizing the recovered ammunition. After the elections were over we arrested Arpan Bezbaruah after a source informed us of one of his hideouts. He was a very committed boy and refused to divulge where he had hidden the AK rifle with which our Sub Inspector was shot and how he had procured it. We could not establish from which weapon the round that killed our Sub Inspector was fired. The murder case of our Sub Inspector had to be closed.

The second incident was horrifying, brutal and pathetic. On the 17th February, the Superintendent of Police informed me that in the heart of Tezpur town, a group of boys had set fire to the PWD office that was designated as a polling booth. The PWD office was an Assam type building with a false ceiling. The three boys had come prepared with petrol or kerosene in cans. Two of the boys broke into the building while unknown to these two the third boy got a ladder and placing it against the wall climbed up on to the framework of the false ceiling. He began splashing petrol on the false ceiling, while the two boys below splashed petrol on the office tables and furniture and set them on fire, forgetting that their friend was on the false ceiling. The furniture caught fire and the flames leapt up and in a trice the false ceiling was aflame, trapping the boy above. He was badly burnt by the time the two boys below could rescue him. The two boys fled leaving their badly burnt friend outside to be rescued by the fire Brigade that came to put out the fire. The SP had gone to the hospital to see this boy, but found him unconscious. He told me that there was little chance of his surviving.

The next morning we went to the airport to meet the Principal Advisor who was stopping at the airport to be briefed on the situation. As I picked up the SP, he informed me that the badly burnt boy had died at night. As we drove out of Tezpur town the countryside was deserted. As we entered the Cantonment area we noticed four boys arranging some logs in a corner of a village field. A little further ahead we noticed six lines of boys and girls coming in single file from different directions towards, the main road. They were strangely silent and we could only hear the shuffling of feet as they reached the main road. We stopped our vehicle and asked the boys and girls in Assamese what had happened and where they were going. We got angry looks but no one uttered a word. Then suddenly we realised that the boys arranging logs and the boys and girls silently marching were organising the funeral for the boy who had died from burns the day before, when setting fire to the PWD office that had been designated as a polling station to prevent the polls from being held. He was a martyr for their cause and hence the military discipline of the funeral!

At the airport we met a haggard Principal Advisor who looked as if he had not slept for days. The terrific tension of the blistering days since the 2nd of February had taken its toll. We told him that in Mangaldoi and North Lakhimpur there was no polling in the Assamese areas and in all interior areas the polling booths had to be established on the highway as the roads were blocked. I also told him that the road to North Lakhimpur was cut off completely and it would take days to reestablish communications.

We left for Tezpur after the Principal Advisor took off. As we drove back we found that the lines of boys and girls had now become a hollow square in the field where we noticed boys arranging logs, and the poor boy who was badly burnt and killed was being cremated. Then suddenly we saw the group raise their fists and shout- "Jai Aie Ahom!" (Glory to Mother Assam.) There were several different stories about the boy who had died. Some said that he was quietly killed at night by his friends so that he could not disclose the names of his accomplices in the arson. Another version was that he was killed to put him out of his misery for he was very badly burnt. The doctors said that he died of excessive third degree burns. We will never know, but his memorial stands to this day in the lonely field outside Tezpur where he was cremated, a martyr to the cause of Assam.

The Polling in Tezpur Sub Division was uneventful. Since it was the District HQs the Police arrangements were fairly satisfactory under the extraordinary circumstances. In the Assamese localities we had to deploy CRPF in strength to protect the Presiding and Polling officers. In these areas there was no polling. In the Tea Garden labour areas like Rangapahar, and Dhekiajuli there was good polling. It was a long day for us. I spent the day patrolling the town and the sensitive areas. When the polling time had closed I returned to the Police Station after patrolling the routes from where the polling parties were returning. Sitting in the Police Station I was monitoring the return of each polling party. It was past 10 PM when the last polling party returned. I was just congratulating all the officers for their extremely hard work, when the telephone rang. It was the Principal Advisor from Guwahati. He informed me that the Prime Minister Mrs. Indira Gandhi was coming by helicopter to Gohpur the next morning and we should receive her there and take her to the refugee camps where the Assamese and the Boros had taken shelter after the clashes between the two communities. I replied immediately that the Prime Minister could not go to Gohpur. The National Highway was blocked in dozens of places and it would take at least a week for the PWD to open the road to traffic. The reply was that the PM has already made the programme to go to Gohpur and then to Nellie where another massacre had taken place and we had to go to Gohpur immediately to arrange for her reception. I quickly thought and said that there was only one organisation that could open the road overnight and that was the Army Engineers. They had Bulldozers and One Tonners with winches and pulleys for removing fallen trees. Till now we had orders not to call the Army for aid to law and order. The Principal Advisor thought for a second and then said that he would talk to the Corps Commander at Tezpur and I should contact him thereafter. Five minutes later I called the Corps Commander and he told me that he had already detailed an Engineers Company to clear the road. They had One Tonners with winches and pulleys, Bull Dozers and Cranes. They would move for Gohpur by 2300 hours. We should give them an hour's time and we should move by 0000 hours of 22 February. I thanked him. I now had the problem of getting at least one Company of CRPF and some District Police officers. All of us had been on the road since 0700 hours and we were on our feet for the last 15 hours. I first asked the CRPF Commandant who was with me since the morning that he should accompany me with a Company, after explaining the emergency requirement. Without a seconds hesitation the Commandant said that he would take a Company immediately and after their dinner, rest them for an hour and he would be ready to move by midnight. We set off from Tezpur exactly at 0000 hours 22nd February. I had confirmed that the Engineers Company had rolled out at 2300 hours. We were just approaching the Zia Bharali Bridge when we saw a number of figures laid out with white shrouds lying on the ground by the side of the approach road to the bridge. My first thought was that the Engineers column had been ambushed. We got down and approached the bridge cautiously on foot. Then we saw an Army soldier on sentry near our end of the bridge and learnt that saboteurs had placed big nails between the bridge and the road and the tyres of the first two vehicles' of the column had all punctured. The rest of the column had advanced, while two vehicles' had returned to their HQs to get fresh tyres. The personnel of these two vehicles' were sleeping on the ground with their bed sheets till their vehicle returned with tyres. Hence the white shrouds. This could only mean that the talk with the Corps Commander had been overheard by someone in the Telephone Exchange and the AASU volunteers alerted to detail a sabotage party.

The Army Engineers column opened the road and we reached Gohpur at 0600 hours. We must now return to the situation at Gohpur.

Gohpur was a small town with a number of villages around it on the National Highway from Tezpur to North Lakhimpur. It was mostly Tea

Garden Country. The people of Gohpur were caste Hindu Assamese, but they were very different from other Assamese Caste Hindus. The Caste Hindu Assamese of Gohpur were known to be short tempered, sometimes a little rude and peremptory in reacting. Gohpur had a famous girl heroine, 14 years old, who in the civil disobedience movement of 1942 led a group in defiance of the police and carrying a National Flag marched at the head of a group of grown up people disobeying the orders of the police. She was shot at point blank range and died on the spot, a martyr to the cause of India's freedom struggle. Her statue carrying the National Flag still stands on the ruins of the old Gohpur Police Station, which has been preserved to this date. Well behind Gohpur, touching and merging with the Arunachal foothills was a magnificent Reserve Forest called the Gohpur Reserve Forest? This forest was encroached by Boro tribals from Darrang district, who had lost their lands to illegal Muslim immigrants from East Pakistan. Despite protests from the Caste Hindu people of Gohpur, the Congress party leaders protected the encroaching Boro tribals and did not evict them. This led to bad blood between the Caste Hindu Assamese of Gohpur and the Boros who had encroached the Gohpur Reserve Forest. Despite all their protests, the Boro encroachment continued aided and abetted by the Congress party in power, until finally the Gohpur Reserve Forest vanished and in place were a dozen villages of Boros tilling the land. When the election was forced on the people of Assam the Boros wanted to take part in the elections. In Gohpur, the Assamese people who lived on either side of the National Highway told the Boros, that they should not vote, to which the Boros in the erstwhile Gohpur Reserve Forest did not agree. Thereupon, the Assamese of Gohpur set fire to all the wooden bridges going to the Gohpur Forest area, where now the Boros were living. The lines were thus drawn between the caste Hindus and the Boros and this was to explode when the polling was to be held.

The ill feeling between the Boros and the Caste Hindus of Assam was smoldering for quite some years. The crux of the issue was that the Mongoloid Boros were kept at the bottom of the caste hierarchy by the Caste Hindus. The issue was further complicated when the party in power decided to play the Boros against the Assamese caste Hindus. This was what the former Minister told me in the circuit house in North Lakhimpur on the 11th February, when he said that something has been done to reduce the pressure on the Police. On 12 February, a mob of several hundred Boros armed with bows and arrows, sticks and batons from the Gohpur Reserve Forest villages suddenly swooped on the Assamese caste Hindu villages and attacked the villagers. It took some time before the Assamese men could organise and retaliate. By that time several people were killed and dozens of houses were set on fire. The Assamese fled before the onslaught towards the Gohpur Police Station. By the time the CRPF from Gohpur Police Station reached the area, the Boros had retreated. Several thousand people, men women and children were accommodated in the Gohpur College. A few Boros who lived in Gohpur were accommodated in a small primary school near the Police Station. The two impromptu refugee camps that came up were without any rations or other supplies as the road from Tezpur was blocked.

The party workers who organised this attack made one miscalculation. They did not take into account the peculiar nature of the Gohpur Assamese caste Hindus. They were a very rough, aggressive, short tempered people. When the news of the attack by the Boros on the Assamese people of Gohpur area spread, a council of war was held by all the Assamese caste Hindu villages from Gohpur to Bihpuriya in North Lakhimpur and on 14 February, a big mob of caste Hindus armed with batons, attacked all the Boro villages in the Gohpur Reserve Forest Area, set fire to all the houses and killed several Boros. The Boros fled into Arunachal forest and were sheltered in makeshift camps by the Arunachal Government. The details of all these events were not known fully by us in Tezpur, beyond the bare facts. In any case we could not move to Gohpur till the polling was over on 21 February. And it was into this disorganized mess that the Prime Minister was going to land on the morning of 22 February.

We went past the Gohpur College where the caste Hindu Assamese were housed in a refugee camp and washed and refreshed ourselves before going to the helipad and organising the security of the helipad. This done, I came to the refugee camp. On first seeing us, the young men in the camp put a chain and locked the gate, but later opened it. We went in and met some elder people in the camp. We told them that the road had been opened and the first supplies of rations would be arriving by afternoon. I told them that the Prime Minister was going to come to Gohpur. All of them said that they did not want to meet the Prime Minister. She was the cause of all the trouble in Assam. She has forced the elections on us without detecting and deporting the foreigners from Bangladesh. I told them that they should tell the Prime Minister what had happened.

The Gohpur College was built as a hollow square. All the rooms were full of people. Sanitation was poor and all the people were angry. I had brought a few Special Branch officers from Tezpur and I asked them to quickly check all the rooms and the people for knives or lathis or any kind of weapon. We had already deployed the CRPF personnel around and inside the college. It was 0900 hours by this time and I got the information on the wireless that the PM's plane had landed and she would reach Gohpur by 1000 hours. I had detailed my staff car to drive the PM from the helipad to the college. I hurriedly ran through the rules in the Blue book that is prescribed for the PM's security. Not a single rule could be implemented!

The PM's helicopter landed and she came down surrounded by the Cabinet Secretary, and other officials. The Cabinet Secretary asked me if it was safe for the PM to go to the refugee camp. I said that she could go to the small refugee camp near the helipad where about 50 Boros were sheltered, but the large camp in the Gohpur College was not safe for her visit. The PM heard this and interrupted- "But I have promised Parliament that I would go to the refugee camps." She moved forward and walked up to the small camp of Boro refugees in the Primary school. The men and women received her graciously and replied in broken Hindi. She condoled with them and then got into the car and we drove up to the college. The Assamese people in the refugee camp had collected at the doors of the college and a few were standing in the corridors. She got down from the car and I followed, uttering a silent prayer and went behind her. She climbed up the stairs and then stopped before the first door and asked the men and women standing there in Hindi "Tell me what happened." All the people addressed had sullen faces and not even one raised their palms in greeting. Neither did they say anything. They just looked at her with sullen impassive faces. The PM was a bit nonplussed. She went further and again asked people at the next door- "What happened here. Tell me." She was greeted by the same sullen faces and silence. No traditional *namaskar*. Mrs. Gandhi was taken aback. She asked me what was wrong, why are they not replying. My answer, that the people were angry, was not very helpful in the circumstances. She turned and went forward and again asked the next group- "What happened here tell me." There was again, the same stony silence and sullen looks. By this time I realised that the refugees had decided that they would not talk to the Prime Minister. Mrs. Gandhi also probably realised this, for now she walked till the end of the verandah, without asking anyone any questions. She turned and quickly covered the next two verandahs of the hollow square. Then she got down and without looking back walked towards the car. She was red in the face. Till now the only sound was the shuffling of feet. As she neared the car, suddenly there was a shrill cry- "Jai Aie Ahom." I wheeled around, reaching for my carbine. A young girl was standing ahead of the others, her hand raised and her fist rolled. Mrs. Gandhi looked unnerved, but she turned and quickly got into the car. We drove off quickly, my mind raced back to Kanaklata Baruah, who had raised her hand carrying the National Flag in 1942 in defiance of the Police and was shot. Mrs. Gandhi got into the helicopter as soon as we returned to the helipad and a few minutes later was air borne heading for Nellie where a worse disaster had taken place.

After seeing off the Prime Minister, I followed up the issue by sending a team to investigate the matter in the Boro areas. The team brought back two Boro boys from Kokrajhar who admitted that they had been briefed by their leaders to move to the Gohpur Reserve Forest and instigate the Boros there to attack the Caste Hindu Assamese of Gohpur as their volunteers had burnt the wooden bridges to the Gohpur Reserve Forest areas and had intimidated the Boros from voting in the election. Two days later the case was transferred to the CID and the two arrested boys were taken by CID officers in their custody. Later I learnt that the case was closed!

The rioting in Nellie was the worst incident that happened in the history of Assam. Nellie was a tribal belt inhabited by one of the smaller Mongoloid settlers of Assam called the Lalungs or Tiwa. There were also some Koch Rajbongshis in the area. The Tiwa are among the more timid of the Mongoloid settlers of Assam. The Tiwa are found in the western belt of the old Nowgong district. This was one of the districts that the British East India Company had selected for settling Bengali Muslim peasants from East Bengal in the beginning of the 20th century. They mainly settled in the Police Station areas of Hojai, Morajhar, Rupohi, Dhing, Lahorighat, and Morigaon in vacant lands. Today they are the majority population in all these Police Stations. The Tiwa are found mainly in Morigaon Police Station area. They are cultivators, growing paddy and related crops like maize and sometimes sesame in winter. Being easygoing, they were no match to the aggressive ways of the Bengali Muslim settlers, who were much more hardworking and continually bought out the Tiwa from their lands. A number of young Tiwa girls were also enticed by Bengali Muslim boys, kidnapped and married by them. The Tiwas were originally animist but had gradually been absorbed into Hinduism. When the Foreigners issue was taken up by the AASU, the Tiwas joined in the agitation. They had genuine grievances that the District authorities had not redressed, of Bengali Muslim settlers being settled on their land that was part of a Tribal Block. A peculiar combination of circumstances led to the incidents in Nellie.

Nellie is near Jagiroad, through which the North East Frontier Railway line runs, going south to Lumding junction via, Khampur, Jamunamukh, Hojai, and Lanka. All these areas were completely taken over by immigrant Bengali Muslims after they were first settled in Nowgong district in the early 20th century. The towns of Jamunamukh and Khampur were the watershed between the Assamese caste Hindu people and the Bengali Muslim immigrants. During the Foreigners agitation, the Assamese caste Hindus were very vociferous and the CRPF deployed in the area became quite unpopular with them because they took strict action against them. As the agitation peaked when the elections were announced, the tension along the fault lines between the Assamese caste Hindu villages and the Bengali Muslim immigrant villages began mounting. There was continual shouting of Allah-u-Akbar from the Bengali Muslim villages at night. It was at this time, after polling was completed in this area that orders were received by the Commandant of the CRPF battalion deployed on the fault lines between the Assamese and Bengali Muslim villages to withdraw and move to the North bank for polling duties there. The Commandant of the CRPF battalion deployed here was my friend and we had worked together earlier. He narrated the sequence of events to me later. He said that he was surprised, when he found after receiving orders to move to the north bank, that the Assamese boys, men and women who had been regularly abusing them during the Foreigners agitation besieged them in their camps and begged them not to go. They told them that if they move out the Bengali Muslim villagers would attack them and set fire to their houses, because they had threatened them not to vote in the elections. The Platoon commanders told the Commandant that the Assamese villagers from being abusive had turned round and were literally begging them not to leave saying that if they left, the Bengali Muslim villagers would definitely attack them. The Commandant then sent a signal to the Deputy Commissioner Nowgong informing him of the changed situation and advised that the battalion should stay on at their posts between the fault line of the Assamese villages and the Bengali Muslim villages. To this he received orders to move immediately. Visiting all the locations the Commandant felt that there would be a communal clash if the CRPF left their location and again advised the Dy. Commissioner that his company's be allowed to stay. By this time it was too late to move to the North Bank and the battalion was allowed to stay. There was a connection with these developments and Nellie that will be seen now.

The location of the Nellie incident was a Public Grazing Reserve-Alichinga Grazing Reserve that had been opened for settlement of Bengali Muslim immigrants in 1943 by the then Muslim League Government. In 1983, there were 9 villages in this Grazing Reserve and all were targeted. The Tiwas had resented the conversion of their grazing Reserve for settling Bengali Muslim immigrants. Their cultivable land had also been designated as Tribal Blocks in 1946. These were however later again occupied by the Bengali Muslim settlers. As per the census of 1971, 39.79 per cent of the population of the area was of Bengali immigrant Muslims. In 2001 the Bengali immigrant Muslims exceeded by more than half, the population of the indigenous people. From interviews conducted after the massacre at Nellie it was found that there were a number of kidnappings of tribal girls by Bengali Muslims and of Bengali Muslims settlers forcibly cultivating lands of the Tiwa tribal and also of some cows of the Tiwas being stolen. On 13 February, the village elders of the Tiwa and Koch villages held a meeting. On 13 February, some Bihari villages in the area were attacked by the Bengali Muslims. On 13 February, the Tiwa and Koch leaders had a meeting again and decided to attack the immigrant Bengali Muslim settlers. The hill Tiwa people had a good relationship with the plains Tiwa people. They were told by the plains Tiwa people of the attack. The hill Tiwas agreed to join in the attack and came down armed with country made 12 bore guns, bows and arrows on the night before the attack. First they went to a village Borbori across the National Highway and attacked the village killing about 300 people. After that they recrossed the National Highway and attacked Muladhari village. Here the attack started at about 1100 hours and continued till 1500 hours. It is clear that the village elders had a leading role in organising the attacks. There was no religious basis for the attacks. It was targeted against immigrants from Bangladesh who had come and occupied their lands.[13] It is very clear that here again it was land and not religion that was the cause of the massacre.

One fact that has not been researched in this issue is that among the 1658 dead bodies found after the massacre, there were very few bodies of young men. All the bodies were of old men, women and children. Where were the Bengali immigrant Muslim young men of Nellie area? It is here that the connection between the incidents at Jamunamukh and Khampur are relevant. All the Bengali immigrant Muslim young men of Nellie area had gone to Jamunamukh and Khampur and were living in the villages of the Bengali immigrant Muslim settlers across the fault lines between them and the Assamese caste Hindus. They were waiting to attack the Assamese villages after the CRPF left. Their plans went awry, when the CRPF did not

---

[13] Agency of rioters, The Nellie Massacre, Makiko Kimura in *Beyond Counter insurgency*. Ed. Sanjib Baruah, Oxford University Press, 2008.

leave. Meanwhile the attack on the Bengali immigrant Muslim villages in Nellie was being planned and was executed on 14 February 1983. No one has researched this issue though it is well known to the Police officers and men who were posted at Jagi Road, Jamunamukh and Khampur and to the CRPF battalion that was deployed between the fault lines of the Assamese caste Hindus and the immigrant Bengali Muslim people of the Jamunamukh and Khampur areas. There are some unanswered questions here. Did the Tiwa and Rajbongshi Koch villagers know that the young men of the Bengali immigrant Muslim villages had gone south to attack the Assamese villagers of Jamunamukh and Khampur? Did they also know that the CRPF were not withdrawing from that area. The Police officers who operated in Jagi Road, Jamunamukh and Khampur probably know of this but they have not spoken out so far.

This then is the story of the brutal election of February 1983, an election that was illegal and unconstitutional that was thrust on the Assamese people by a central political party that was only blindly interested in coming to power and creating a vote bank for future elections and whose leadership had no statesmen who could see fifty years into the future.

The Congress was declared elected, though polling had been countermanded in most of the Assamese constituencies. Also, in almost all the mixed constituencies, polling booths were not set up as per the election laws. In many polling booths the results were declared with only a few hundred votes polled, though the electorate was more than a lakh. The election was obviously illegal. Yet the Chief Electoral Officer declared the results of all these partial polls. Immediately after the polling was over and the Assamese people lifted the unofficial curfew there was an attempt in many Police Station areas by Assamese youth to try and forcibly snatch the 12 bore guns of people. This became so serious that the district administration had to ask all citizens to deposit their licensed arms.

You have seen that a left wing extreme group had been set up after the CPI ML extended their activities to Assam from West Bengal. This group turned chauvinist from its left wing origins due to the Foreigners Agitation and formed the Assam Peoples Liberation Army (APLA). But a more serious development had taken place. In 1979 a group of people from Upper Assam, led by two elders, Bhim Kanta Bargohain from Saikhowa *Ghat*, and Badreswar Bargohain from Sonari, both Ahoms had proposed organising a group they called the *Samjyukta Mukti Bahini Ahomor* or United Liberation Front of Assam (ULFA) after discussions about the situation in Assam, mainly of the organised immigration of Bengali Muslims from Bangladesh. This small group of Morans and Ahoms from Upper Assam met for a picnic on 4 July 1979 in *Rangghar* a stadium built by the Ahoms at Simalguri, and decided to raise this armed group and fight for the liberation of Assam from India. This remained dormant for four years. It was the brutal election of February 1983 that galvanized the group to take to arms. Soon after a small group left for Dimapur where the newly formed Nationalist Socialist Council of Nagaland (NSCN) was based and asked for help. Thuingalen Muivah and Isaac Swu, the leaders of the NSCN warmly welcomed the group and advised them on the formation of an insurgent group. They suggested that the ULFA should have a Civil Wing and an Armed Wing. They had already contacted the Kachin Independent Organisation in Burma to train the NSCN cadres. By 1985, the first cadres of the ULFA were on their way to Kachin for training.

Meanwhile the party in power had a *coup-de-grace* for Assam. They amended the Foreigners Act of 1946 making it applicable for all states in India except Assam and enacted a fresh act called the Illegal Immigrants Determination by Tribunal Act applicable exclusively for Assam State only. This act stipulated that all cases of suspected foreign nationals must be referred to a Tribunal for detection and deportation. It also stipulated that under this act it is for the prosecution to produce evidence that the suspect is a foreigner! In acts concerning detection of foreigners in all countries in the world it is for the suspect to produce evidence that he is a national of that country. To add insult to injury the considerate party in power in Delhi stated that this new act was being notified in Assam to make the process of detection of foreigners easy! Obviously the act was to make the detection of foreigners almost totally impossible. The IMDT Act was clearly illegal and unconstitutional and it was imposed on the Assamese people deliberately to punish them for daring to oppose the Party in power in Delhi. A leading MP from Assam immediately filed a public interest litigation in the Supreme Court of India. Regrettably, the Supreme Court took 22 years to dispose of this petition calling it illegal and unconstitutional! The perfidy of the party that legislated this illegal and unconstitutional act can be seen by the way they behaved. They were in power in 2005 when this act was struck down by the Supreme Court. Assam was going for Assembly polls in 2005. To safeguard their votes from their vote bank of illegally settled immigrant Bengali Muslims in Assam, the party in power amended the Foreigners Tribunal Order under the Foreigners Act. The amendment annulled the original Foreigners Tribunal Order that was applicable for the whole country and introduced two Orders, one for Assam only and one for the rest of the country. The original Foreigners Order under the Foreigners Act had stipulated that a State *may* appoint a tribunal for considering cases under the Foreigners Act. The amended order meant only for Assam stated that the State *shall* appoint a Tribunal for all cases under the Foreigners Act, while the Tribunal Order for the rest of the country stipulated that they *may* appoint a tribunal for cases under the Foreigners Act. What could be a more unholy act than this? Assam was being punished for not silently bearing the burden of the immigrant Bengali Muslim vote bank. The same MP, who had filed the earlier public interest litigation, again filed another one before the Supreme Court. This time the Supreme Court heard the case expeditiously and struck down this amendment of the Foreigners Order quickly stating that it was illegal and unconstitutional.

The United Liberation Front of Assam

The fact that the ULFA was born in 1979 is not correct. It is true that the concept and idea was discussed on 4 July 1979 in a picnic that some of the leaders of the Organisation had in the Rangghar near Nazira. I had interrogated a number of front line leaders of ULFA during my tenure as Inspector General Operations in Assam between end 1990 and early 1993.

All of them confirmed my view. The Indian Intelligence agencies and the Central Government however continued with the fiction that the ULFA was born in July 1979. It was the horrifying election that was forced on the Assamese population and the resultant blood bath in February 1983 that triggered off the creation of ULFA.

In 1983 the Congress formed the Government after the fraudulent election. In 1984 Mrs. Gandhi was killed. When Rajiv Gandhi became the Prime Minister he was guided by a group of advisors. The talks with the AASU and the other groups were resumed. The Prime Minister's advisors probably put across the idea to the Prime Minister that the AASU should be persuaded to accept the illegal cut off year of 25 March 1971, if the Congress Government were directed to step down on the presumption that the election of 1983 was not really a legal election and fresh elections could be called for after this. Then the AASU and the other groups could form a new party and stand for election. The AASU leaders fell for this bait! They forgot that 25 March 1971 had no legal basis for being made a cut off year. They forgot that they had steadfastly refused to change the cut off year 1950 that was enshrined in section 6 of the Indian Citizenship Act through 5 years of agitation. Obviously they were attracted by the thought of coming to power that made them agree at last. The Assam accord was then signed after the AASU office bearers agreed to 25 March 1971 as the cut off year for detection of illegal immigrants from Bangladesh. The ink had not dried on this agreement made in 1985, when the Home Ministry promptly submitted papers to Parliament to amend section 6 of the Indian Citizenship Act. Section 6 A, the amendment stated that the new date for seeking citizenship as Indians was now 25 March 1971! The leaders of such a historic and brutal agitation tamely succumbed to the temptation of money and power.

There is one other very pertinent point. How can an agreement signed between a student body-the All Assam Students Union be the basis for changing the cutoff date enshrined in the Indian Citizenship Act? It is not only the state of Assam that is affected. The whole of India is affected by this change of the cutoff date. Patently, this was an illegal action by the then Government and they had no legal basis to amend the Indian Citizenship Act.

In the two years that the Congress ruled from February 1983, there was no indication of the ULFA. It was in 1985 that the NSCN was established. It was in 1985 that the ULFA leadership went to Dimapur and contacted the NSCN leaders and a link was established. When the Government of India signed an agreement with the Naga National Council in 1975, a section was in China undergoing training. This section was led by Thuingaleng Muivah, a Thangkhul Naga from Ukhrul in Manipur and Isaac Swu, a Sema from the Sema area of Naga Hills. Both had studied in the Union Christian College in Umiam in Meghalaya, a Baptist college with links to the Baptist church in the United States. Isaac Swu was a very devout Baptist Christian. Angami Zapu Phizo the architect of the Naga insurgency had taken the Underground Naga army to East Pakistan in 1960 and the Pakistan Army had helped the rebels, armed them and trained them. The passage to East Pakistan was by crossing the border Sub Division of Paren in Naga Hills, entering the North Cachar Hills, traversing it and crossing the short plains section into the forested Jaintia Hills and then into Sylhet district across the Jaintia Hills border. The Indian Army that was by then deployed in the Naga Hills got a good taste of guerrilla warfare from the well trained and very well motivated Nagas. Subsequently the Naga Underground decided to approach China for help and a group set out crossing the Naga Hills border into Burma. Across the border in Burma lived the Hemi Nagas, who were then animist. The Burmese Government had been taken over by the Burmese Army in 1968 and they were fighting a running battle with the groups in the hills surrounding the plains of that country. To the east none of the different Mongoloid groups like the Kachin, Wa, Karen, Shan, were happy with the Burmese Army controlling the Central Government. These groups were fairly advanced. The Nagas who lived on the eastern borders of India opposite Naga Hills and Manipur were still very backward. The Burmese Government sent annual expeditions in the winter to control them, but left them alone in the summer when it rained from March to September. The Burmese Nagas welcomed the Indian Nagas, who after establishing a base there moved further north and east and befriended the Kachins, who for a price led them across the border to China. Initially the Chinese refused help but later relented and trained and equipped them. The first Naga group came back to Naga Hills, with Chinese arms and accessories after paying the Kachins in the early sixties. In 1975 when a section of the Naga National Council was won over by the Indian Government, Thuingaleng Muivah and Isaac Swu were just returning from China. They were furious with the leaders of the NNC who had signed the accord. They tried to persuade the NNC to annul the accord and they kept trying for five years. In 1980, fed up with the NNC, Muivah and Swu formed the National Socialist Council of Nagaland (NSCN) along with S.S. Kaphlang a Hemi Naga from Burma.

It was in 1985 after the brutal election that the ULFA approached the NSCN in Dimapur and were warmly welcomed by Muivah and Swu. It took some time for the arrangements to be made with the Kachins to train the NSCN and ULFA cadres. The first groups began their trek from Kanubari tea estate in Sonari from where a track led up between the border of the Naga Hills and Khonsa district of Arunachal Pradesh, wild, hilly and thickly forested country. To the best of my knowledge, the Assam Government got no clue of the organising of ULFA into civil and military wings and the recruitment of its cadres from the interior villages. I was posted in Tezpur till end 1893 after the elections of February 1983. During this period, the AASU continued its agitations.

Very little was heard of the ULFA during the remaining period of the Congress government in Assam till 1985. The Group who went to meet the NSCN in Dimapur included Paresh Baruah, the self styled Commander in Chief, Golap Baruah the General Secretary, both from Jheraigaon near Tinsukhia, Aurobindo Rajkonwar and Pradeep Gogoi both from Lakwa village near Sibsagar, the Chairman and Vice Chairman of ULFA. The first group of cadres crossed into Khonsa district of Arunachal Pradesh through Kanubari Tea Estate near Sonari, trekked along the border of Khonsa district and Nagaland to the trijunction of Arunachal Pradesh, Nagaland and Burma at Longwa and crossed into Burma. From here there was again a long trek to the Head Quarters of the NSCN in Burma. They were given a very warm welcome from the NSCN cadres. The Peoples Liberation Army (PLA) Manipur were also there. The March to the Kachin camp was also arduous and took many days. The Kachins are a battle hardened group who fought the Japanese tenaciously for the British. When the British Army was forced to retreat before the Japanese in 1943, the Kachin soldiers were given advance pay of several months and left behind to organise a resistance for the British. They played a significant role behind the enemy lines in the British fight back. The Kachins were also known for their cruelty. I had interrogated a number of Kachin trained ULFA boys. Physically they were better than any of the Assam Police Battalion personnel. The Kachins were known to tie up a turncoat and kill him slowly by getting all the cadres in that group to inflict one knife cut on the victim. One of the ULFA cadres who had been won over by us was found out by their group commander. He was tied to a tree and both his hands were cut off. He was left to die, the stumps of both arms spouting blood. Luckily for him, a Police party on patrol chanced to reach the place and rescued him and saved his life.

It was only when the Ahom Gana Parishad won the elections and formed a Government that the ULFA really began operating. Their first task was to collect money, for the Kachins charged them heavily for training and for supplying weapons. The extortion net started operating only after the AGP government was established. The cadres of the ULFA were the same boys who had fought pitched battles with the Boros and the immigrant Bengali Muslims who wanted the elections to be held. For the purpose of conducting insurgent operations and extortion of money the State was divided into districts, with district commanders in charge. The homework for extortion was carefully worked out. The ULFA district commanders contacted the Chartered Accountants and Income Tax assessors and had all the information of each big Marwari businessman before he was called for making the demand! The Tea Garden managers were ideal targets for extortion as they were situated far away from towns' and therefore from Police Stations. The ONGC and Oil India were also good targets. With the Assam Gana Parishad in power, the Police were asked to look the other way, so the ULFA cadres had a free run. The result was that the ULFA were not blooded like other insurgent groups.

Knowing that the Government was behind them, they set up a base camp in a forest in Tinsukhia district called Lakhipather. This camp was tactically poorly sited. The forest was surrounded by rich paddy fields.

This meant that they could be easily surrounded. Lakhipather Reserve Forest was the military wing HQs of the ULFA for some years. When I joined as Inspector General Operations, I asked the Deputy Inspector Range Guwahati and the Superintendent of Police Tinsukhia why they had not encircled this base camp with the BSF or the CRPF. The reply was that the Government would not allow this.

The extorted money was reportedly carried to Bombay by one Rebati Phukan a close friend of Paresh Barua from Jheraigaon village. Both Paresh Barua and Rebati Phukan were known football players and the latter was a qualified football referee too. Rebati Phukan was known to deal in *Hawala* business, illegal trading in dollars and Middle East currency. The dollars were brought back to Assam and taken to Kachin for payment for weapons and cost of training. The Kachins drove a hard deal for both sales of weapons and cost of training.

The Naga National Council had managed to get some groups trained in China. After the cease fire, and when the NSCN was formed five years later, they again went to China for procuring weapons. This time the Chinese did not help. Paresh Baruah also went to China from Kachin trying to get support from them for the ULFA. He was not successful either.

On the eastern frontier of Burma, south of the Shans and the Was lived a very bright group called the Karens. They were closest to the British, when they ruled Burma and at the time of independence, they were promised by the Burmese leaders that they would get a measure of autonomy. There was bad blood between the Burmese and the Karens. When Burma became independent, the Burmese refused to give anything to the Karens. The Karens were the first to take to arms against the Burmese Government. Across the border from Karen country was the town of Changmai in Thailand. India's External Intelligence Agency had an office in Changmai. Operating from here Indian agents managed to influence Bransein, the President of the Kachin Independent Organisation (KIO) to withdraw support to the NSCN, ULFA and the PLA.[14] This was managed sometime in 1989-

---

[14] Information from interrogation reports of arrested ULFA cadres.

90. Both the NSCN and the ULFA were also refused help by the Chinese at about this time. It was at this time that the NSCN and the ULFA leaders decided to again approach Bangladesh for getting weapons and help in training their cadres as had been given to the old Naga underground.

The support given to the ULFA can also be gauged by the following episode. Hirak Jyoti Mahanta was the Vice Chief of the ULFA. He was a strapping young man of Guwahati full of bravado when he joined the ULFA. He was trained in Kachin and was made the deputy chief of ULFA's armed wing. He was one day returning from Jalukbari towards Guwahati in a rickshaw and was noticed by a Sub Inspector who was on patrolling duty below the Kamakhya hill. The Sub Inspector stopped the rickshaw and challenged the occupant, who instantly grappled with him and managed to fire his revolver at the Sub Inspector. The SI was slightly wounded but the SI did not let him go and ultimately with the help of a constable managed to hold Hirak Jyoti Mohanta, and disarm him. A police party took him to Guwahati Police Station, where he was quickly interrogated and forwarded to court and remanded to custody and sent to Guwahati jail. The ULFA leadership could come to know the whole matter only after Hirak Jyoti Mohanta was lodged in jail. This was a big blow to them and they tried their best to get him released. The ULFA leaders met the Chief Minister and the Home Minister in their houses and pressurized them to release Hirak Jyoti Mohanta. The Home Minister is reported to have suggested to the ULFA leaders that they may try and kidnap either the General Manager of the North East Frontier Railway at Maligaon, or the General Manager of the Guwahati Refinery at Noonmati and ask the Government to exchange Hirak Jyoti Mohanta in place of either of these two General Managers.[15] The ULFA leaders did exactly as suggested. They tried to kidnap the General Manager of the NF Railway, but could not due to good security by the Railway Protection Special Force, but succeeded with the GM of the Noonmati Oil Refinery. In exchange, Hirak Jyoti Mahanta was released from the Guwahati jail. He was picked up by the ULFA and whisked away straight to their Lakhipather camp.

---

[15] Information from interrogation of senior ULFA leaders captured later.

With the AGP Government looking the other way, the ULFA had a free run of the State of Assam. A pall of fear descended on the State. Since the State was behind the ULFA, the private sector could not fight back when the ULFA demanded money from them. A few who refused to pay were shot. One was an important Marwari trader from Guwahati. The other was an owner of several Tea Gardens in Assam. After this the Government of India arranged evacuation of a number of Tea Garden managers from Doom Dooma in Tinsukhia district. The saddest part of this chapter was the miserable state of the Assam Police. There were some officers who collaborated with the ULFA. There were others who fought to maintain the rule of law. A few gallant officers paid with their lives for standing up to the ULFA. The epicenter of ULFA's operations and movement was Dibrugarh and Tinsukhia districts. The first Superintendent of Police who took strong action against the ULFA was S.N.Mallick, a very brave and upright officer. The ULFA decided to assassinate him. He used to frequently visit Tinsukhia to meet friends. This was noted and the ULFA put a surveillance net on him. One evening he decided to go to Tinsukhia, but stayed back at the last moment. Mrs. Malick however went with her two small children. The ULFA team selected to assassinate the Superintendent of Police of Dibrugarh district was based in Jheraigaon village. The team was led by Chakra Gohain, the then arms controller of the ULFA. The hit team was positioned in a car that was parked on the dirt road leading from Jheraigaon village to the national highway from Dibrugarh to Tinsukhia. An ULFA surveillance party was also positioned near the house of the SP Dibrugarh. As soon as the Ambassador car of the SP left his residence, they informed that the SP had left. In those days, the cars of the Deputy Commissioner and SP were given the number plates ASL 1 and ASL 2. The surveillance party noted that the car with number plates ASL 2 had left. They did not notice that the SP had not gone in the car. At the point where the road from Jheraigaon joined the national highway an ULFA watcher was waiting. As soon as the SP's car crossed, he informed the hit team who were sitting in a car under a big *semul* tree on the road from Jheraigaon village to the national highway. It immediately started and drove to the road junction and began chasing the SP's car. The SP's driver was however driving at high speed and the ULFA hit car could not catch up. When the SP's car reached Panitolla, the hit car turned back as the road was now in a populated area. After a discussion in Jheraigaon, it was decided that they would try again in the evening as the SP always returned to Dibrugarh after his visit to Tinsukhia. In the evening before last light, Mrs. Mallick left Tinsukhia with her two small children. A gunman was sitting beside the driver. Watchers detailed informed the hit team at Jheraigaon that the SP had left. Again they went by the number plate ASL 2. They did not know that the SP had not even come to Tinsukhia. The hit team at Jheraigaon had positioned a watcher at the junction of the road from Jheraigaon and the national highway. As the SP's car went by, the watcher signaled with his torch that the SP's car had crossed. The hit team waiting under the semul tree on the Jheraigaon road immediately took off, reached the highway and chased the SP'car. They soon caught up and began overtaking it. As they drove level with the SP's car, the two ULFA cadres sitting on the left front and left rear seats fired bursts from their AK rifles into the front and rear seats of the SP's car. The driver, gunman in the front seats and Mrs. Mallick on the rear seat were instantly killed as the burst of AK fire hit them on their faces and heads. The two small children of the SP were sleeping on their mother's lap and miraculously survived. The SP's car sputtered to a stop on the side of the road. The hit car stopped and checked up and found that the SP was not there. They took the weapon of the gunman and returned to Jheraigaon.[16]

The second such case was a repetition of the modus-operandi of the first one, which only spoke about the sad lack of professionalism in improving the defences of the State Police. Daulat Singh Negi a brave upright officer was posted as SP Dibrugarh after a period when the SP had compromised the district Police Force by looking the other way on ULFA's operations in the district. After joining, Daulat Singh Negi immediately tightened the Police in the field and the ULFA found they were again hampered as happened during the tenure of S.N.Mallick. Daulat Singh had after recceeing the roads in the district made a plan of setting up check gates at strategic intervals.

[16] Information from interrogation reports of several ULFA cadres arrested.

With the setting up of the check gates the movement of ULFA with weapons was completely stopped. The ULFA decided to eliminate Daulat Singh Negi also. The team was headed by Saurabh Gogoi, the district commander of ULFA of Dibrugarh district, Ajay Kalita and Jewel Gogoi. Besides there were three other cadres, one to drive the Maruti 800 car that was to be the hit car and two to be on a scooter that was to work as the advance pilot. After briefing the team, Sourabh Gogoi took them on a trial run with a dummy acting as the SP's car. The plan was to position the pilot scooter with two unarmed ULFA cadres on the outskirts of Dibrugarh town on the Tinsukhia road. As the SP's car came up, the advance scooter was to drive well ahead of it and stop at the first check post, located a short distance beyond a dirt road branching off to Mohanbari. They would be let off quickly, as they had no weapons. Then they were to drive ahead and turn into the dirt road going to Rohumari. Here the advance scooter pilot was to turn into the Rohumari Mohanbari dirt road and drive well ahead of the SP's car, cross the Mohanbari check gate and wait well ahead for the SP to reach the Mohanbari check gate. As soon as the SP finished checking this post, the scooter advance pilot would drive to rejoin the Tinsukhia Dibrugarh road. Meanwhile, the hit car with Saurabh Gogoi on the left front seat, Ajay Kalita on the rear left seat, and Jewel Gogoi on the rear right seat would follow the SP's car and stop well behind when he stopped at the check post at the turning of the Mohanbari dirt road. Then they would drive a little ahead of the dirt road branching off to Mohanbari, reverse and wait for the SP to come after checking the gates at Rohumari, and Mohanbari. From where they were parked, they could see the advance pilot scooter coming from Mohanbari and joining the Tinsukhia Dibrugarh highway, the indication that the SP's car was following. The moment the SP's car came on to the highway, they would follow and overtake the SP's car and while overtaking, fire bursts and kill him, his guard and driver.

First, they placed the SP on surveillance. They already had personnel in the Police Station and Police Reserve who passed on all information of the movements of the SP and other marked officials. They placed a recently returned, Kachin trained boy, Ajay Kalita to watch the SP at his official residence. Opposite the SP's official residence were two or three small shops, of which one was a book shop. The young Kachin returned ULFA cadre was asked to sit in the small book shop opposite the SP's house and watch him. The SP had a daily morning routine. This was to start at about 1000 hours and drive on the Tinsukhia road. A little distance from Dibrugarh town was the first picquet that he had set up. He would check up this picquet, then proceed a short distance towards Tinsukhia and then turn left onto a dirt road towards a Police post- Rohumari. After checking the second barricade that he had put, he would then follow the dirt road to Mohanbari where the Dibrugarh airport was located. After checking the post at Mohanbari, he would then drive along the Mohanbari road to rejoin the Dibrugarh, Tinsukhia National Highway and then return to Dibrugarh. The team did two more dry runs to ensure that there would be no lapse on the D Day.

A few days after the ULFA cadre was posted to the book shop opposite his residence, he was asked by Saurabh Gogoi, the District Commander of the ULFA of Dibrugarh district to get ready for the important assignment. Meanwhile Ajay Kalita had been sitting at the book shop opposite the SP's residence and watching him. After watching him for some days, he began to feel some affinity with him. He decided to warn him and then drafted a small note to him saying that his life was in danger and he should be careful. He sent the note to him through a small boy and watched him deliver it to the SP's guard.

When the hit team met Saurabh Gogoi, he informed them that they would carry out the assignment the next day. The next morning, the team positioned themselves along the Tinsukhia road. Then the call came that the SP had left. As the SP's car left the town, the pilot scooter took off well ahead followed by the hit car. Sourabh Gogoi, Ajay Kalita, and Jewel Gogoi were carrying AK 47 rifles in the hit car. As rehearsed, the pilot scooter stopped well ahead of the first check post well beyond the point where the Mohanbari dirt road branched off. The SP's car stopped at the check post and Daulat Singh got out, checked the post register and talked to the policemen posted there. Then he got into his car and drove off to Rohumari out post where the second check gate had been made. The pilot scooter drove on and stopped after crossing the Mohanbari check gate and waited well ahead. The hit car meanwhile had gone a little beyond the point where the Mohanbari dirt road branched off from the Tinsukhia road. It then reversed and parked at the side now facing Dibrugarh and waited for the pilot scooter to come from Mohanbari side followed by the SP's car. The pilot scooter as rehearsed came on to the Dibrugarh road and drove ahead. The SP after checking the Rohumari and the Mohanbari check gates came on to the Dibrugarh road. The hit team had braced themselves as the pilot scooter came from the Mohanbari road. They followed the SP's car and then accelerated and began overtaking it. As they came level with it both Saurabh Gogoi and Ajay Kalita fired bursts into the front and rear windows of the SP's car. Daulat Singh Negi, his gunman and driver took the bullets on the side of their faces and heads causing instant death. The SP's car slewed to the right and hit a pile of stones on the side of the road and stopped. The hit car stopped at the left side. Saurabh asked Jewel Gogoi to go and collect the weapons and brief case of the SP and check if all were killed. As Jewel Gogoi opened the doors and took out the carbines of the SP and his gunman, Saurabh Gogoi was clearing his AK rifle. By mistake a round was left in the chamber. It went off as Saurabh cleared his rifle. Carelessly Saurabh cleared his rifle without pointing it upwards. The round went off and hit Jewel Gogoi, drilling a hole through his neck. Meanwhile a bus had come from Dibrugarh side and stopped seeing the SP's car and the dead persons inside. Saurabh Gogoi and Ajay Kalita picked up Jewel Gogoi after menacing the bus that had stopped. They drove straight to a Tea Garden nearby to show Jewel Gogoi to a doctor.[17]

I was posted as Inspector General Operations in November 1991 after the AGP government was dismissed. One of my first tasks was to supervise the investigation of the assassination of Daulat Singh Negi. I had reconstructed the incident in detail. My conclusion was the poor professional standard of the Police. The killing of Daulat Singh could have been easily avoided by having an escort car with trained personnel in it. Regrettably no one thought of this simple measure.

---

[17] Reconstructed from interrogation of Ajay Kalita who was arrested in 1992 and interrogated by the author.

The cumulative incidents of the murder of a leading Tea Garden official and the killing of the SP Dibrugarh led to the centre arranging the airlifting of several Tea Garden Managers from Doom Dooma without informing the State Government. The obvious next step was to dismiss the State Government for failing to maintain law and order. The Army was simultaneously called in to assist the State. The Army operation was called OP Bajrang. This operation commenced on 28 November 1991. I was posted in the Central Bureau of Investigation in Delhi at that time. I was called by the Home Secretary on 26 November 1992 and directed to go to Assam for posting as the Inspector General Operations. I joined in this post on 28 November 1992, the day the State Government was dismissed and Presidents rule imposed. For the next two and a half years I crisscrossed Assam, conducting operations, liaised with the Army, collected intelligence, supervised cases against ULFA cadres, interrogated important ULFA cadres and came to understand this insurgent organisation fairly well.

The first operation the Army did was to encircle Lakhipather, the base camp of the ULFA. Regrettably, they did not take the State Police into confidence as they did not trust them. Also, the information of the declaration of Presidents rule was leaked out presumably from the State Assembly. The leaders promptly left Lakhipather and scattered. The Army probably went by the map in posting cutoffs. Actually there were several dirt roads, leaving from the Lakhipather forest, some made after the last survey. When the encirclement was done, several dirt roads were not covered. I learnt from interrogations of arrested militants later, that about 20 odd ULFA cadres escaped. None of the first or second line cadres were arrested in the first flush of operations. The effect of the Army operations was however very successful as the ULFA scattered, many escaping to the interior villages.

The first major arrest was by the Army in Dibrugarh district. They managed to find Sourabh Gogoi, the district commander of the Dibrugarh unit of ULFA. He was handed over to the Police after he was arrested, but taken back by the Army after the Police took him in custody. During interrogation by the Army he disclosed a big sum of money of several lakhs that he had hidden. He led the Army and they recovered this amount. After this, his remand period was over and he went into judicial custody in the district jail at Dibrugarh. Shortly after, he managed to escape. This led to a reexamination of the jails and 4 special jails was set up in four districts located in the Army cantonments, guarded by CRPF and managed by the Jails department. This prevented further escapes.

Our first breakthrough after Army operations started came when the SP Guwahati T.P. Chakravarty's source gave a clue to the kidnapping of the General Manager of the Noonmati oil refinery, which was carried out by the ULFA during the AGP rule to get their deputy leader Hirak Jyoti Mohanta released. The source revealed that ULFA had a campus on a hill top further east from Noonmati near Chandrapur. The SP organised a raid on this hill top with the CRPF and two ULFA cadres were arrested. After Army operations had started, this area had not been looked into. The ULFA camp had been closed down and only two of their cadres were kept there. The two who were arrested readily admitted that the General Manager of the Refinery was taken to their camp after being kidnapped. They cooperated fully with the Police team and led them in reconstructing the kidnapping. After kidnapping the General Manager from his car at gun point as he left the Refinery, he was taken straight to this camp. From there he was taken towards Chandrapur, ferried in a small boat across the Kolong River and then on foot further and finally ferried in a boat across the Brahmaputra to North Guwahati. Here he was kept in the house of respectable Assamese people. As the negotiations for the release of Hirak Jyoti Mohanta were going on, he was shifted daily and kept in 14 houses of respectable people by rotation. This fact exploded a myth that was being built up in interested quarters that the Assamese people did not support the ULFA. Promptly the SP Guwahati requested that a Magistrate do a local verification of the confession of the ULFA cadre. This request was granted and the next day a Judicial Magistrate accompanied the ULFA cadre who led him from his base camp across to the point where he crossed the Kolong River, then to the point where they crossed the Brahmaputra to North Guwahati and then to the 14 houses where they had kept the kidnapped General Manager of the Refinery. All the 14 families admitted that the ULFA had kept the kidnapped man with them. The case was charge sheeted, but the General Manager refused to come to Guwahati to testify in the case and the accused had to be let off!

The wave of Army operations scattered the ULFA first and second line leaders. Information was scarce. The movement had the backing of the people. The pall of fear that had settled on the people of the state had however been lifted. Markets were running normally and shops in towns and cities remained open till late at night. Just as the operations were zeroing on the ULFA frontline cadres, a peculiar incident happened. Every morning we used to have a meeting of the Unified HQs at Guwahati attended by the Army, Para Military, Police and Intelligence officials. Our Principal Advisor a strong sycophant of the party in power in Delhi never attended this meeting. One morning just a few months after President's rule was imposed, he attended the meeting. After all the officers had their say, he suddenly spoke up and said that the Army should be immediately withdrawn. Everyone present was taken aback by this surprising announcement. I objected strongly and said that just when the Army was gaining momentum and the ULFA was disorganised and on the run it would be disastrous to withdraw the Army. Besides the BSF and CRPF were far less in number and could not fill up the space left by the Army's departure. The Principal Advisor was however adamant and said that the Army must withdraw and we should go for elections. None of us present could understand this including the Army, who had no inkling about their withdrawal. We dispersed, disheartened but could do nothing about this.

Shortly thereafter, the elections were announced. I was expecting a surge in insurgent activity, but was surprised, by complete inactivity by the ULFA. This was inexplicable. After the elections were announced, we were surprised by the creation of a new political party headed by Rebati Phukan, the same person from Jheraigaon, a cousin of Paresh Baruah, who was based in Bombay doing *Hawala* business and who had converted the extorted money of ULFA into dollars for payment to the KIO in Burma for weapons and training charges. My colleague T.P. Chakravarty was the Superintendent of Police of Kamrup district. He and I were working closely together. When he heard of this news, he met me and said that as soon as Rebati Phukan surfaced as the leader of the new political party, he would arrest him. I agreed immediately. Meanwhile our Director General of Police B.D.Kharakwal was suddenly changed and Prakash Singh, an officer of the Uttar Pradesh cadre was posted as the Director General of Police. I could guess that this was to cater for the elections soon to be held as B.D.Kharakwal was not amenable to Hiteshwar Saikia, the leader of the Congress party. Shortly after this, Prakash Singh called me and told me that the Principal Advisor had told him that Rebati Phukan, who had recently formed a new political party, should not be arrested. I immediately disagreed and said that Rebati Phukan was related to Paresh Barua and he was converting the extorted money of ULFA into dollars for payment to the KIO in Burma. Prakash Singh then told me that I should send the SP Guwahati to him. When T.P.Chakravarty met him, the DGP gave him the same orders. Since he was junior, he had to agree after remonstrating first. T.P.Chakravarty then came to me and told me that this direction was wrong. We knew that Hiteshwar Saikia was behind this but could not understand what the game was. We discussed and made a plan. We decided that Rebati Phukan would be arrested as part of several raids organised at night. The next night we put our operation into action. Several raids were conducted and in one of them Rebati Phukan was picked up. He was whisked away to a hideout and quickly interrogated. He sang quite fast and the whole mystery of the Army being suddenly recalled was solved. Late at night the DGP called me and said that the Principal Advisor was told by Hiteshwar Saikia, that Rebati Phukan had been arrested. I said that I had not agreed to the direction that he should not be picked up, but I shall find out from the SP. I checked up from the SP and then reported to the DGP that several people had been picked up and maybe Rebati Phukan was one of them. Since no one was found to be suspected, they were all released.

The quick interrogation of Rebati Phukan revealed that shortly before the morning meeting in which the Principal Advisor had abruptly announced about the withdrawal of the Army, Paresh Baruah was trapped in a an encirclement by the Army in Saraipung Reserve Forest on the Khonsa District border. He managed to send a message to Rebati Phukan in Jheraigaon, that he should immediately meet Hiteshwar Saikia and tell him to get the Army withdrawn immediately and in return, he would ensure that the ULFA would not interfere in the elections! And this is exactly what happened in the run up to the elections and during the actual elections too!

After we got this interesting piece of information, I checked up from all my contacts and found that the ULFA first and second line leaders had disappeared from the scene. They were reported to be in remote interior villages and the cadres were told to lie low till the elections were over. None of our sources in ULFA knew why this step was taken. With the announcement of the withdrawal of the Army, all their ongoing operations were closed, including the wide cordon that they had established in the Saraipung Reserve forest, thereby narrowly missing capturing Paresh Baruah!

The elections were peaceful, with not a single untoward incident by the ULFA cadres. The Congress won by a good margin. The date for the swearing in was fixed on 30 June 1991. Suddenly and without a whisper of information, the ULFA struck on 29 June, kidnapping 14 officials, 13 of the Assam and Central Government and a Russian mining engineer, who probably resisted and was killed when he tried to escape after being kidnapped. Neither the Central Intelligence Agencies nor the Special Branch of Assam Police had a clue to the simultaneous kidnapping across the State. It was a message from the ULFA chief that the truce between the ULFA and Hiteshwar Saikia was over. The ULFA chief had requested that the Army operations be called off and in return they would not disrupt the elections. He had kept his side of the bargain. Now that the elections were over he had struck. The operation of arranging and executing the kidnapping of 14 officials across the State was meticulously done. And all of the 14 kidnapped officials appeared to have vanished into thin air.

I was in Upper Assam along the Noa Dihing River conducting an operation, on the day when the kidnapping took place. When I returned to Guwahati, the next day, I had to meet the DGP as soon as I returned. He was angry and frustrated and told me that neither, the Special Branch, nor the Intelligence Bureau had a clue to the kidnapping. He asked me if I had good sources and if I could find out any clues of the kidnapped persons. I said that I would try my best to find clues of where the kidnapped persons were being kept. I spent the next few days in visiting all my contacts in a wide circumference around Guwahati, but I could not get a clue. The 14 kidnapped persons appeared to have simply vanished. I guessed that they were being shifted from house to house, like the General Manager of the Refinery had been shifted. I reported back to the increasingly frustrated DG, that I could not get a clue. My remark that the people were totally supporting the ULFA did not help improve the DG's feelings. After a few days, the ULFA's message was conveyed to the Chief Minister. They wanted about 20 odd ULFA second and third line cadres who had been arrested from December 1990 to May 1991 to be released.

The Chief Minister told the DGP that he should allow the cadres to be released on bail. The DGP refused and put in his papers. He could afford to do this as he was from another cadre. S.V.Subramaniam who was the DGP during the AGP government returned as the new DGP. All the second and third line cadres of the ULFA, who were in custody under the Terrorist and Disruptive Activities Act (TADA) were released on bail. All the 13 kidnapped persons were released by the ULFA. They did one dastardly act however. While an engineer of the ONGC who had been kidnapped was released near the Simalguri railway gate, he was shot by the ULFA as he was crossing the gate after being released. The reason for this unpredictable behavior could not be ascertained.

Shortly after he took over the Chief Minister called in the Army. This time the operation was named OP Rhino. Meanwhile I had taken out a leaf from Frank Kitson's The Bunch of Five, about his experiences in tackling insurgency in Malaya and Kenya. He had managed to convert a number of cadres after they were arrested to the Government side and use them as his eyes and ears. Whenever ULFA cadres were arrested in lower Assam districts, we brought them to an interrogation centre located at Kahalipara where 4 Assam Police Battalion was located. Here T.P. Chakravarty, the SP Guwahati and I used to interrogate the arrested cadres. Most of the boys were dropouts from school, but were quite committed and refused to be won over. We persisted and soon for every ten boys we interrogated one would agree to work for us. We recruited these boys as constables in the Special Branch. They were deployed in the roads of Guwahati town with a company of an Infantry battalion in civil dress, armed with only pistols. Whenever one of our boys noticed an ULFA cadre moving along the main road connecting North Guwahati with Khanapara at the east end of the city he would indicate it to the leader of the Army section with him, who would alert a cut off positioned well ahead, who would then suddenly cordon the road as they noticed the target approaching. In this way we were able to arrest a number of low level ULFA cadres and sometimes second level cadres too. In turn we were able to win over some of them.

It was this team of converted militants who gave us a surprising gift. One evening one of these boys met me after telling me that he had some urgent information. He told me that a group of ten ULFA cadres led by a second level leader from Kamrup had gone to Pakistan for training via Bangladesh. They had come back because of some differences with their leader Paresh Baruah who was in Dacca and they wanted to surrender. They had told them about me and T.P.Chakravarty and they wanted to meet us. At first, I suspected that this was some ruse. I did not believe that ULFA cadres could go to Pakistan for training. I knew that Angami Zapu Phizo had gone to East Pakistan in 1955 and they had trained and equipped the Naga Underground Army. I did not believe that the ULFA could have gone to Bangladesh for the same purpose, when the cause of their insurgency was the illegal migration of Bengali Muslims from Bangladesh. My contact was however adamant. I called in T.P. Chakravarty and we jointly talked to our contact. Finally we agreed to meet the group who was supposed to have gone to Pakistan and had returned after training.

The next evening the leader of the group who had gone to Bangladesh was sitting with us together with some of his Pakistan returned colleagues. He told us that, Paresh Baruah was told by the leader of the Kachin Independent Organisation sometime in 1990 that they could not train any more ULFA cadres. He had then gone to China and asked the Government there for help. They refused him. After this Paresh Baruah had a discussion with Kaphlang, the Hemi Naga leader who had formed the Nationalist Socialist Council of Nagaland (NSCN) along with Thuingaleng Muivah. They decided to send a group to Bangladesh asking for help.

When Bangladesh was created with India's help in December 1971, the Naga Underground leaders were arrested from Dacca by the Indian Army. The Mizo National Front managed to flee from Bangladesh to the Arakhans when they found that Pakistan was going to be defeated. It was only in 1977, when General Ziaur Rehman took control of Bangladesh and reestablished links with Pakistan that the MNF could go back to Bangladesh and reestablish camps in the Chittagong Hill Tracts. When the Naga National Council signed a peace treaty with the Government of India in 1975, Thuingaleng Muivah and Isaac Swu were returning from China via the Kachin area and Kaphlang's area in Northern Burma. They then tried to persuade the NNC to reverse their decision. Having failed in this they created the National Socialist Council of Nagaland (NSCN). Since then they had been training their cadres with Kaphlang or the KIO. When the KIO chief withdrew support to the NSCN and the ULFA, they decided to try and revive the Bangladesh connection.

The group of ULFA contacted the Directorate General of Forces Intelligence (DGFI) and with their help was taken to the Pakistan embassy where they met an ISI official. After discussions, the DGFI official made identity cards for them in Bangladeshi names and then got them Bangladeshi passports. They were kept in a safe house and then put on a Bangladesh Biman flight that took them to Karachi. There officials of the ISI were waiting, who took them on a Pakistan military plane to Peshawar, from where they were taken to a training camp of Gulbuddin Hekmatyar's *Hizb-e-Islami*. Here they were trained in weapons of different kinds-AK-47, RPD 7.62 LMG, grenades and preparing Improvised Explosive Devices (IED). After their training was over, they were returned to Dacca by the same route. Here they had a meeting with ISI and DGFI officials, in which Paresh Baruah was present as by that time several ULFA leaders had crossed over to Bangladesh. A few days after returning from Pakistan, they were summoned for a special meeting in which ISI and DGFI officials were present. They were briefed that they had to set off explosives in a big industry in Guwahati on their return. After the briefing, the Pakistan and Bangladesh officials left and Paresh Barua told them that the target was the Indian Oil Refinery at Noonmati. After Paresh Baruah left, the group discussed the task given to them and decided that they would not blow up their refinery in Noonmati. That night, knowing that Paresh Baruah would force them to do this job, they decided to run away. They slipped away from their safe house and managed to return to Guwahati and they now wanted to surrender.

After informing the DG of this development, I informed a friend of mine who was in India's external Intelligence agency about this transaction. At first he would not believe that ULFA had gone to Bangladesh or Pakistan, but when I narrated all that had been told to me, he immediately flew down to Guwahati and had a session with the group who had gone to Bangladesh and Pakistan. This officer had worked in Dacca and therefore could quickly cross-examine our new friends about their movements in that city. After a thorough briefing my friend confirmed the veracity of the facts narrated by the group. He also told me that the Chinese had refused to sell arms to both the NSCN and the ULFA, but they directed them to get in touch with the Khmer Rouge in Cambodia. The weapons brought by coastal steamers to Cox's Bazaar were purchased through black market dealers who got them from the Khmer Rouge.

Shortly after this, our group of converted militants gave us another good break. They noticed two ULFA cadres, one a first line and a second line cadre going on a scooter along the Guwahati Shillong road in the heart of Guwahati town. They alerted the stop who had been stationed ahead. When they tried to intercept the two as they drove up, the two ULFA cadres tried to swerve and drive away. A quick well aimed shot from a pistol hit the driver on his leg and the two crashed to the ground. The pillion rider was unhurt, while the driver had a bullet on his thigh. The two were picked up and I was informed. The injured ULFA cadre was taken to the Military hospital while the unhurt cadre was taken to our interrogation centre. Within half an hour I and T.P.Chakravarty were interrogating him. The subject was suspicious when he first saw me, but soon relaxed when I spoke to him in Assamese and was completely taken back when I put him at ease and spoke in friendly terms as an equal. By the end of the day, I had won his confidence. He and the group who had returned in a hurry from Bangladesh surrendered to the Government.

From further detailed interrogation we learnt that Paresh Baruah and the NSCN leaders Thuingaleng Muivah and Isaac Swu had also gone to Bangladesh and met the DGFI and the ISI officials. They had a meeting in the Sayeman hotel in Cox's Bazaar, where it was decided to get arms purchased from the illegal arms bazaar of Thailand, probably from the weapons surrendered by the Khmer Rouge from Cambodia who had recently surrendered, ferry them by coastal steamer to Cox's Bazaar and from there take them to Bandarban in the Chittagong Hill Tracts, where the NSCN was allowed to set up a transit camp, and then carry them to Nagaland via Burma.

Shortly after this we had another break. On a tip off from an Intelligence Agency, the Calcutta Police were informed that Golap Barua, the General Secretary of the ULFA was on a flight from Dimapur to Calcutta. The Calcutta Police followed him on arrival at Calcutta to the house of an Assamese boat builder and then arrested Golap Barua, the boat builder and his wife. T.P.Chakravarty and I went to Calcutta to take Golap Barua in custody. We had a long session of three days with Golap Barua in Calcutta. Golap Barua was an exceedingly cunning person and despite prolonged interrogation did not give any information that we did not already know. He was then taken to New Delhi and interrogated by personnel from the Central Intelligence agencies and then brought back to Guwahati. A senior Intelligence official from Delhi then came and met him in the Special jail where he was lodged. Later there was a conclave with the Chief Minister in which we were not associated. A select group of surrendered ULFA leaders were then taken to Delhi by an Intelligence Agency. I do not know what transpired there or who met them. Then I was called and told that it was decided that Golap Barua would be given a car and allowed to go and meet the ULFA leaders who were in Nowgong area. I immediately consulted a couple of senior ULFA leaders who had been arrested and discussed Golap Barua and the plan of allowing him to be set free so that he could consult the other ULFA leaders. The advice I got was clear. "Never trust him. He is an extremely cunning man. He will never let you know what he is thinking in his mind. He will never look you in the eye." Then to cap it, one of them told me – "Sir, Do not ever trust him. When he was born, a hundred jackals died in the forest!" This last was a typical piece of rustic Assamese humour. I immediately conveyed all this to the Director General of Police and told him to tell the Chief Minister that if he was set free, that was the last we were going to see of him.

Golap Barua was taken out from the special jail after giving him bail in a dozen cases and then given a Maruti car and allowed to go towards Nowgong. That was the last we saw of him. I do not know whether he talked to the Chief Minister or the senior official from the Central Intelligence Agency, but after three days, the Chief Minister told the DGP that Golap Barua had betrayed him and had sneaked across to Bangladesh. I was told to hurriedly go to Nowgong area and conduct a cordon search operation for the Council leaders of ULFA whom Golap Barua had reportedly met. There was no clue as to where the council leaders of ULFA had met. No Intelligence agency had any clue to this also. I went for a wild goose chase and came back without a sign of any of the top ULFA leaders not yet arrested. Very obviously they had all left long ago and scattered all over Assam! We also got no clue of the Maruti car that was given to Golap Barua. It had vanished into thin air!

A few weeks later, in early 1992 I got a call from Kiran Bedi the DIG of Police Mizoram, stating that a column of Nagas were marching along the Tiddim road in the Chin Hills of Burma located to the east of Mizoram. They had obviously come from Nagaland through Manipur and crossed into Burma across the south of the Manipur border in Churachandpur district. After the Mizo accord all Para Military forces had been withdrawn from the Mizoram border with Burma. The only post manned at the southern tip was Parva, held by the Border Security Force. Parva was a trijunction of the Chittagong Hill Tracts (CHT) to the west, Mizoram to the north, and Burma to the east. There were only an Assistant Sub Inspector with four or five constables in the posts on the Burma border; where earlier there were at least a company of Central Para Military Forces (CPMF). These undermanned posts reported that the NSCN troops were well armed and would cross into Mizoram and buy some chickens or pigs from the local villagers, camp for the night and push off the next morning. They were tracked all the way from Champai in the north east corner, a junction between Mizoram and Churachandpur district of Manipur right upto Parva.

When I got these signals I immediately realised that this was the final sequel to the discussions held in Sayeman hotel in Cox's bazaar, between the ULFA, NSCN and Pakistan ISI for procuring weapons from Thailand and bringing them to Cox's Bazaar and then carrying them overland to Nagaland by the NSCN. I informed the senior Intelligence Officer in Delhi immediately. Then we had a lucky break. A few days after the NSCN group had passed Parva, ten cadres of the NSCN, ran away from their camp, intending probably to try and return to Nagaland. They were chased by their leaders, but managed to reach Parva and surrender to the BSF. They were taken immediately to their base at Massimpur in Silchar and debriefed. They stated that they had set forth from their camp in Benin in Tamenglong in Manipur and had trekked south through Churachandpur district crossed into Burma on the Tiddim road axis and walked south skirting the eastern border of Mizoram ,then turned west and skirting Parva had reached a place called Bandarban in the CHT. Here the NSCN had made a transit camp. A few weeks later, the DIG Mizoram again reported that the big group of Nagas, who had skirted the eastern borders of Mizoram and gone into Bangladesh, were now returning and this time most of the Cadres were carrying two weapons each! This confirmed the information given by the ten boys of this group who had surrendered at the Parva post of the BSF. The DIG Mizoram again tracked the movements of this group, this time in reverse going towards Manipur. Regrettably despite this excellent job done by the Mizoram police, nothing was done by the Centre to intercept this group at the point where they would be entering India, or on their movement from the Manipur Burma border inland through Manipur and Nagaland.

A few months later, I had gone to Cachar district to verify information of the NSCN operating in that district, extorting money from the Tea Gardens in the low hills to the north of Cachar, and bordering North Cachar hills. I found it was true and also that the NSCN had even attempted robbing a bank in a small town to the east and north of Silchar. I had also arranged a meeting at Silchar between the Director General of Manipur and the DIG of Mizoram, Kiran Bedi. In the meeting she described vividly how she had tracked the big group of NSCN men going to Bangladesh and later returning from there with weapons.

The situation in Assam had meanwhile badly deteriorated. The group of ten ULFA cadres who had returned from Bangladesh, and several others who had been arrested all surrendered formally to the Chief Minister, who passed verbal orders to the DGP that in future all surrenders should be to the Chief Minister only! Shortly after, I heard that Saurabh Gogoi, the district Commander of the Dibrugarh district of ULFA and Chakra Gohain had surrendered to the Chief Minister. Saurabh Gogoi was the killer of Daulat Singh Negi, the SP of Dibrugarh district and Chakra Gohain was the killer of the wife of Mallick, the SP of Dibrugarh district. I was the Inspector General Operations and when I heard this I strongly objected to this arrangement. I told the Director General of Police that they should be handed over to us for interrogation and recovery of the weapons used in the killing, so that they could be matched against the empties recovered. The DG informed me that the Chief Minister had allowed them to keep their weapons and they would not be handed over to the Police for interrogation! This was a blatant case of obstructing the investigation of two heinous murder cases one of assassinating a Superintendent of Police and the other of the assassination of the wife of a Superintendent of Police. By this time the case of the assassination of Daulat Singh Negi had been handed over to the CBI. They did nothing to get the accused arrested.

Earlier in 1985 when the Sangram Parishad had formed the Ahom Gana Parishad and winning the elections had formed the Government, they had a problem to settle hundreds of volunteers of the All Assam Students Union (AASU), who found themselves at a loose end after their party, formed the Government. The AASU leaders had resettled these dozens of hangers on, in a coal mafia. They were given sales tax forms illegally by the Sales Tax department and they collected sales tax from all the trucks, carrying coal, as they transited through Assam from Meghalaya on their way to Bihar Uttar Pradesh and Delhi. This was illegal as they had already paid sales tax in Meghalaya. This group was taken over by the Congress when they won the elections of 1991, only now they were called a cooperative. The public at large knew them as the coal mafia. The ULFA cadres who surrendered to the Chief Minister were formed into "cooperatives." They were in actual practice an illegal body who were allowed to retain their weapons when they surrendered. Initially they were given loans for their "cooperative societies." After some time they were allowed to move around in their vehicles that they had stolen at gun point, and were again demanding and collecting money from the big business companies in the towns and cities of Assam. Since they were working under the patronage of the Chief Minister, the Police were asked to look the other way. They were soon given the title of Surrendered ULFA or SULFA sarcastically. From 1994 to 1996, this arrangement continued under the Congress government. In 1996, their old patrons the Assam Gana Parishad came back to power and the unholy system continued under the patronage of the Assam Gana Parishad. In 1998, I had visited Assam as the Director General of the BSF, to visit the BSF battalion that was deployed along the Bhutan border. When I came to Guwahati, I contacted a senior ULFA leader who had also "surrendered" to the Chief Minister in 1991 after he had been arrested. As the Inspector General Operations then, I had interrogated him extensively after he was arrested. I called him to the BSF mess at Patgaon, and asked him whether the SULFA were keeping their weapons and were collecting money from local businesses. He said that he would call a group of them to meet me at the BSF mess and I could talk to them myself. A short while later, a car drove upto the gate of the BSF mess at Patgaon and a boy got out and asked to see me. When informed I asked the BSF guard to disarm all the boys if they had weapons frisk them and then let them in. Five AK rifles with two magazines each were taken from them and they were let in. I met all of them and told them that they should be ashamed at what they were doing. They had no answer. They had the Chief Ministers patronage and the Police had no face to show the people. I told them to go back and stop this game. They went back sheepishly, but naturally continued the game! The insurgency had been reduced to a farce!

The worst phase of the Insurgency was yet to come. The SULFA were used to eliminate the members of the families of known ULFA insurgents. The SULFA were utilized to tell the close relations of leading ULFA cadres that they should force their relative who was a leading ULFA cadre to surrender, else they would be eliminated! Naturally none of the ULFA cadres who were threatened to surrender did so. In retaliation the SULFA cadres brutally shot dead innocent relatives of the ULFA cadres. There was a hue and cry in Assam but regrettably no one was punished for these cold blooded murders. The SULFA cadres concerned, the Police officers and the politicians who masterminded these dastardly acts went unpunished. This was a standing disgrace in the history of counterinsurgency, of policing and State politics.

The Bodo Insurgent Groups-the Boro Liberation Tiger Force and the Boro Security Force

At this stage I have to digress and narrate the rise of two new insurgent groups in Assam. This is inextricably linked with the ULFA; hence this has to be narrated at this juncture. In the Foreigners Agitation, the AASU had included a Youth leader of the Boros in the movement. The Boros were part of the original migrants from Northwestern China who came into the Brahmaputra valley several thousand years ago. They settled in the plains of lower Assam, though some of them also migrated into the Karbi Anglong Hills. They are mainly found in the western districts of Assam-Goalpara, Kamrup, and Darrang. The Koch-Rajbongshis and Rabha had also migrated either along with the Boros or had come before or after them. Of these, the Koch Rajbongshis also settled in North Bengal or Kamtapur. The Koch Rajbongshis are as much tribals as the Boros genetically. However over the years they have been assimilated into Hinduism and have also lost their original dialect. The Koch Rajbongshis of North Bengal speak Bengali, while the Koch Rajbongshis of Assam speak Assamese. Among the Boros, there is a group called the Saraniya Boros. They have taken *sharan* (shelter) with the Hindu Assamese. They are therefore considered as caste Hindus, but at the bottom of the Hindu caste scale. The main Boro tribals look down on these *Saraniya* Boros.

When the Foreigners agitation took place, the All Boro Students Union supported the AASU. This was because the main sufferers of lands occupied by the Bengali Muslim immigrants were the Boros. Many of their tribal blocks were occupied by the Bengali Muslim immigrants. The Boros were however not with the Assamese on other issues. They felt that the caste Hindu Assamese looked down on them as tribals. They refused to accept the Assamese alphabet for the Boro language, preferring the Devanagiri script. In the violent election that was forced on the Assamese people, the Boros did not oppose the election. The polling was good in the exclusive Boro constituencies. However when the Assam accord was signed and fresh elections were held, that the Assam Gana Parishad won, the Caste Hindu Assamese pulled a dirty trick on the Boros. They offered no post to the leading Boros who were elected including their charismatic young leader-Upen Boro. This upset them. After the AGP formed the Government, the ULFA had organised themselves and began to operate. Upen Boro was taken to the Political leaders in Delhi by a Congress leader, after they were sidelined. A plan was launched to get the Boros organised to start a movement against the Assamese. The All Boro Students Union (ABSU) was a product of this planning. The planning was taken further, when the ABSU was converted into the Boro Liberation Tiger Force (BLTF). Soon Assam Police picquets were being attacked. There was a wave of Improvised Explosive Devices (IED) blasts on Assam Police vehicles. The *Coup de Grace* was the demolition of a span of the Manas Bridge on the National Highway. I later talked to Army Engineers, when the BLTF blasted the Gourang Bridge on the Dhubri road. I was the Inspector General Operations and I was the first to reach the bridge after it was blasted. I had done training in Guerrilla warfare and been taught how to blow up big bridges. The Army Engineers told me that only a professionally trained group could have blown up these bridges. When the country's Intelligence Agencies play such mischief they forget that a good interrogation of a trained cadre will reveal where he received this specialized training. I had in the course of my work interrogated dozens of ULFA and BLTF cadres. It was during the interrogation of BLTF cadres that I could conclude that the country's Intelligence Agencies had trained the BLTF to counter the ULFA. This was a dirty war. The operations of the BLTF, led to several ambushes and land mine blasts on Assam Police vehicles in the Boro inhabited areas. Many Policemen died or were injured in these IED blasts.

In 1991 we heard of a new guerrilla group called the Boro Security Force. This was raised in Udalguri in 1986 and had set up camps across the border in Bhutan in 1990-91. The Bhutan border was Tea Garden country and the BdSF got its first extortion money by kidnapping the Assistant Manager of the Badlapara Tea Garden. Our enquiries revealed that this group was set up by Boros who had converted to Christianity. Their leader Ranjan Daimary had studied in Union Christian College in Barapani in Shillong. Very soon we heard that the ULFA had a meeting with the BdSF. In this meeting it was decided that the ULFA would join the BdSF in setting up camps in Bhutan. Starting with three camps in Bhutan opposite Udalguri Sub Division, it led to establishment of a number of camps both in Eastern Bhutan, but also in Western Bhutan opposite Kokrajhar area, and even opposite North Bengal. In fact in this area, the safe route into Bhutan was through North Bengal border with Bhutan. In a few years time, ULFA shifted their Council HQs and GHQ into Bhutan. The ULFA particularly had a very good relationship with the district officials, carrying out deals with them. This led to an official of the Defense Ministry of Bhutan signing an indent for purchase of AK rifles, RPD 7.62 Kalashnikovs, RPD 7.62 LMGs and 60 mm mortars from the Chinese Government arms factories for equipping the ULFA cadres.

Delivery of these weapons was made across the Bhutan border with China. At least two such consignments were received by ULFA.[18] A large number of Bhutan Government officials were kept quite happy by the ULFA and BdSF cadres, particularly at the district level. After senior officials in the Bhutan Government found out about the indents signed by officials of their Defense Ministry this practice was stopped.

In 1992, a bomb was placed in a suit case that was kept in a crowded line bus that was parked at its terminus near Paltan Bazaar Police post.

---

[18] From Interrogation reports of captured ULFA cadres.

Within minutes of the blast the Guwahati SP and I were at the spot. It was a bad case and more than 20 persons were badly injured. The case was solved quite fast, when sources revealed that a Boro doctor working in a Government dispensary near Paltan Bazaar had placed the suitcase with a bomb in the bus. He was picked up and this led to a "mechanic" who had come to Guwahati, bought the materials required to make the bomb and prepared the bomb in the house of a lady Boro member of the State Assembly. The Mechanic was arrested and the Member of the State Assembly questioned about the container for the IED. The case was solved. It is interesting here that the information about the Doctor being involved in this case came from political sources. This clearly indicated that the monster that had been created- the BLTF had gone out of control. The Politicians who were in the know realised that matters had gone out of hand and decided to pass on the information of the persons involved in the case to the Police.

Meanwhile the BdSF spread to the Kokrajhar area. They set up a number of camps across the border in Bhutan. The worst case that the Assam Police suffered was the looting of arms from the Battalion HQs armoury of an Assam Police Battalion in Saraikhola forest in Kokrajhar district in 1992. A group of BdSF militants came to the Battalion HQs at about midnight. The night sentry at the front gate of the Quarter Guard was a Boro who was a BdSF sympathiser. He quietly opened the gate of the Quarter Guard. The Guard commander and the rest of the constables were sleeping in one room of the Quarter Guard. The BdSF militants fired on the sleeping guard and injured all of them in one burst. One of the BdSF men went behind to silence the rear sentry. This sentry had his LMG fixed to fire to the rear. Hearing the firing at the front of the Quarter Guard he swiveled his LMG and waited for anyone to come behind. As soon as the lone BdSF militant came to the rear, this brave sentry fired a burst that killed the militant instantly. By this time the BdSF militants in the front had removed 160 odd Self Loading Rifles (SLRs) and 5 Light Machine Guns. When they saw that their man who had gone behind to kill the rear sentry was dead, they did not try to attack the rear sentry, but quietly retreated from the camp. There was a guard sleeping behind the Quarter Guard across a small nullah. They had an LMG with them. Regrettably, they did not fix their LMG and fire at the militants who were fleeing with 160 rifles and 5 LMGs. Instead of rousing the men and chasing the group, the unit simply informed the SP in Kokrajhar, who naturally replied that it was for the battalion to organise and chase the group. The whole episode was a blot on the unit and a shame for the Assam Police. By first light, the gang must have crossed into Bhutan.

There were interesting developments in the months that followed. The ULFA also opened several camps in Bhutan across the border of Kokrajhar district. The BdSF changed its name to the National Democratic Front of Boroland (NDFB). The ULFA shifted its Council and Armed wing HQs to Bhutan. In West Bengal, the Koch Rajbongshis, the counterpart of the Koch Rajbongshis of Assam had formed a group called the Kamptapur Liberation Front (KLF). They established a link with the ULFA, who gave them arms and training and also set up camps for them in Bhutan across the border from Kokrajhar district. The NDFB meanwhile was taken by the ULFA and the NSCN IM to Bangladesh and Ranjan Daimary established his base in Dacca. The NDFB also were helped by the Pakistan ISI and the Bangladesh DGFI to procure arms from Thailand and Burma. After the first land trek by 250 NSCN IM cadres from their camp in Benin, Tamenglong through Churachandpur, Tiddim, and the Chin Hills and into the CHT, in 1992, two more such treks were undertaken by the NSCN, ULFA and the NDFB in 1993 and 1994. Finally in 1995, when the group had gone into the CHT, the Indian Army in conjunction with the Burmese Army ambushed the combined group of the ULFA, NSCN IM and the NDFB east of Parva. In the ambush 58 cadres were killed and as many arms were captured. Unfortunately the day after the interception, an announcement was made in Delhi by the Indian Government giving an award to Aung San Suu Kyi, the head of the National League for Democracy in Burma, who had won an election, but was not allowed to form the Government. The Burmese Army promptly withdrew support in the middle of the mopping up operations and moved to their rear locations. The Indian Army had perforce to withdraw from Burma.

After the ambush on the combined group of the ULFA, NSCN IM and the NDFB in 1995 we learnt later that the group changed their route. The first indication of this came in 1999. In that year, there was an attack by the Mizo Zirlai Pawl (Mizo Students Union) on the Reangs (Brus) of Mizoram and several thousand of them fled to Tripura. A company of Assam Rifles was deployed in the Longai Valley, across the border of the CHT in the South and Tripura in the north to control this disturbance. One night a villager of the area came to the Assam Rifles camp and informed them that a number of tribals in camouflage uniform were camping for the night near the location of the Assam Rifles camp. The Officer in charge of the Assam Rifles detachment sent a detachment to investigate. They came upon an encampment of NSCN boys camping for the night. Surprised, the NSCN party fired on the Assam Rifles detachment. There was a firefight, in which six NSCN boys were killed and one injured. Seven weapons were recovered. The rest of the group managed to escape. I was Director General BSF and I got a copy of a sitrep (situation report) of the encounter and the capture of the weapons from an NSCN group in the Longai valley. I was keen to interrogate the NSCN cadre who was injured and therefore went to Agartala the next day. When I contacted the Brigadier of the Assam Rifles at Agartala, I learnt that the injured NSCN cadre had died. A team of NSCN personnel from Dimapur had come to Agartala and demanded that the weapons seized from the NSCN group who were ambushed by the Assam Rifles in the Longai valley be returned to them! They said that there was a ceasefire and their weapons could not be seized! The Assam Rifles Brigadier told me that they refused to hand over the weapons. What was interesting was what were the NSCN doing in the Longai valley, which is in Mizoram adjacent to the Mizoram-Chittagong Hill Tracts in Burma far away from Nagaland? It was only later in 2001 that the mystery was solved.

In 2001, I was posted as the Advisor to the Governor of Manipur during President's rule. In the winter of 2001-2002, a party of NSCN IM along with other groups allied to them was trekking to Bandarban in the CHT when a group of 8 to 10 NSCN IM cadres deserted their camp in Bandarban and ran back towards Parva. The NSCN IM cadres chased them and managed to kill two or three of them. Five NSCN IM boys managed to reach the BSF camp at Parva and surrendered. I got a copy of their interrogation reports. These reports stated that after Operation Golden Bird, the NSCN IM, ULFA and NDFB had abandoned the route from Bandarban via Parva, the Tiddim road, entering Manipur through Churachandpur and then going to Benin in Tamenglong. From Bandarban, instead of going east via Parva, the groups carrying weapons struck north to Kagrachari and then going further north, slipped between the BSF BOPs at Tuipuibari and Amchurimukh on the Mizoram-CHT border and entered the Longai valley. Going up the Longai valley, they hit the road coming from Kanthlang, the last BOP in Tripura and going to join the Aizawl-Silchar road. Here vehicles of the NSCN were waiting for them. The NSCN IM cadres with weapons were taken in these vehicles and driven via Silchar, Jiribam, Khonsang, Tamenglong to Benin, the NSCN IM camp. The five boys who had surrendered to the BSF at Parva stated that they had carried weapons by this route in the winter of 2000. I had earlier learnt through a good source in the NSCN IM that they had opened a camp in Aizawl. The vehicles for ferrying the weapons from the Longai valley near Kanthlang were based in the NSCN IM camp at Aizawl. In fact the camp was opened in Aizawl only to facilitate the movement of arms into India! I informed the Home Secretary of this new route and of the camp of the NSCN IM in Aizawl. Later when I asked an Intelligence Agency of India about the NSCN IM camp in Aizawl, they flatly denied that there was a camp of theirs in Aizawl! I discussed this with my good friend Subir Bhowmik, the BBC correspondent in Calcutta; he told me that he had visited the NSCN IM camp in Aizawl at their invitation! I did not understand what game the Intelligence Agency was playing.

The ULFA continued to keep the insurgency alive by bomb explosions. Extortion continued but not on the scale between 1985 to 1990. The SULFA continued its activities. In 1999, the Pakistanis managed to infiltrate troops of the Northern Light Infantry dressed as *Mujahideen* across some sections of the Line of Control in the Kargil Sector that were manned neither by the Pakistanis nor by us because of the difficult terrain. The intrusion was discovered in April 1999 and the Indian Army had to engage the enemy in a minor war. Since the terrain in the three subsectors-Mushko, Drass and

Batalik was very mountainous there were a number of casualties. When the war was on, Paresh Barua the SS Commander of the ULFA made a public statement that they supported the Pakistanis in this mini war. Young officers from Meghalaya, Nagaland and Assam had died in the Kargil heights. This announcement of the ULFA chief came when an emotional farewell was being given to a young Assamese captain who had sacrificed his life on the Kargil heights, fighting the invaders from Pakistan. This naturally had a very bad effect on the popularity of the ULFA among the Assamese.

For years, the Government of India was trying to convince the Government of Bhutan to take action against the camps of the ULFA and the NDFB inside Bhutan. The district officials in Bhutan were quite happy with the ULFA and the NDFB cadres. This was because of the money generated by these cadres in buying ration for themselves.

However after persistent persuasion, the Bhutan Government finally acted in December 2003. They attacked camps of the ULFA and NDFB inside Bhutan simultaneously. All the arms of the two groups were seized and the cadres were arrested and handed over to the Indian Army. It appeared that the two groups were surprised by the sudden action of the Bhutan Army. The leaders of the two insurgent groups never expected the Bhutan Government to attack their camps and they were taken by surprise. This was a big blow to the ULFA and the NDFB. They lost a very large number of their weapons.

This however did not deter them. Their supply from the arsenal of the Khmer Rouge was continuing to come. They now opened eight camps in Mymensingh district bordering Garo Hills district of Meghalaya. Drishti Rajkhowa was made the commander of the Mymensingh area. The biggest camp was located in Halughat quite close to the border of Garo Hills. The ULFA leaders continued to stay in Dacca, where they reportedly had twelve safe houses.

One of the founders of ULFA-Bhima Kanta Bargohain was arrested from a camp in Bhutan and handed over to the Indian Army. He was in jail in Guwahati till a few months ago. He was released after all the top office bearers of the ULFA were handed over to the Border Security Force in

2010 after Sheikh Hasina came to power in the 2008 elections. They were arrested and were in the Guwahati jail till they were released on bail in early 2011. Four top ULFA commanders-Robin Neog, Ashanta Bagh Phukan, Bening Rabha and Robin Handique were handed over by the Bhutan Army but have not been produced in court so far.

In between, the ULFA had sent hit teams who fired and killed innocent Bihari labour in several areas where they had settled temporarily. It is not clear why the ULFA did this, for Bihari labourers are no threat to the Assamese people. They occupy a very small niche in the agricultural landscape of Assam. It is possible that there was some direction from the handlers in Bangladesh to confuse the issue in Assam. Besides this the ULFA also set off several IEDs in different towns of Assam during the Republic day function. On one occasion, the IEDs set off in Dhemaji killed innocent children who had come for the parade.

The biggest reverse after the Bhutan disaster was the very successful operation of the Assam Police in getting two companies of the 28 battalion of ULFA based in Dibrugarh, and Lohit district of Arunachal Pradesh to surrender. They have not handed over their weapons so far. The personnel of these two companies are being kept in a safe house.

The NDFB never recovered after its Bhutan camps were attacked. Ranjan Daimary continued to camp in Bangladesh. The group in Udalguri however sued for peace. The Government of India agreed and placed them in designated camps. This was done several years ago. Recently there was a clash between Bodo groups and immigrant Muslims in the area. Government intervened and set up refugee camps for the people of both sides whose homes were burnt. Meanwhile the NDFB cadres who were kept in a designated camp elected a new leader. After some time Ranjan Daimary issued a statement claiming that he was still the leader. Soon after he made this statement, Sheikh Hasina came to power and had all the ULFA leaders returned to Assam. Ranjan Daimary continued to stay in Bangladesh. The NDFB group in Udalguri removed Ranjan Daimary as their leader. There was a series of bomb blasts in Kokrajhar, Guwahati and Maligaon in 2009 in which several people were killed and many badly

injured. It is learnt that Ranjan Daimary's group in Bangladesh had
masterminded these blasts. The Bangladesh Government handed over
Ranjan Daimary to the BSF on I May 2010 and he has been handed over to
the Assam Police. The Government of Bangladesh has kept its promise of
handing over all the wanted insurgents who had been hiding in their country.

Recently in November 2010, the NDFB group in Udalguri fired on
some Bihari traders in an area bordering Assam and Arunachal Pradesh.
These Bihari petty traders have been trading in this area for many decades.
They have not purchased lands but live in rented houses trading in petty
goods. They were by no means a threat to the Boro people there. They
have been made a target out of sheer frustration. It is the Bengali Muslim
farmers who are the threat to the Bodos. Dalgaon in Mangaldoi district is a
tribal block, but the whole area has been transferred to Bengali Muslim
immigrants by petty bureaucrats of the district administration. The Bodos
are not attacking the Bengali Muslim farmers as they fear retaliation by
them and the Government. Killing a few Bihari traders will not invite
retaliation by them. The Government of Assam should identify the Tribal
blocks that have been taken over by the Bengali Muslims and revert these
lands to the Tribals.

The ULFA got its first weapons from the Kachin Independent Army
(KIA). They had to pay for these in dollars. Many weapons sold to them by
the KIA were weapons captured from the Burmese Army. Later, the ULFA
were able to buy some Chinese weapons like the M 22, the equivalent of
the Russian AK 47 from the Kachins. Still later the KIA withdrew support
from the NSCN, PLA and the ULFA. This was probably on the instigation
of India's external Intelligence Agency based in Changmai. It was at this
junction that Paresh Barua decided to send a team to Bangladesh and request
the BD Army to help them. The Bangladesh Directorate General of Forces
Intelligence (DGFI) welcomed the ULFA delegation and brought in the
Pakistan ISI to take part in the discussions. By now the NSCN had also
joined the ULFA in Bangladesh. It was in a historic meeting held in Sayeman
hotel Cox's Bazaar that the deal to purchase weapons from the arms market
of Thailand was taken. Later the NSCN was also able to purchase arms

from the Chinese arms factories set up in the Yunnan area. This was probably done through the good offices of the Wa State Army, who probably had an understanding with the Chinese for purchase of arms. When I was posted as Advisor to the Governor of Manipur in 2001-02, I was able to get information about the clandestine arms deals of the Wa State Army and the Chinese Arms factories in the Kunming area. The ULFA had a base in Bangladesh opposite the Garo Hills border where they had kept a good number of arms.

The Chittagong Arms Haul

Paresh Baruah almost pulled off one of the biggest arms hauls at the Chittagong harbor in April 2004. He was supervising the unloading of a huge consignment of arms at the Chittagong Urea Fertilizer Limited jetty along with Anthony Shimray of the NSCN IM when the Bangladesh Police arrived and seized the weapons.[19] The weapons included T-56-1 Sub-Machine guns-690, 7.62mm T-56-2 SMGs-600, 40mm T-69 Rocket Launchers, 40mm Rockets-840, 9mm Semi Automatic Rifles- 400, Launching Grenades-2000, Hand Grenades-25,020, SMG and other Magazines-6392, SMG cartridges-7,00,000, 7.62 caliber Rifle ammunition-7,39,680, Cartridges of other weapons-4,00,000.[20] It is obvious that such a large consignment of weapons and ammunition could not be purchased second hand from the KIA or any other insurgent group. This must have been arranged from the ordnance factories in the Yunnan area.

The 2008 elections in Bangladesh and the reversal of policy in Bangladesh

The biggest blow to the ULFA was the reversal of policy by the Sheikh Hasina Government after the 2008 elections, when the Bangladesh National Party (BNP) and the Jamaat-e-Islami lost very badly. Sheikh Hasina won the election because the Army chief interfered and removed the partisan

---

[19] Troubled Periphery-Crisis of India's northeast. Subir Bhowmik. Sage. 2009.
[20] Ibid.

officials of the Interim Government and later guided the country in enumerating the electoral rolls and getting voter identity cards issued. After she won the elections, the BNP and the Jamaat tried to interfere in the revolt of the Bangladesh Rifles and destabilise Sheikh Hasina. After she got the revolt quelled, she transferred the head of the DGFI and appointed a neutral officer in that post. Then she ordered the new chief of the DGFI to withdraw the false identity cards and the passports issued to the ULFA leaders in Dacca and to tell them to return to India. Aurobindo Rajkhowa, the Chairman, Chitraben Hazarika, Sashadhar Choudhary and several other leaders were escorted to the Indian Border. Meanwhile the BDR had informed the BSF, who received these leaders and handed them to the Assam Police. All of them were arrested and were in jail, till recently, when they were released on bail to facilitate talks with them. Golap Barua is reportedly still in jail in Bangladesh. Paresh Barua probably saw the writing on the wall and had already left for Burma. He is reportedly living in Kachin area and sometimes moving to Kunming area. He probably has links with the Kachins and the Wa people and through them to the Chinese also. A number of Assamese ULFA cadres are also reportedly sheltering with the Kachins.

It appears that the long journey is nearing the end of the road for the ULFA. The cause for which they had the support of the Assamese people though is still very much there-the continued illegal migration of Bengali Muslims from Bangladesh. Though three companies of the 28 battalion of ULFA made a partial surrender, the remaining battalions in Lower Assam and Upper Assam are still in the field. Paresh Baruah camping in the Kachin area and sometimes reported to be moving in the area of Kunming is not likely to come in. The Chinese are likely to continue to help him indirectly. The talks that had been attempted by the Assamese Litterateur Madame Indira @ Mamoni Raisom Goswami a few years ago petered out inconclusively. The crucial issue for the Assamese people is the looming threat of Bengali Muslim migration from Bangladesh. Unless the illegal cutoff date of 25 March 1971 which was imposed on the Assamese people and the rest of India is struck down, there is not going to be any fruitful talks between the ULFA and any group in Assam. The Bangladeshi people who have been given citizenship on the basis of the illegal date of 25 March 1971 obviously cannot be sent back. They will have to be given work permits and allowed to stay. Their progeny will also be entitled only to work permits and will have to choose between staying or going back to Bangladesh. It is natural for the Assamese to want to keep the political leadership with them, the majority population of the State. If Bangladesh immigration be allowed to continue, the political leadership will go into the hands of the Bangladeshis. The cutoff date is therefore the crucial issue and unless the original date of 26 January 1950 as per section 6 of the Indian Citizenship Act is restored, there can be no peace in Assam. There is also one more significant point in the agreement signed by the Government of India and the All Assam Students Union in 1985 when the AASU student leaders agreed to accept 25 March 1971 as the cutoff date as proposed by the Government of India. The moot point is who is the AASU to accept this new cutoff date? What is the locus standi of a student body to accept an illegal cutoff date? Obviously the Government of India had no business to sign an agreement with a student body to foist an illegal cutoff date on the people of India! There is no doubt that changing the cutoff date from 1950 as per section 6 of the Indian Citizenship Act 1955 to 25 March 1971 was both immoral and illegal. There should be therefore no hesitation in annulling this amendment to the Indian Citizenship Act.

The Naga Insurgency

The Naga Insurgency is the oldest insurgency of independent India. It has its roots in the way the British handled the hill districts of Assam when they ruled India and also in the way the Government of India handled the Nagas in the years immediately preceding independence and also immediately after independence. A careful study of the origin and history of the Nagas will make this issue clear. The Nagas declared independence on 14 August 1947 and took to arms in the nineteen fifties. They fought bitterly and tenaciously till 1997, when they agreed to a ceasefire. Unfortunately the Government of India has dragged on the peace talks for more than 12 years. In the process the terms of the ceasefire have been seriously violated by the Nagas on several points, the main being the bringing in of arms from outside the country. Today from an estimated 2000 odd weapons, they have more than 7000 weapons of different calibers and ammunition for all these weapons.

History and origin of the Nagas

The Nagas like the other Mongoloid tribes who now inhabit the Northeast of India, migrated to this area several thousand years ago. They probably came from Northwest China and travelled across what is now Burma, crossing into the hills to the south of the Brahmaputra valley across the Patkai Range. There is no recorded history of this movement, since the languages of all the different tribes of the Nagas are dialects and none had a written script. Now however each of the tribes is recording the stories that were passed from father to son over the years and an indication is coming that they did migrate from China. One of the legends of the Mao and related tribes that live south of the Naga Hills in North Manipur is that just north of the Manipur Nagaland border in the area where dwell the Chakesang tribe there exists a sacred stone called *Khjezekenoma*. It is believed that all the Naga tribes migrating into Manipur and the Naga Hills came to this sacred place first and then moved on. Today the Naga tribes are in the Naga Hills, now Nagaland State, in Ukhrul, Senapati, Tamenglong and part of Chandel districts of Manipur. A few Rengma Naga villages are in Karbi Anglong district of Assam. There is a small percentage of Zemei Zeliangrong Nagas in North Cachar Hills district of Assam, less than 20 per cent of the population of that State. The Naga leadership also claim that there are Naga tribes living in Khonsa district of Arunachal across the eastern border of Nagaland State. This is not true as these tribes are not Nagas, but akin to the other tribes of Arunachal. There are Hemi Nagas in the northern part of Burma, bordering Ukhrul district of Manipur. This part of Burma is the most neglected part of that country.

The interesting feature of the Nagas is that all the forty odd different tribes speak dialects that are totally different from each other. The language of the Nagaland Assembly is Nagamese, a corrupted form of Assamese, mixed with English, Hindi and some Naga words. The main tribes of Nagaland are the Aos, Semas, Angamis, Lothas, Chakesang, Rengma, Khimungan, Pochuri, Sangtam, Yimchunger, Konyak, Phom, and Zeliangrong. This last tribe consists of three sub tribes, the Liangmei, Rongmei and the Zemei. In Manipur, the main Naga tribes are the Thangkhul in Ukhrul, the Mao, Poumei, Thengal and Maram in Senapati district, the Zeliangrong in Tamenglong and a number of small tribes like the Anal, Loyong, Monsong, Maring, Chote, Chiru and Tanao in Chandel district, whom both the Mizos and Nagas claim as their own.[1] The physique and appearance of the different Naga Tribes differ, their cultural practices also differ. Curiously, there never was a grouping of all Naga Tribes as one nationalistic group. For the majority of the tribes the entity was the village and each village was independent of the other. In general a Naga village was considered to be self sufficient and by and large maintained its sovereignty. Any interference, trespassing or encroachments by members of other villages in its territorial jurisdiction

---

[1] Zalengam, the Kuki Nation.P.S.Haokip Published by the Kuki National Organisation- 1 April 1998.

usually provoked inter village war where head hunting would follow. The ritual of most Naga tribes was the same for young boys attaining manhood. He had to bring the head of a man of any adjacent village. The head of a woman was prized as the women were always kept in the inner circle of the village.

The first organised group of people who came in touch with the Nagas was the Meiteis of Manipur. The Meiteis were also a Mongoloid people who migrated into Manipur earlier than the other groups. They settled in the fertile valley of Manipur and took to wet cultivation. They developed a fine civilization with a written script Meiteis Mattock for their language. Their kings ruled depending on their strength and extended their sway right upto the foot hills of Assam in the North and also into the Kebaw Valley in the South. All the Naga tribes who lived in their kingdom spoke Meitei. In 1835, the forest between the Dayang and the Dhansiri rivers was declared as the boundary between Manipur and Assam.[2] Further in 1835, the forest between the Dayang and Dhansiri rivers was again declared to be the boundary between Manipur and Assam.[3] Mackenzie writes in this book- "The Government was and is still inclined to regard the Manipuri as the defacto master of the hills." There are numerous references in the recorded history of Manipur of relations with the Naga tribes, of tributes being paid by Naga tribal chiefs. Nagas were regularly recruited in the army of the Manipuri kings. Many of the Naga tribes spoke Meitei, the language of the Meiteis. Many Naga villages had Manipuri names in addition to their own. Whenever a Manipuri visited a Naga village, he was treated as an honoured guest, at a time when a British subject could not venture into the interior without risk of being murdered. Many Naga villages paid annual tribute to the Manipuri kings.

When the Ahoms under Sukapha crossed the Patkai range and moved towards the Brahmaputra valley, they passed through Naga dominated areas as they came down the Naga Hills into the valley below. The Nagas fiercely

[2] My Experience in Manipur and Naga Hills. James Johnston. Sampson, Low, Marston and Company Ltd. London.1835.

[3] The Northeastern Frontier of Bengal. Alexander Mackenzie. 1884. Mittal Publications Delhi, 1929

resisted this movement. Later when the Ahoms settled down and established their capital near the Naga Hills border at Gargaon, there were several clashes with the Nagas over collection of salt from the salt licks which were all in the Naga Hills. According to Verrier Elwin the Ahom kings regarded the Nagas as their subjects and took taxes from them in the form of slaves and elephant tusks.[4]

The British Period

The Burmese invaded Assam and Manipur in 1822 and laid waste the plains of Upper Assam and Central Manipur. The British East India Company was requested for help, by the Ahom princes. The British sent their Army and defeated the Burmese who retreated to Burma. The treaty of Yandaboo was signed in 1826. After this the British established their rule over Upper Assam, the erstwhile kingdom of the Ahoms. After a while the British discovered that tea grew well in Upper Assam. They drafted suitable land regulations and soon a large number of tea gardens were set up on the low foothills both on the north as well as on the south bank of the Brahmaputra River. It was then, on the south bank, where the Tea Gardens had been set up on the low foothills of the Naga Hills that the British came into clashes with the Naga villages. The fiercely independent Naga villages objected to their village lands being encroached by the Tea Gardens and resisted fiercely. At first the British sent punitive expeditions against the concerned Naga villages, but this did not work and then they had to send stronger forces to subdue the fierce Nagas.

The route from Manipur to Assam passed through the Naga Hills. The British had gone upto Manipur from Jiribam on the Barak River in the Surma Valley. Soon they had to establish a land route from Manipur through the Naga Hills to Golaghat. In January 1832, Captains Jenkins and Pemberton led a group of 800 Manipuri troops from the Manipur Valley to a town called Mohandijua on the bank of the Jamuna River below the Naga foothills. Their march was strongly contested by two Naga tribes, the Angamis and

---

[4] Nagaland. Verrier Elwin. 1961. Shillong. Advisors Secretariat.

the Zeliang. After several such skirmishes the British decided to bring the Naga Hills directly under British control. After several expeditions, the British subdued the Nagas to some extent and established a district, the Naga Hills district with HQs at Samagooting (Chumukdima) in 1866. This HQ was later shifted to Kohima in 1878. The policy of the British in administering the Naga Hills district was one of defense and conciliation, not of coercion.[5] The British then promulgated a law that they felt was necessary for protecting the culture and way of life of the Nagas. This was the Inner Line Regulations. This was the first law promulgated in Assam under the authority conferred on the Government for summary legislation for backward tracts. Since it would not be correct to call Naga Hills district as backward, it was decided to call these areas "excluded" areas. Also, the Naga tribes were by a regulation of 1880 excluded from coming under such laws as may be complex, or in any way unsuitable to them. Unwittingly the germs of separation were laid with these regulations, though they were passed with the best of intentions and for the good of the Nagas.

The Nagas were exposed to the outside world for the first time during the First World War. About 2000 Nagas were recruited in the Pioneer Corps and served in France. When these troops returned, their exposure to the western world set them thinking and they felt that they would prefer to be under the British as their rights would be protected by them.

The British allowed their Protestant Missionaries to enter some of the Naga areas to set up their missions. One of the first missionaries to go into the Thangkhul areas in Ukhrul district of Manipur was John Pettigrew. By the beginning of the 19th century several Naga tribes had seen conversions. One of the tribes that remained animist was the Zeliangrong group consisting of the Liangmei, Rongmei, and the Zemei. Even today, the majority of this tribe is animist. In the beginning of the 19th century, a young Naga born in a Rongmei village called Kambiron in Tamenglong district became a mystic. His name was Jadonang and very soon he was preaching an animist religion.

---

[5] The Northeastern Frontier of Bengal. Alexander Mackenzie. 1884. Mittal Publications Delhi, 1929.

He gathered a small following. One of his ardent followers was a young Zeliang girl called Guidinliu. Jadonang's preaching soon took on some of the unfair practices of the British rule. He was implicated in a murder of four Meiteis traders and tried and hanged. Actually, he was not even present when the traders were murdered, but his preaching led to boycott of several orders of the British rulers. Jadonang's movement was carried on by Guidinliu. She was imprisoned by the British and she was released only after India became an independent country. When the Naga insurgency broke out Guidinliu reorganised her followers and bitterly opposed it even collecting weapons and fighting against the Naga Underground. Her services were recognised by the Indian Prime Minister, who began to address her as *Rani* Guidinliu. She was no Queen as there is no royalty in the Naga hierarchy. The name however stuck. To this day all her followers in the Zeliangrong tribe continue to be animists.

The Nagas, who returned from France after World War 1, organised a Naga Club in 1918, drawn from a number of Naga tribes. The most significant act of this club was the representation submitted by them to the Simon Commission, wherein they stated that they wished to be left out from the Reformed Scheme for India. They did not want the scheme to be extended into their areas, thereby again making it clear that they did not want the laws and practices of mainland India in the Naga Hills. The Government replied stating that the Naga Hills were declared excluded areas already.

At this stage the Governor of Assam Sir Robert Reid made a suggestion to the British Government that certainly gave ideas to the Naga leadership. Sir Robert Reid had been a Deputy Commissioner of the Naga Hills district. He suggested that all the tribes of the hill districts of Assam and the tribes in the hill areas of Burma should be clubbed together as a Trust Territory and kept under the British. He suggested this because he felt that the tribals of the hill areas in Assam and Burma were ethnically and culturally different from the plains people of India and Burma. The Nagas however opposed this idea.

A short while after this the Second World War broke out. The Japanese invaded Burma and pushed the British across the Patkai Range into Assam and also crossed into Manipur from both Ukhrul and Chandel. The British resisted stiffly and finally turned the tide in the Battle of Kohima and then pushed the Japanese back into Burma and finally counterattacked in Burma and pushed them south into Malaya. The Nagas were fully involved in the fighting and particularly in the Battle of Kohima. A few joined the Indian National Army and fought against the British. After the war, the Deputy Commissioner Kohima set up a Naga Hills District Tribal Council to repair the war damages. In April 1946, at its meeting in Wokha, the Nagas rechristened the District Council as the Naga National Council (NNC) and in June, the same year submitted a memorandum to the British Cabinet Mission who had come to prepare the ground for granting independence to India. The main points were as follows:-

- The Naga National Council stands for the solidarity of Naga tribes.

- The Council strongly protests against the grouping of Assam with Bengal.

- The Naga Hills should be constitutionally included in autonomous Assam, with local autonomy and due safeguard for the interest of the Nagas. The tribes were represented through a system of proportionate representation. At its inception the Council consisted of 29 members.

The Conflict with India

Jawaharlal Nehru, the then Congress President replied to this rejecting any independent status for the Nagas. In 1947, the NNC sent a memorandum to Lord Mountbatten, the Viceroy requesting setting up of an interim Government for the Nagas for a period of ten years, after which they would choose a form of Government that they wished. A meeting with the Advisory Committee for Aboriginal Tribes also ended in a deadlock. Nehru then sent Sir Akbar Hydari the Governor of Assam to discuss the issue with the Naga leaders. A nine point agreement was signed. The ninth point was not happily worded and was interpreted differently by the NNC and the Government of India. By this time the NNC had a diehard and a moderate group. A diehard leader had emerged in the NNC, Angami Zapu Phizo. He led a team of the NNC to Delhi in July 1947. Their interpretation of the 9th point in the agreement of Sir Akbar Hydari was differently interpreted by Delhi and the team returned disappointed. Phizo set to work and on 14 August 1947 declared the independence of Nagaland with a good gathering. School children took part in the Independence Day function in Kohima and Mokokchung. The celebration of India's Independence Day on 15 August 1947 was boycotted by the people of Naga Hills district.

The Naga National Council in this uncertain period adopted the view that the British should go and that the Central Government of India should act as the "guardian power" for a period of ten years, after which the Nagas would decide their own future. In the mean time the Government of India set up a committee on the Aboriginal Tribes. The Sub Committee visited Kohima to find out the wishes of the Nagas. The NNC put forward the following terms to be conveyed to the Government of India.

1. The interim Government of the Naga People will rule over all the people of Nagaland, having full powers in respect of Legislature, Executive and Judiciary.

2. Nagaland belongs to the people of Nagaland and will be inalienable.

3. The interim Government of the Naga people will have full powers in the matter of raising revenue and expenditure, an annual subvention to cover the deficit to be given by the Guardian Power.

4. For defense and aiding civil power in case of emergency, a force considered necessary by the Naga National Council will be maintained in Nagaland by the Guardian Power.

Shortly after the visit of the members of the Sub-Committee of the Advisory Committee, Sir Akbar Hydari, the then Governor of Assam visited Kohima to discuss the matter in detail with the Naga National Council. The meetings were held on June 27, 28 and 29, 1947, and an agreement was concluded with the Nagas, the Nine point Hydari agreement. Article nine of the agreement proved controversial and it has become the crux of the

Naga political problem. The article entitled Period of Agreement reads,-
"The Governor of Assam as the agent of the Government of the Indian
Union will have a special responsibility for a period of ten years to ensure
the due observance of this Agreement; at the end of this period the Naga
National Council will be asked whether they require the above Agreement
to be extended for a further period or a new Agreement regarding the
future of the Naga People arrived at."

Not very long afterwards, a dispute arose between the NNC and the
Government of India regarding the implication and the interpretation of the
Agreement. It cannot be denied that clause 9 was vaguely and weakly
worded and has been the cause of a very long and tiresome quibbling as to
what it does or does not mean. The NNC has consistently maintained that
it has given the Nagas the right to claim independence and to secede from
the Indian Union and that they are free as of 1958, i.e. ten years after the
Agreement was signed. On the other hand the Government version
interpreted the Agreement to mean that after ten years there would be a
review of the situation and a fresh agreement more widely acceptable to
the Nagas would be arrived at. The Government denies that autonomy for
the Naga Hills was even vaguely on its mind and resents the insinuation that
there was ever any question of granting the Nagas any right of separation
from the Indian Union. It is difficult to say whether the talks preceding the
signing of the Agreement had unwittingly encouraged this feeling among
the Nagas or whether the far from clear clause nine inspired a brilliant
afterthought in the mind of a Naga leader, but the fact remains that the
arguments over this issue strained Indo-Naga relations to the snapping point.
As far as the extremists were concerned, the ambiguity of the 8th point,
which they consider to be deliberate, had rendered the Agreement inoperative
long before 1958.

In 1948, the draft Constitution of India was published. The nine point
agreement was not mentioned in it. A moderate group of the NNC then
visited Delhi. They were assured that all constitutional safeguards were
provided in the constitution for tribal districts. The team returned disappointed.
In December 1950, Phizo was elected as the President of the NNC. The

NNC had a grand conference with representatives of several tribes in May 1950 in which a resolution was passed to have a plebiscite for independence. This was conducted in May 1951. The plebiscite was only partial, but this led to the boycott of the first general election of India in Naga Hills district in 1952. Not a single vote was cast on the polling day. Phizo realising that the Government of India will now impose its will on the Naga Hills, formed the Naga Home Guards in Tuensang armed from Second World War weapons that had been cached by the British during the Second World War. The moderate faction of the NNC had resisted the movement for independence. They included T. Sakhrie, J.B.Jasokie, T.N.Angami and Dr. Imkongliba Ao. They resigned from the NNC. As disturbances broke out, the Indian Army was deployed in the Naga Hills district in 1955. The Assam Disturbed Areas Act 1955 was notified for the Naga Hills District.

In 1955, the NNC set up the Federal Government of Nagaland (FGN) and drew up a constitution of a Parliament of 100 *Tatars* (members of parliament) and a *Kedhage* (President) with a cabinet of 15 Kilonsers (Ministers). In addition Deputy Commissioners and other officials were appointed. A parallel administration both civil and military had been set up by the NNC. The Naga Army had also aggregated to 15,000. In January 1956 T. Sakhrie was shot dead, the first major casualty. He was killed for cooperating with the Indian Government.

It was at this stage that Phizo slipped out of the Naga Hills and crossed over to East Pakistan. The Paren area of western Naga Hills borders the North Cachar Hills of Assam. In the North Cachar Hills district of Assam lives a small population of Zemei Nagas. On the west the North Cachar Hills district borders the Jaintia Hills, then the Jowai sub Division of the United Khasi and Jaintia Hills district of Assam. The whole of the North Cachar Hills is thickly wooded and it is easy to traverse the district and slip into the Jaintia Hills. To the south of this district is a thick forest bordering the plains of East Pakistan? Even today, there is no border road in this last stretch of the Megahlaya border with Bangladesh. It is through this axis that Phizo must have crossed into East Pakistan. Pakistan was smarting from being cheated of Kashmir. The Indian Army had defeated and dispersed the raiders who entered Kashmir in October 1947. When Phizo surfaced in East Pakistan, they seized the chance at getting back on India and promptly agreed to help him. They agreed to train the Naga volunteers and arm them to fight against the Indian Army in the Naga Hills. By 1962, when the Chinese war broke out more than a thousand Nagas had been trained and equipped by the Pakistan Army. They infiltrated into the Paren area of the Naga Hills through the Jaintia Hills and North Cachar Hills in small batches between 1956 and 1962.[6]

In 1956, two divisions of the Indian Army had been deployed in the Naga Hills. The Assam Government had also promulgated the Assam Disturbed Areas Act, a draconian act for that time. It was during this period that the Government adopted a very wrong policy, the grouping of villages picking it up from the example of Malaya. In Malaya, Chinese Communist Cadres had slipped into Malaya and lived among the Chinese immigrant rubber tappers. They lived on the edge of the forests in shanties. The British Army grouped all these settlers into improvised villages at the edge of the forest, so that they could be watched and prevented from slipping rations to the communist guerillas living in the thick Malayan jungles. In Nagaland, the Naga lived in villages, generally located on the summits of the hill features. The villages were very old and each village had its sacred groves. Cultivation was on the slopes of the hills well below the villages, or on the narrow valley at the bottom of the hills. Water was also fetched daily from the streams way down the hill slopes. Removing the Naga people from their ancient villages and grouping them in clustered shanties was a grievous mistake. This clearly aggravated the situation and hurt the psyche of the Nagas.

Pakistan meanwhile helped Phizo to move to Britain. From here Phizo tried to internationalise the Naga cause. In this he was aided and abetted by the Baptist church of the United States. Phizo's attempts to get the United Kingdom and the United States to influence the Indian Government did not succeed, but his Underground Naga Army gave a running fight to

[6] My Years with Nehru. B.N.Mallick. The Chinese Betrayal. Bombay Allied Publishers. 1971.

the Indian Army in the Naga and Manipur Hills. The Indian Army also deployed forces in a garland across the North Cachar Hills to intercept the Naga groups going for training and returning trained and battle hardened with weapons from East Pakistan. One of their ablest commanders was self styled (SS) Commander Kaito Sema. In the mid sixties he was trained to use plastic explosives, and he used them to very good effect by setting up bases on the hills overlooking the stretch of the Brahmaputra valley from Diphu to Amguri, along which was the single rail track going to Dibrugarh and sneaking down, blowing up the rail track, derailing the Assam Mail. The Army had to deploy two special battalions of the Railway Protection Special Force to patrol the rail track.

The counter insurgency operations led to severe alienation of the Naga people. There was a small group of leaders who had not gone along with Phizo and the NNC. They began to realise that it was better for the Nagas to work out a deal with the Indian Government. The Indian Government had protected the Naga way of life and allowed the customary laws to operate for the Naga people. This moderate group organised an all tribes Naga Peoples Convention in August 1957 attended by 1765 delegates and 2000 visitors representing every tribe. The convention adopted a resolution for a negotiated settlement of the Naga issue and for setting up the Tuensang division of the North East Frontier Agency in the Naga Hills district and for placing the Naga Hills district under the supervision of the External Affairs Ministry. The Indian Government agreed to this.

A Manipur Naga Council had been set up in 1956 by the Naga tribes of Ukhrul, Tamenglong, Senapati and Chandel districts. This group merged with the NNC. Meanwhile, the Naga Peoples Convention intensified their activities and organised meetings in 1958 and 1959 at Ungma and Mokokchung, despite threats from the underground. In the last convention they drafted a 16 point resolution for the creation of a separate State to be called Nagaland. The Government of India accepted this resolution with little modification and the new State of Nagaland was inaugurated in December 1963. The Underground opposed it vehemently and the NNC refused to recognise the new State.

Meanwhile in 1962, India clashed with China all along its borders with Tibet and China in Ladakh, Himachal, Uttar Pradesh and Arunachal sectors. This came about as a result of wrong policies of the Central Government. China had generally been having some measure of sovereignty over Tibet. During the Chinese revolution and the protracted internal war with the Nationalist Army of Chiang Kai Shek, this sovereignty had been considerably diluted. Generally the Indian Prime Minister had been favouring China's long guerrilla war. After the Chinese Red Army defeated the Nationalists and drove them to Taiwan, they turned their attention to Tibet. Meanwhile the United States had been talking to the Tibetan religious leader, the Dalai Lama and quietly went about collecting about 5000 Khampas, the wild Tibetan tribe who made up the fighters in the Tibetan Army of the Dalai Lama. They came across the Arunachal border to Kalimpong in 1956, and were then taken by train to Calcutta and then airlifted to Taiwan. After training the Khampas were air dropped into Tibet by the US Air Force.[7] Obviously India's Intelligence Agency must have been involved in all these movements of the Khampas. Besides in all such clandestine introduction of rebels trained and equipped, they will naturally be interrogated in the event of capture. The Chinese must have found out that India had an indirect role in this transaction.

Besides this fact, the Government of India naturally helped the Dalai Lama when he fled to India along with about three lakh Tibetans in 1959 and gave them sanctuary. Thirdly, the Government of India should have negotiated with the Chinese Government about the border between India and Tibet/China and set about demarcating the border instead of operating a forward policy along the Tibetan Frontier, when on the ground neither the British nor the Indian Government had really held any ground on this rugged frontier. These were the three factors that led the Chinese to attack India on two fronts, in Ladakh and Arunachal Pradesh. The Nagas probably knew nothing about all the above intrigues. However on 29 May 1963, Kughato Sukhai, the *Alo Kilonser* of the Federal Government of Nagaland wrote to the Chinese Premier Chou En Lai, copies of which were sent to

---

[7] The President's Secret Wars. John Prados. Quill Willam Morrow, New York. 1987.

Phizo, the British and Indian Prime Ministers to recognise the territorial rights of the people of Nagaland. This was a major step for the Christian Nagas to approach an atheist country for help. Phizo acknowledged the step as he felt there was no encouragement from the western countries. Three years later the first Naga group led by Thinoselie Medon Keyho and Thuingaleng Muivah consisting of a detachment of 353 guerillas reached China. The Chinese were informed of the movement of this detachment by the FGN liaison cell in Dacca. This cell had been regularly informing the Chinese diplomats in Dacca. A second detachment of 300 Naga guerillas led by Isaac Swu and Mowu Angami reached China passing through the Kachin State in Eastern Burma. By end 1968, three groups of Naga guerillas had been trained and sent back equipped with weapons suitable for guerrilla warfare.[8]

The Indian Army fought a pitched battle for four days at the Jotsoma knoll with a big group of China returned guerrilla fighters. The Indian troops suffered a number of casualties. [9]

Meanwhile in the Naga Hills, India's Intelligence agency had been working on tribal rivalry among the Nagas. They succeeded in winning over a Sema faction, who formed the Revolutionary Government of Nagaland (RGN), led by self styled general Kaito Sema. A group of the underground Nagas who were not aware of the split and formation of the RGN, walked into the RGN camp by mistake, when they returned from China and were detained and handed over to the Indian Army.[10] The underground got their revenge when SS General Kaito Sema was ambushed and killed by them on 3 August 1968.

The Chinese coordinated their actions with the Pakistanis in the Chittagong Hill Tracts (CHT) The Chinese and Pakistanis even planned to build an airstrip near Rangamati, the HQ'S of the CHT.

---

[8] *Insurgent Crossfire*, Subir Bhowmik, Lancer. 1996.

[9] Ibid.

[10] Ibid.

The NNC had boycotted the elections of 1952 and 1957. After the State was formed in 1963 they had to take part in the elections. Two parties were formed, the Democratic Front and the Nagaland National Organisation. The first wanted the independence of Nagaland, while the second spoke of peace and economic progress of the State. The NNO won 28 seats and the Democratic Front 12. The fighting however continued without let up. The third Baptist Convention in its meeting at Wokha requested the Central Government to set up a Peace Mission. The Government of India constituted a Peace Mission. With the help of the Baptist leaders the Peace Mission met the Underground leaders. This led to a ceasefire being declared in September 1964. Several rounds of talks were held but they did not lead to any fruitful result.

The RGN then surrendered to the Government in August 1973. They were later absorbed as three battalions in the Border Security Force.

The situation however escalated and there was an attempt to ambush the Chief Minister Hokishe Sema. The ambush was probably arranged to protest the transfer of the Naga Hills district Affairs from the External Affairs to the Ministry of Home Affairs. The Nagaland Church leaders and Sarvodaya leaders met and formed the Nagaland Peace Council. They interacted with the Naga Underground Army leaders. After several months of ground work they succeed in mellowing down several of the leaders They finally arranged for talks between six Underground leaders and the Government of India. The Naga group was led by Kevi Allay brother of Angami Zapu Phizo. After discussions a Peace Accord was signed at the Raj Bhavan Shillong 11 November 1975.[11] There were three paras:

(a) The Underground of their own volition accept without condition the Constitution of India.

(b) The arms now underground would be brought and deposited.

(c) The leaders of the Underground would formulate other issues for discussion and final settlement.

[11] *Naga Insurgency*, M. Horam, Cosmo Publications, New Delhi,1988.

The Unlawful Activities Act that was enforced after the ambush on Hokishe Sema was abrogated. Later the FGN met at Dihoma and the SS President Zashi Huire, SS Home Minister Biseto Medom and the SS Chief of the Army Vijalie Mehta endorsed the agreement.[12]

At the time of the run up to the Shillong Accord, Isaac Swu and Thuingaleng Muivah were on their way back from China. When they returned and found what had happened they were furious and strongly denounced the accord. They also asked Phizo to denounce the accord. Strangely Phizo did not respond, but privately remarked that the signatories were puppets. Muivah and Isaac Swu returned to Burma and camped with Kaphlang the Hemi Naga from Burma who was their contact enroute to China. They tried to reverse the Peace Accord. They kept persuading the NNC but the Naga polity was by now clearly divided. Finally after five years, Thuingaleng Muivah, Isaac Swu and S.S. Kaphlang, the Hemi Naga from Burma formed the Nationalist Socialist Council of Nagaland (NSCN) in 1980. The word Socialist in the designation was in deference to the Communist Government of China who was their mentor.

The friendship with Kaphlang however did not last very long. The Hemi Nagas clashed with the Thangkhul. The differences smouldered for some time and then broke out into a severe firefight. The Thangkhul had to precipitately flee from Kaphlang's HQs. Several were killed and the rest were literally hunted all the way to the Burmese Ukhrul border. There was to be no reconciliation between the two groups. It was probably because of this fight with the Hemi Nagas that Muivah could not activate the Chinese link for some time. Earlier in 1984-85, the ULFA had approached the NSCN to train and equip them to fight the Government in Assam. The Peoples Liberation Army (PLA) in Manipur had also passed through Kaphlang's territory in northern Burma to go to the Kachin country for training and purchase of arms and ammunition. The NSCN took both the PLA and the ULFA to the Kachin Independent Army led by Bransein. Both the ULFA and the PLA were trained by them. The PLA already had contacted the

---

[12] Ibid.

Communist Party of China in 1977 and had been trained by them. The ULFA however was refused help by China. It was in the late 1980s when this happened. It was then that Paresh Baruah the SS Commander of the ULFA sent a team of ten cadres to Bangladesh to see if the Pakistan ISI could help them out. The team went in late 1990 to Bangladesh and struck gold. After the coup that placed Gen. Ziaur Rehman as the head of the Bangladesh Government, he had reversed the policy of the Awami League and reestablished relations with the Pakistan Government. The Directorate General Forces Intelligence (DGFI) immediately took the ULFA cadres to the Pakistan embassy who in turn sent them to Karachi and then to Peshawar for training in the camp of Gulbuddin Hekmatyar, the Hizb-e-Islami chief. Very soon Muivah was also in Bangladesh and a deal was struck with the ISI for purchasing arms from the weapons released to the black market by the Khmer Rouge of Cambodia. According to the confessions of a captured Finance Secretary of the NSCN Khayao Huray, Pakistani diplomats in Dacca had handed over I million dollars to the NSCN Muivah faction between 1993 -94.[13]

The NSCN Muivah faction was now called NSCN Isaac/Muivah or NSCN IM. This faction developed links with several insurgent groups in the Northeast. Earlier, the Naga Underground did not have links with any other insurgent group. This benefited the NSCN IM greatly as the extorted money from the people and the business community was now shared with the NSCN IM by each of the different insurgent groups. The NSCN IM befriended the Hmar Peoples Convention (HPC) an insurgent group of Mizoram, who felt that the Mizos had let them down after getting statehood from Delhi. Very cleverly, the NSCN befriended the group in the North Cachar Hills, where they had no grievance as the Hmars were a minority and were not discriminated too. They developed links with a Meiteis insurgent group called the Kanglei Yawol Kanna Lup (KYKL) although the Meiteis were no friends of theirs. They also befriended a small group of Paites in the southern border of Churachandpur. The Paites were part of the Chin-

---

[13] Insurgent Crossfire. Subir Bhowmik. Lancer. 1996. As told to the author by NSCN SS Brigadier Medom Keyho.

Kuki-Mizo group of Mongoloid tribals. Living far away from developed areas, the Paite and related groups called the Zhou or Zomi raised the Zomi Reunification Army (ZRA). Later when the Kukis fought with the Zhou, their friendship with the NSCN IM helped them. The NSCN IM also established links with two disgruntled Kuki factions the United Kuki Liberation Front (UKLF) based in Chandel and the Kuki Revolutionary Army (KRA) based in Kangpokpi and Saikul area. Extortion by all these groups brought handsome dividends for the NSCN IM. They befriended two minor insurgent groups, one in Khasi and Jaintia Hills and another in Garo Hills. These two groups were ostensibly for creation of an independent Khasi and Jaintia country and a Garo country. They were in actuality nothing better than brigands, who liberally extorted money from the Marwari traders who controlled most of the business in Meghalaya. These last two groups got sanctuary in Bangladesh. The NSCN IM frequently used the Meghalaya border to exfiltrate into Bangladesh. Hence their acquaintance with these two groups. The major allies of the NSCN IM were the ULFA and the NDFB, both of whom contributed money for purchase of arms from Cambodia.

With the sanctuary in Bangladesh, the NSCN, ULFA and NDFB went on a buying spree for arms. After buying arms from the defunct Khmer Rouge of Cambodia, these three groups were able to purchase arms from the arms factories in Yunnan. The Chinese Government had set up a number of arms factories besides opening up this region to several industries to enter the South East Asian market. They even looked the other way when several Methyl Amphetamine factories were set up in this area. Opium from the Kachin, Wa and Shan areas of Burma was the raw material for these factories. The NSCN IM managed to purchase arms from Ms. Norinco an arms manufacturing company of the Chinese Government in Yunnan. A cheque signed by Angelous Shimray the Finance Secretary of the organisation in the name of Ms. Norinco was traced. These arms were brought to Cox's Bazaar by coastal steamer and then overland to Bandarban in the CHT, where, the NSCN IM had been allowed to establish a transit camp. They also had set up camps in the following places-Jortan camp near Cox's Bazaar, Vaital camp near Rangamati, Galilee camp near Alikadam, and Mauni transit camp near Sylhet. The NSCN IM also had an office in a four storey building in New Market Dacca. Initially they carried three consignments by marching 200 to 300 cadres from Benin a big camp of theirs in Tamenglong district of Manipur south to Churachandpur and then across into Burma close to the Tiddim road, then to Parva at the southern tip of Mizoram and thence to Bandarban. After collecting the arms and ammunition from here, the party marched all the way back on the same route to Benin. All this was informed to the Intelligence Bureau. In 1995, the Army planned an ambush with the Burmese Army in the Chin area between Parva and Tiddim. 58 cadres of ULFA and other groups were killed and as many arms captured. Unfortunately in the midst of this encounter when the Indian and Burmese Army were mopping up and forming up to chase the fleeing groups, the Government of India announced an award for Aung San Su Kyi, the leader of the party that had won the elections in 1990 and had been imprisoned and not allowed to rule the country. Hearing this, the Burmese abruptly withdrew from the operation and retreated. After this the NSCN reviewed the route and instead of going east from Bandarban, struck north to Kagrachari and thence managed to slip between Amchurimukh and Tuipuibari posts of the BSF on the Mizoram border with the CHT. Vehicles of the NSCN IM based in the office, they opened in Aizawl, then came to the Kanthlang trijunction of Tripura, Mizoram and the CHT, picked up the arms and ammunition and drove to Silchar, Jiribam, Khonsang and then to Benin in Tamenglong district of Manipur. This was discovered in 2001-2002 by the author in the winter of 2001-2002 and informed to the Home Secretary of India. The information of the NSCN IM opening an office in Aizawl was also informed to the Home Secretary, though the Intelligence Bureau stoutly denied that the NSCN IM had opened an office in Aizawl. I have yet to understand what game the Intelligence Bureau was playing? Consignments were brought probably till about 2004, when a very large consignment that was being unloaded in Chittagong port by Paresh Barua, the SS Army chief of ULFA was seized by the Bangladesh Police. Paresh Barua was arrested and later released. I understand that it was India's Intelligence agency that tipped off the Bangladesh Police at Chittagong port.

The extortion net of the NSCN IM in the nineties and early 2000 was reported to be as follows-

Gas Cylinder truck per trip	=	Rs. 2000/-
Oil tanker per trip	=	Rs. 3000/-
Truck MS rods	=	Rs. 3000/-
Cement truck	=	Rs.1000/-
Rice to FCI	=	Rs. 500/

In addition tourist buses, gas cylinder trucks and petrol tankers had to pay Rs. 7000/- to Rs. 12,000/- per year, while gas cylinder trucks had to pay Rs.1,00,000/-

Besides this there was and still continues a big gold mine, the transport of wheat from the railheads to the capitals of all the hill states. Wheat is supplied to the Northeast as per the population census, by the FCI. The people of Northeast are however not wheat eaters. Yet the supply continues. All the flour mills in the northeast are owned by the *Marwaris*. A small quantity of wheat is downloaded to be ground as wheat flour and supplied to the different states for sale to the bakeries. The rest which is easily 90 per cent is then sold in the black market for supply to other states. To add insult to injury, the wheat is shown as transported to all the hill states and the fake transport charges are claimed. The NSCN naturally takes a major share of the fake transportation bills.

The Naga Kuki clashes

In 1992, a very shameful episode of the Centre's dealing of the insurgencies in the Northeast was played out. With the supply of weapons for the NSCN IM through Bangladesh finalized, the first consignment had come in 1991/92. It was in 1992, that one of India's external Intelligence agencies stirred a hornets' nest in the Northeast. The Nagas and Kukis were ancient enemies. The Meiteis kings had played the Kukis against the Nagas by allowing Kuki villages to be settled as a bulwark between the Thangkhul and Meiteis villages. However during the run up to the independence of India, many

Kukis had sided with the Nagas in the Naga struggle. There were even Kuki officials in the Naga self styled administration. Notwithstanding this, there was a divide between the Naga and the Kuki. The British had also used this distrust between the Naga and the Kuki in their administration. Now, taking a leaf from these two earlier examples, India's Intelligence agency decided to play the Kuki against the Naga to weaken them. They encouraged the Kuki National Organisation (KNO) to set up an armed group called the Kuki National Army (KNA). It was the Indian Intelligence Agency's office in Changmai, in northern Thailand, that arranged the training of the KNA by the Karen underground group that had been fighting against the Burmese ever since independence in 1947. The trained cadres of the KNA were set up against the NSCN IM. The result was disastrous. The NSCN IM cadres were battle hardened through years of fighting the Indian Army. They made short work of the KNA. The real disaster was yet to come. There were isolated Kuki villages in Tamenglong district among the Zeliang villages in that district. The Nagas now attacked these isolated villages. Whole villages were wiped out with men, women and children indiscriminately killed. Several thousand Kukis were rendered homeless and became refugees in their own state. There were also retaliatory attacks against isolated Naga villages. This stupid experiment had just the reverse effect than what was intended. The NSCN IM became more battle hardened. A bitter trail of distrust and hate was left in the wake of this thoughtless experiment. This also had a fallout. The fact that the Indian Government used the Karen National Union, ancient enemies of the Burmese in this experiment angered the Burmese Government. The Indian Intelligence agency obviously had handsomely recompensed the Karen group for the training undertaken by them. They also probably were given some weapons for their help. The Burmese Government retaliated by allowing several militant groups of Manipur to shelter in the Chin and Naga areas east of Manipur and Assam. These included the PLA and UNLF. There was an additional fall out. The ZRA had links with the NSCN IM. When clashes took place between the NSCN IM and the KNA, The ZRA sided with the NSCN IM as they had an earlier connection. This angered the KNA and they attacked the Paites, Zhou and Zomis. Several Zhou villages were burnt and hundreds rendered homeless.

In 1992, when I was IG Operations, my good friend Mr. Prabhakara who was the Hindu correspondent in Guwahati for many years, had travelled to Tamu across the border from Moreh and met the chief of the KNA there. He confided to Prabhakara about the raising of the KNA to fight against the NSCN IM.

Ground Rules

In 1997, the NSCN IM came forward for talks. An interlocutor was appointed for the talks and he continued for ten long years. There was nothing to show for ten years of negotiation. The worst part of this deal was the continual transgressions of the terms of the cease fire. Starting from about 2000 weapons in 1997, the NSCN IM has today more than 7000 weapons all kept at their Hebron camp near Dimapur. Agreed Ground Rules for the ceasefire were finalised between the Government of India and the NSCN IM on 12 December 1997. One of the conditions was that forcible collection of money would not be done. This clause was observed more in the breach than in observance. The collection of money as noted above from gas carrying trucks, oil tankers and other such transport vehicles continued and continues till today. In the Chandel district of Manipur, in 2001, NSCN IM cadres detained the Deputy Commissioner and five Block Development Officers and forced them to sign receipts for a total of Rs. 44 lakhs on cheques sent by the Central Government for Rural Development Schemes and took away the money. When the matter was referred to the NSCN IM HQs they demanded an explanation for this open misdemeanor from the NSCN IM unit at Chandel. The blatant reply was that the NSCN IM did not do this. The so called ground rules were just a farce.

Conclusion

The Naga demands for inclusion of the North Cachar Hills, Karbi Anglong and parts of Tirap district just cannot be conceded. The Naga presence in Karbi Anglong is just two villages of Rengma Nagas. In North Cachar Hills district, the Zemei Naga population is less than 15 per cent of the total population. Besides the Dimasa Cachari who is more than 50 per cent of the population, there are Kukis and Hmars and Hwrangkhals. To whom can you give this district? Certainly not to Nagaland. In Tirap district of Arunachal Pradesh the tribals are not Naga but peculiar to that district. Many of them have been converted to Christianity by the Nagas. That does not make them Nagas. So, ultimately what can you give the Nagas? Frankly nothing more than the State they have. The Nagas have no unique history as they claim. They were animist tribes who separately migrated and settled in the Naga Hills, part of the hills of Manipur and in the hills of Burma. Here they have never lived as a tribe. Each village was an entity by itself. There is nothing more that the Government of India can give them.

The main challenge of Nagaland is the rampant corruption that has become endemic in the state. Right from the time that Naga Hills was made a State, the Central Government instituted a policy of corrupting the administration of the State. I remember that as Superintendent of Police CBI in Shillong in 1979, I was called by the Governor of Assam and Nagaland Mr. L P Singh and met Mr. Vizol, the Chief Minister of Nagaland at the Raj Bhavan, Shillong. Mr. Vizol handed over a complaint of corruption against his Deputy Chief Minister. When I visited Kohima to seize files in connection with the complaint, the Deputy Chief Minister had got the concerned offices of the Secretariat set on fire and all the crucial files were burnt! The continual corruption has created a set of people, the politicians and the bureaucrats and their respective families, who are well heeled and live a life of luxury. For years many contractors of Nagaland who lived in Shillong, used to tell me that all items supplied to the Nagaland State were much less than the concerned invoices. The ordinary people of the villages are still very poor. The main task before the Government of Nagaland would therefore be to see that corruption is eliminated and improve the lot of the common people.

Manipur's Multifaceted Insurgencies

Geography

Manipur is probably the most beautiful of all the Northeastern States. This is because it is situated up in the hills. Its landscape is unique, as it has a verdant plain with a beautiful lake and sparkling rivers in the middle which is surrounded by ranges of hills that extend north-south on either flank, five to the east and six to the west. The ranges of hills extending north-south in the east are the Nupita, Chinga, Malain, Angoshing, and Yomadung. To the east of the last range are the northern hill tracts of Burma. These are inhabited by Hemi Nagas, who are close to the Konyak Nagas of eastern Naga Hills. There are also Thangkhul villages just across the border. The Hemi Nagas were animist till recently as the British never sent missionaries from Rangoon to the distant north. They also did not build roads into this area. The Burmese when they got independence neglected this area. Because of the lack of roads into these thickly forested hills, the area was inaccessible in the rainy season. It was only in winters that units of the Burmese Army were reluctantly pushed to this area to try and subdue the recalcitrant Nagas. Beyond the Naga area were the more difficult hills where the Kachins live. This fierce tribe was very loyal to the British when they ruled Burma and a large number became Christians. When the Japanese invaded, they found the Kachins were even crueler than them. When the British retreated, the Kachin scouts who worked with them were given advance salaries and directed to return to their villages and await the return of the British. They were the eyes and ears of the British behind the enemy lines and were invaluable when General Stillwell constructed the Stillwell road.

The ranges to the west are the Uningthon, Khoupum, Kobru, Haopi, Kalang and the Nungjiabong. The last range overlooks two streams –the Jiri that flows north-south from the watershed to the north and the Barak that flows north from Tipaimukh. The Jiri flows into the Barak as it turns west at Jirimukh and then flows through Cachar and then into Bangladesh. These eleven ranges are thickly wooded and ideal guerrilla country. The hill ranges to the east have been the sanctuary of the old Naga Underground and then of the NSCN IM for years. The hill ranges to the west have been the sanctuaries of the Naga underground and then of the NSCN IM in the northern half. In the southern half, they have been the sanctuaries of the Peoples Liberation Army (PLA) and the United National Liberation Front (UNLF) and the Hmar Peoples Convention (HPC) for years.

History

The Meiteis were Mongoloid people who migrated from Northwest China like all the other Mongoloid people of the Northeast. They were probably the first to migrate into Manipur and finding the plains uninhabited settled there. The Nagas probably came later and settled in the hills to the east, north and south east. The Kuki, Chin Mizo, it is generally accepted came last and settled in the south and west. They also settled further west in the Mizo Hills. The Meiteis having settled in the central plains of Manipur took to wet cultivation and developed a civilization and a written language, Meiteis Mayak. They have even a recorded history of two thousand years of their development-the Cheitharol Kumbaba. The Meiteis unlike the Naga and the Chin-Kuki-Mizo developed a system of kingship. The Meiteis developed a religion of their own, the cult of *Sanamahi,* which developed and became institutionalized with temples dedicated to their gods. Over the years, the Meiteis travelled west through Cachar and reached Nabadwip in Bengal from where they brought back Hinduism to Manipur. Over the years, Hinduism developed in Manipur and many Meiteis embraced the caste system of the Hindus. The Meiteis who became priests became *Brahmins,* while the princely group became *Kshatriyas*. Some of the lower and poorer people even became scheduled castes! During the reign of Garib Nawaz, probably under the influence of Bengali Brahmin priests, the King declared

Hinduism to be the State Religion. He even ordered the destruction of Sanamahi temples. After independence, and after the Meiteis became disenchanted with the Governance of India, there is a return to the cult of Sanamahi and a revival of the old Sanamahi temples and of the old religion.

During their travels to and fro from Manipur to Nabadwip and back, many Meiteis settled in East Bengal. Thus you have a Meiteis community in Sylhet district in Maulvi Bazaar and Banaguch. Meiteis also settled in the Kebaw valley to the south of Chandel district. This happened because the Meiteis kings had held the Kebaw valley and this area was handed over to Burma by the British before giving independence to India. There are also many Meiteis who have settled in Rangoon, Mandalay and other Burmese towns. The troubles for Manipur started from the time the British allowed the Marwaris to settle in the British area in Imphal. It was similar to the British allowing the Marwari to settle in Assam, who after some time permeated every sphere of commerce in Assam and finally captured the whole economy of Assam. It was also akin to the British bringing the Chettiar from Madras to Burma, who captured the economy of Burma. When Burma became independent, they got rid of the Chettiar. But in Assam and Manipur, the Assamese and the Meiteis could not get rid of the Marwari.

There was a renaissance in Meiteis Mayek literature in the 1920's. In1933 the Nikhil Hindu Manipuri Mahasabha (NHMM) was inaugurated with Hijam Irabot as the head of the reception Committee. He was a social reformer and literary person. In three sessions, the first in Imphal and the third in Mandalay, the links with Hinduism were discussed. The fourth session of the NHMM saw a clear parting of the ways and a turning point in the politics of Manipur.[1] A determined effort to bring the Meiteis within the Aryan Hindu tradition was being made by a section of the Meiteis. In opposition to this a movement had arisen to rediscover and reassert the religion of the past and to purify it from Hindu influence. This movement came to be called the Sanamahi movement. This movement was led by

---

[1] *Wounded Land, Politics and Identity in Modern Manipur.* John Parrat, Mittal. New Delhi, 2005.

Naorem Phullo. He founded the *Apokpa Marup* in Cachar. After a long struggle against the brahminical opposition, the Apokpa Marup was formed in Imphal as the Manipur State Metei Marup. Its objective was to revive the Meiteis culture, and to revive the archaic script. They also determined to recover the ancient *lai* from Hinduism by getting rid of the Hindu names of the traditional Meiteis Gods. The fourth session of the NHMM was now held at Chinga Hill near Imphal with Irabot as President. The new Brahmins were absent. The NHMM was developing into a political movement to oppose feudal rule and religious opposition. Also, the word Hindu was dropped from the name of the organisation and it became Nikhil Manipuri Mahasabha (NMM). At the convention two resolutions were passed which struck at the heart of the feudal and colonial governance of Manipur. The first resolution addressed the separation of the Hills and the Valley under the British administration and the second called for the curtailing of the feudal system of governing by the Maharaja and his durbar. A third resolution demanded the setting up of an elected legislature. At first there was strong resistance to these proposals, but within a year the Maharaja Chura Chand was himself suggesting for an elected assembly of an elected Prime Minister and 27 members.

In 1936 a Krishi Sammelan had been set up under the umbrella of the NHMM. This was a peasant movement to improve the productivity and trading opportunities of the farmers. Hijam Irabot took over as its president in 1946, and renamed it as the Manipur Krishak Sabha and began to pursue a radical programme in the interest of poor farmers. He campaigned for three items - fair prices for the produce, reduction of land tax, and compulsory land rights for those who tilled the soil. Its urban counterpart was the Manipur Praja Sangha. These two organisations were to play a crucial role in the dramatic events of 1947-49.

The British often remarked on the high status that the Meiteis women had in Manipur. They controlled the food supplies and the markets and were therefore a dominant economic force. The first *Nupilan* (Women's War) in 1904 began as a protest by the women against the ruling by the Political Agent Maxwell that the Meitei men should rebuild colonial officers' bungalows destroyed by arson. Maxwell had to compromise and reversed his orders. The second *Nupilan* began in 1939. The bulk of the paddy was husked by hand by women and then sold in the markets. Most of the rice was exported as the trade was in the hand of the *Marwaris*. Originally, the permit for export could only be issued by the Political Agent. It was later delegated to an agent. The Marwaris exploited the agent and began to increase the export of rice from the 1920's. In 1939, the paddy harvest was reduced due to excessive rainfall. As the shortage of rice began to be felt, the women took the law into their hands and attacked and overturned several carts carrying rice. They later demanded that a telegram be sent to the Maharaja, who had gone to Nabadwip. A British officer was virtually kept in the custody of the women agitators, until he was rescued. The second Nupilan eroded the authority of the British Resident and the Maharaja. This revolt represented a dramatic popularisation[2] of the struggle for release from the burdens of feudalism. The main force behind the second Nupilan was Hijam Irabot. He dominated Manipur's political development in its most traumatic years between 1931 and 1951. Throughout his life his sympathy was with the urban and rural poor. His objectives were largely frustrated by the superior power of the feudal system and British colonial control over Manipur until 1947 and by the ruthless march of Indian integrationism thereafter, his legacy remains strong within Manipur today specially in the continuing activity of the Meiteis insurgency movements.[3]

The merger with India and the roots of Insurgency

The rule of Bodhchandra the penultimate Raja of Manipur before the state was merged with India was a reign of incompetence, corruption and nepotism. The educated Meiteis who had control of the Manipur State Congress met the day the Chief Commissioner took office expressed their gratitude to India and organised a solidarity march. The bulk of the population and the other political parties were full of misgiving seeing in it the end of Manipur's two thousand years' history. The Assembly that had been elected was summarily dismissed. It was only in Manipur and Travancore Cochin that

---

[2] Ibid.

[3] Ibid.

the ruler had held elections and Assemblies were constituted before formal accession. Contrary to the agreement many Manipuri employees of the Government were dismissed and replaced by civil servants from India. The Chief Secretary and the Home Secretary were dismissed. The purge of Manipuri officers extended to the Police also. The first three Chief Commissioners appointed were unmitigated disasters, particularly with reference to the integration of the State with India. The first years of Indian rule had brought into Manipur a degree of unaccountability, financial corruption and nepotism that the State had not seen since the heyday of Churachand's rule.[4]

It was at this stage that the Naga insurgency broke out in full force. Angami Zapu Phizo as the head of the Naga National Council (NNC) had declared the independence of the Naga Hills district of Assam on 14 August 1947 itself. It took some years for this to grow into an insurgency. By 1955 the NNC established contact with East Pakistan and obtained weapons and were also trained by the Pakistan Army. There were four districts of Manipur where there were Naga tribes.These were Ukhrul with the Thangkhul, Senapati with the Mao, Maram, and Thengal, Tamenglong with the Zeliangrong, consisting of three sub tribes, the Rongmei, Liangmei and the Zemei and Chandel with the Anal and several small tribes. The insurgency of the Nagas in the Naga Hills naturally spread to the Naga tribes in Manipur. The Thangkhuls and Maos were closely associated with the insurgent Naga tribes of the Naga Hills. Many of the Zeliang did not join the insurgents. The Manipur Rifles a State Armed Police Battalion of Manipur, recruited mainly from the Meiteis people of Manipur was deployed against the Naga Underground groups along with the Army and other Armed Police Battalions of Assam and other States. The standard of the Manipur Rifles was very good and they performed very well against the Naga Underground. This led to some uneasiness in the relations between the Meiteis and the Thangkhul and other Naga tribes of Manipur.

The first years of Indian rule very badly alienated the people of Manipur. Firstly there was a very considerable increase in corruption after the elected

---

[4] Ibid.

State Assembly was dismissed and several top administrators removed and Indian counterparts brought from Delhi. The main issue was the attitude of the new Government officials brought from outside the State. The people of Manipur were ethnically and culturally very different from the plains people of India. The new Indian officials did not try to understand this ethnic and cultural divide. Probably, the only exception to this was R. Constantine who came from far away Bangalore as the news editor of All India Radio. He fell in love with Manipur and its people and after a lifetime spent in Manipur wrote a wonderfully charming book-Manipur, Maid of the Mountains, which is the first book that anyone who wishes to study Manipur should read.

In 1950, the Government of India set up an Advisory Council. In 1952 Manipur was declared a Part-C State. A limited political representation was now possible. Two members could now be elected to the Lok Sabha. In 1956, Manipur was declared a Union Territory. An elected Territorial Council assumed office. Its powers were limited to the rural areas outside Imphal. This led to calls for the Council to be abolished. In March 1960, a group of Manipuris set up an Assembly Demand Coordination Committee. Delhi did not heed this demand.

Several factors led to the raising of the first insurgent group in the Valley. These were the way the centre ignored the elected Assembly of Manipur when the Maharaja was forced to sign the instrument of accession in Shillong. Secondly a host of unfeeling bureaucrats from Delhi were hoisted on the Manipur Government. Besides being totally insensitive to the local Meiteis people and the local administration, they were also corrupt. The Centre had made the Naga Hills district of Assam a State, after separating it from Assam. Manipur an older kingdom with a 2000 year history was made a Union Territory getting it directly administered by Delhi. Behind the rise of the first insurgent groups was the spirit of Hijam Irabot. The first group consisted of a shadowy pan Mongoloid group followed by another group that called itself as the Revolutionary Government of Manipur.

These groups slipped into Sylhet district and tired to meet the East Pakistan Government to ask for help as the Naga National Council had done. There were about 200 youths who were taken to East Pakistan led by Oinam Sudhir, Nameireikpam Bisheshar, R.K.Sanatomba and Dhaneshwar. Oinam Sudhir the leader had come first to contact the East Pakistan authorities to arrange for the training of their cadres. The Naga Underground had earlier been helped by the East Pakistan authorities. Strangely the East Pakistan Government and its Army did not favour these groups. Oinam Sudhir did manage to set up a camp and some arms were given by the Pakistan Army. The group also underwent some training. The project fizzled out when the Liberation war started in East Pakistan. The Pakistan Army pushed the Meiteis group back across the border into Tripura into the arms of the Indian Army. They were jailed in Tripura and later released when the Manipur Government gave them amnesty.[5]

A little later a group was formed by Arambam Somerendra, a graduate of the Tata Institute of Social Sciences, called the United National Liberation Front (UNLF). It started as a social group and remained so for some years before it took to arms. In 1976 Rajkumar Meghen @ Sanaiyama who was earlier with the groups that had gone to East Pakistan joined the UNLF, established contact with the Naga Underground and left for Burma. He established contact with the Burmese Nagas and returned to Manipur in 1977. It was only in 1985, when the National Socialist Council of Nagaland was established by Thuingaleng Muivah, Isaac Swu and S.S.Kaphlang, that he again went to Burma to the NSCN HQs with some new recruits. By this time Somerendra, the founder of the UNLF had abandoned the martial line. During the seventies, support for the UNLF had grown very fast. Rajkumar Meghen alias Sanaiyama was a descendent of Tikendrajit Singh, a crown prince, the tragic hero of Manipur's conflict with the British in 1891. Sanaiyama was a graduate in International Relations from the Jadavpur University. The NSCN was formed in 1985 by Thuingaleng Muivah, Isaac Swu and S.S. Kaphlang, a Pangmi Naga from Upper Burma, after the old Naga Underground had signed an agreement with the Government of India in 1975. It was in Kaphlang's HQs in Burma that the NSCN was set up. The PLA from Manipur were the first group outside of the Nagas to join the

[5] Insurgency Movement in Northeastern India.Phanjoubam Tarapot.Vikas.1993.

camp for training. Later the ULFA from Assam also sent their cadres for training. Still later the NSCN established links with the Kachin Independent Organisation (KIO) headed by Brawnsein and the cadres of the ULFA were attached to the Kachin Independent Army (KIA) for training. More than a thousand ULFA cadres were trained by the KIA. I had seen and interrogated several ULFA cadres who were Kachin returned. I found them physically and mentally very tough. The ULFA cadres who were Kachin trained were brutal, sometimes cruel and physically completely changed from the usual Assamese young men. In two occasions I know of personally, ULFA's Kachin returned cadres preferred to kill themselves rather than be captured.

In all these years, the UNLF had remained a social organisation. It was only in 1976 when Rajkumar Meghen joined the UNLF that they decided to take to arms. Even then it was after many years on 15 December 1991 that they attacked a security patrol in the Loktak area. Their ambush on the CRPF patrol was successful. Five CRPF personnel were killed. It was shortly before this ambush on 22 May 1990 that the UNLF announced the formation of the Indo Burma Revolutionary Front (IBRF). This organisation comprised three groups, the NSCN, UNLF and ULFA. Their main objective was to get independence for Assam, Manipur and for the Naga areas in Burma and India.

Nameireikpam Bisheshar formed the Peoples Liberation army (PLA) in 1978. He along with some associates slipped into Tibet through Nepal and met the Chinese authorities who took them to Beijing and trained and indoctrinated their cadres. One other group was formed in 1977-78 called the People's Revolutionary Party of Kangleipak (PREPAK) headed by R.K.Tulachandra. The PLA, after their return from China and the PREPAK both sought to snatch arms from the Police and Para-Military forces. They started with a series of attacks on banks and Police Stations, the first to collect money and the second to get arms. The attacks of these two insurgent groups were fierce and determined. The valley was under severe tension for weeks in 1978. Imphal city was always tense and the tension was palpable to anyone visiting Imphal. The PLA group that went to China through Tibet returned after indoctrination by the Chinese and with some weapons.

The group set up several camps in and around the Imphal valley. They also started extorting money from the Government departments and officials. They also captured arms by ambushing Police patrol parties. One of their major successes was the attack on the Manipur Rifles post at Mongshangei. The PLA group got away with 10 Self Loading Rifles and 1 Light Machine Gun. It was around this time that the PLA decided to ask for help from the KIO for a safe hideout and for training their cadres. The KIO received them well and the PLA thus got a base in the eastern part of Burma with the KIO.

One of their famous attacks was on a jeep of a Para Military force that had come to the district court in Imphal for some work. The jeep was parked in the court compound and the driver was sitting behind the steering wheel. There were two constables sitting behind with their rifles. Another was sitting to the left of the driver. Two young men covering themselves with shawls came up to the jeep. One asked the driver some question and the other asked something from the person sitting to the left. As they were answering, both the persons whipped out pistols from behind their shawls and shot dead the driver and the person sitting to his left. Simultaneously two other young men also wearing shawls appeared behind the jeep and each of them pulled out pistols from behind their shawls and simultaneously shot dead both the constables sitting behind. In a trice the four young men had pulled the dead bodies of the four personnel that they had shot, snatched their weapons and jumping into the jeep drove off. The Police reacting gave chase in the direction in which the jeep had driven off. They could not locate the route taken by the hijacked jeep. Meanwhile, while driving fast; the jeep collided with a truck. Kunjbehari Singh one of the hijackers was badly injured. He had broken his leg. The jeep immediately changed direction and drove to the main hospital in Imphal, where Kunjbihari was taken to the surgery and operated. The Police got no clue of this and Kunjbihari recovered and went out without the Police knowing about him. Such was the clout of the PLA in Imphal city at that time.

The PLA was in full flow from 1979 onwards. The number of people killed in 1979 was 14, 36 in 1980 and 50 in 1981. Incidents of ambushes of Security Forces increased from 77 in 1980 to 116 in 1981 Attacks and ambushes on the CRPF led to clashes of the Para Military forces with civilians after the CRPF personnel were ambushed and their survivors took revenge on the nearby civilian population. There were a number of such incidents. This only led to the promulgation of the Disturbed Areas Act over the whole of the Imphal valley and the hills surrounding it. On 26 April 1980 a very bad incident took place at Patsoi a town west of Imphal. In an ambush on the CRPF by an insurgent group suspected to be of the PLA, 3 CRPF personnel were killed. Enraged by this incident, a group of CRPF personnel from a nearby camp went berserk and beat up civilians and damaged household properties worth lakhs of Rupees. The CRPF personnel also fired indiscriminately at the crowd killing two men and two women. A Parliamentary Committee enquired into these incidents and confirmed the misbehavior of the CRPF party. On 26 October 1981, the Government of India issued notifications declaring the PLA, People's Revolutionary Party of Kanglieipak (PREPAK) and the Kangleipak Communist Party as Unlawful Associations under provisions of the Unlawful Activities Prevention Act which was promulgated in 1967.

The situation had deteriorated so fast that the Army had to be called in. Gen. V.K.Nayyar was the GOC commanding the 8 Mountain Divisions in Kohima. He set up a Tactical HQs in Kangla Fort in the heart of Imphal and oversaw the Counterinsurgency operations in the Imphal valley. He had an excellent technique to control human rights violations. He had strict orders to all his lower formations operating in the valley against the PLA. Any one detained by them was to be produced before the Tactical HQs located in Kangla Fort in Imphal immediately. There, his next of kin were to be informed to come to the Tactical HQs. When they came the arrested boy was produced before them with seized weapons if any and they were told if there was a case against their ward. If there was no case he was handed over to them. In this way all subordinate formations were controlled and no custodial killings took place. Gen. Nayyar was revered by the people of Manipur. Regrettably no commander after him followed his methodology. He was later Governor of Manipur for a short time and resigned because of political interference. After his departure, the history of insurgency in Manipur is one long story of custodial deaths and fake encounters.

Bisheshar, the leader of the PLA was ill at their camp near Tekchan village located south-east of Imphal. With him were Kabichandra, Rajen Macha, Indrajit, Khogen, Shanti, Biramongal, Inao and Sarat On a tip off that some insurgents were camping in the area of Tekchan, an Army patrol led by Second Lieutenant Cyrus Pithawala surrounded the camp near Tekchan at first light of 6 July 1981 and ordered the inmates of the camp to surrender and lay down their arms. The PLA group answered the call to surrender with a hail of bullets. The encounter lasted for nearly 2 hours, at the end of which, Kabichandra, Rajen Macha, Indrajit, Khogen, Shanti, Biramongal and Inao were killed. Bisheshar and Shanti were captured alive. Major Gen. V.K.Nayyar announced the arrest of Bisheshar, leader of the PLA. This breakthrough broke the back of the PLA. They revived, but many years later. Among the Lhasa trained PLA only Soibam Temba Singh, Thoidam Khunjbihari and Manikanta were alive now. The PLA drifted without regrouping firmly and a little less than a year later, the main group led by Kunjbihari were surprised in a house near Kadampokpi, where they were sheltering by an Army patrol. In the ensuing firefight, Kunjbihari, Paka Singh, Th Loken Singh, Kameshwar, Naorem Rajendra and Kundrekpam Rajen were killed. The Army captured four PLA cadres and seized several foreign made rifles and ammunition. The only main leaders of the PLA alive were Temba Singh and Manikanta.

The PLA remained in the wilderness for some years. But they revived. It was under the leadership of Soibam Temba Singh and hardcore cadres like Irembam Bhorot, Manoharmayum Pravin Kumar alias Ngouba and Ahanthem Mema that they crossed into Burma via Kamjong east of Kasamkhullen and trekked to Lonkho village in eastern Burma. This was in early 1983. From here they moved to the Kachin Independent Army (KIA) camp.

In Burma, differences arose between the Thangkhul tribe of Manipur who were the main group of the Naga tribes in the NSCN and the Burmese Nagas. Sometime in 1988, these differences boiled up and the Burmese Nagas suddenly attacked the Thangkhul Nagas from Manipur who were in the NSCN camp in Eastern Burma. It is reported that Rajkumar Meghen the leader of the UNLF who was in the camp at that time knew about the impending attack, but did not warn Muivah the leader of the Thangkhul Nagas in the camp. Though surprised, Muivah managed to escape with some of his close confidantes and most of the Thangkhuls. Quite a few of his loyal Thangkhuls were killed in the attack. Muivah and his group retreated towards, the border of Manipur, but they suffered severe privations. It is reported that Muivah nursed a grudge against Rajkumar Meghen. The two never crossed trails after this. Muivah and Isaac Swu set up the HQs of the NSCN IM inside Indian Territory near the Burma border. The NSCN K formed the Indo Burma Revolutionary Front with the ULFA and the UNLF. It was round about this time that the ULFA leader Paresh Barua had gone to China to ask for Chinese help in training the ULFA cadres. The Chinese probably refused or placed some difficult conditions which Paresh Baruah was not in a position to comply? After consulting with Muivah, Paresh Baruah sent a probing team of ten ULFA cadres, led by Munin Nabis to Bangladesh to contact the Pakistan ISI in their embassy in Dacca. With the Bangladesh DGFI collaborating, the Pakistan ISI sent the team to Karachi and then to Peshawar for arms training in the camp of Gulbuddin Hekmatyar. Subsequently, officials of the Pakistan ISI and the Bangladesh DGFI met in Sayeman Hotel in Cox's Bazaar and after discussions, the Pakistan ISI agreed to fund the NSCN IM, ULFA, and the PLA of Manipur to buy weapons from the arms bazaar of Cambodia and Thailand. The ISI advanced the funds for the purchase of arms to the group. The NSCN IM also opened a series of camps along the route from their camp in Benin in Manipur's Tamenglong district, south traversing the Churachandpur district, crossing the border into Burma on the axis of the Tiddim road, and then along the eastern and southern border of Mizoram to Parva, the trijunction of Mizoram, Burma and the Chittagong Hill Tracts of Bangladesh. The NSCN IM set up transit camps at Ali Kadam and Bandarban in Bangladesh on the axis from Cox's Bazaar to Parva. The first consignment of arms were purchased with the funds given by the Pakistan ISI from the arms bazaar of Cambodia/Thailand loaded on a steamer that sailed north and anchored off the coast at Cox's Bazaar. The arms were unloaded in boats and landed at Cox's Bazaar, from where they were collected by the NSCN group that had marched all the way from the Nagaland border with Manipur. From here the arms were carried on foot all the way to the Benin camp of the NSCN. From here they were distributed to the ULFA, the PLA taking their quota, enroute in Burma itself.

The PREPAK was broken up by some scintillating intelligence work by the then Inspector General of Police, which ended by the leader Tulachandra, being captured. The organisation however revived and is now operating in full strength. The UNLF set up base camps in south Chandel district in thick jungles where there were no roads. From here they could always slip into Burma into the Chin Hills if attacked by the Indian Army and where the Burmese Army did not have a reach.

In 1985, when the NSCN IM took the ULFA to the Kachin Independent Organisation (KIO), the PLA were already there. Later the PLA also took some cadres to Sylhet district and contacted the Bangladesh Army and their Directorate of Forces Intelligence (DGFI) to help them. This they probably did after the ULFA had sent a group to Bangladesh to help them after the Chinese had refused help. The PLA probably got its first consignment sent to them by the Pakistan ISI through Cox's Bazaar and Bandarban in 1992-93. In 1995 when the Indian Army ambushed the combined column of ULFA and NDFB in Burma in conjunction with the Burmese Army, the PLA were also probably part of the group.

Two other insurgent groups that were formed were the Kanglei Yawol Kanna Lup (KYKL) and the Kangleipak Communist party (KCP). The KYKL attained notoriety for attacking Government officials who accepted bribes. Their modus operandi was to pick up such targets and maim them by shooting them in the leg. The interesting fact about this shadowy group was that they developed a link with the NSCN IM. In fact they gave a part of their extortion funds to the NSCN IM. The KCP also notorious for extortion has now broken into several factions. Reportedly one faction is working with Intelligence agencies. Other factions have degenerated into extortion as a means of livelihood.

In 1998-99, the PLA and the UNLF went into Churachandpur and occupied four Sub Divisions-Henglep, Thanglon, Parbung and Singhat. The Sub Divisional officer and his staff all fled to Churachandpur. In Imphal, the Civil Supplies department had been corrupted badly by the State

Government officials. Rice, sugar, kerosene oil, petrol and diesel were being diverted to the black market. In this the politicians were a major share holder. Seeing this, insurgent groups stepped in and began taking a major share of the supplies. Part of these they carried to their jungle camps and sold to the local villagers at very low prices to get a Robin Hood image, while the rest were sold to the black market dealers. In 1999, as the Director General BSF, I was asked by the Home Ministry to open up the four Sub Divisions that were occupied by the militants. We made an elaborate plan setting up a base in Churachandpur. The Border Roads had built a highway from Churachandpur to Tipaimukh, 230 kilometres long that wound across five ranges that straddled north south between Churachandpur and Tipaimukh. This highway had been abandoned by the PWD for several years. Thanglon and Parbung were on this highway. Henglep was north of this highway form a place called Singmun which was about 70 kilometres from Churachandpur. We sent foot columns along the abandoned highway, with our vehicles carrying stores coming behind. The militants kept firing and retreating disappearing into the jungles to the north and the south of the highway. To reach Henglep, we sent two columns on foot, one from the penstock of the Loktak dam and one from Singmun to Henglep. The two columns advanced simultaneously, with the insurgent groups firing and retreating. We occupied the three Subdivisions Henglep, Thanglong and Parbung. A similar strategy was adopted to occupy Singhat, which lay about 20 kilometres on a road from Churachandpur south to the Chin Hills border. Thus we occupied all the four Sub Divisions within a week of starting the operations without any casualties. We then approached the Deputy Commissioner Churachandpur to direct the civil Supplies contractor to load rice and other essential commodities in their trucks. We volunteered to escort the trucks to the 4 Sub Divisions. The DC after some promises backed out and said that no civil supplies of rice, sugar etc was being sent from Imphal. We learnt later that the Chief Minister was reported to have links with the PLA and the UNLF and did not want to see the Central Government succeeding in carrying supplies to these remote areas. We held these four Sub Divisions till 2000 November. We suffered one ambush during our stay when a column was ambushed near Senvon, a village near Parbung, where we lost three personnel. In 2001, the Chief Minister got the

Central Government to withdraw the BSF from the four beleaguered Sub Divisions.

Shortly after this a dastardly crime took place in the Loktak Project area. The General Manager of the Loktak Hydroelectric Project was from North India. He was brave fearless and efficient. An insurgent group the Kanglei Yawol Kanna Lup (KYKL) had begun operating in the valley in the 1990's. It specialized in extorting money and though a Meiteis group was linked to the NSCN IM. The KYKL demanded money from the GM of the Loktak project, which he refused to pay. He complained to the CRPF who were guarding the project. It is reported that the KYKL met the Chief Minister and told him to change the force guarding the Loktak project. The Chief Minister called the Director General of Police and directed him to change the force guarding the Loktak project. The DGP replaced the CRPF with the State Manipur Rifles. A few days later a gunman of the KYKL entered the room of the GM and shot him. This was clear proof of the link between the Political leadership and the Meiteis Insurgent groups. In the enquiry that followed, the Home Ministry sent an Additional Secretary of the Home Ministry to enquire into this incident. The Director General of the State Police who had replaced the CRPF with the State Police to guard the Loktak Project on the orders of the Chief Minister refused to appear before the Additional Secretary of the Home Ministry as he had retired. The enquiry could not be completed because of lack of evidence.

The State Government had created a Commando Platoon by taking selected personnel from the district Police and the Manipur Rifles. This Commando Platoon was based in Imphal under an Inspector General Operations and used to operate in the four plains districts of Imphal East, Imphal West, Thoubal and Bishnupur. Initially it worked well and the Platoon had several successes against the PLA, PREPAK and the Kangleipak Communist Party (KCP) another insurgent group that was formed in the early 1990's. Unfortunately the Platoon picked up the bad habit of extorting money from the Bazaars of Imphal where the Marwaris and outsiders had their shops. In one such episode, the driver of the officer heading the Commando Platoon was caught by some shopkeepers in Paona Bazaar. The shopkeepers were beating him, when, the district Police intervened and rescued him. Hearing this, members of the Commando Platoon came and rescued him. Later his body was found thrown by the road side in the city. The finger of suspicion naturally pointed to the Commando Platoon, but the case was closed without any further information forthcoming. This episode naturally besmirched the reputation of the Commando Platoon.

Sometime after 2001, when attempts to dislodge the PLA and the UNLF from South Chandel did not fructify, Rajkumar Meghen was interviewed by a TV Channel reporter from Delhi. The TV interview of Rajkumar Meghen saw him demanding that India should vacate Manipur and the United Nations should be asked to decide on Manipur's future. It was around this time that UNLF cadres were shown holding an Air Defense Gun. Presumably this weapon must have been supplied by China to the rebels.

The scourge of corruption in the Northeast

One of the main Factors for the growth of Insurgent groups in Manipur was the enormous corruption patronised by the Party in power in Delhi. I was posted as the Superintendent of Police Central Bureau of Investigation in Shillong in 1979. Prior to this posting I was the Superintendent of Police of Khasi Hills for three and a half years. I found out about the corruption in Nagaland, Manipur, Mizoram and Arunachal Pradesh during my tenure as SP CBI Shillong looking after the six Northeastern States. Almost all the big contractors operating in all the Northeastern States had a base in Shillong and for some peculiar reason many of them were visitors to my office when I was the SP Khasi Hills. They used to openly tell me of the huge pickings in the hill states of Nagaland, Manipur, Mizoram and Arunachal Pradesh. Many of the contractors who used to supply stores to Nagaland Police or hospital equipment used to drop in at my office and tell me that they were going to Kohima or Aizawl to collect payments. They would blithely tell me that they had supplied ten thousand numbers of a particular item and billed for one lakh numbers. Such juicy bits of conversation were told to me most casually. When I was hearing all these juicy bits of gossip, I had no idea that I would one day end up as SP CBI Shillong. When I did, it was very easy for me to get cases registered in Nagaland or Manipur. My pleasure at getting cases in these States however turned sour very soon, for I found that in all cases where the contractor or supplier was a crony of the party in power at Delhi, the cases though absolutely fool proof were always closed by CBI HQs. It was only then I realised why so many insurgent groups had sprung up in the Northeast.

The NSCN IM had a standard rate for all trucks carrying goods to Kohima or Imphal from Dimapur. The rates were fixed for POL tankers, trucks carrying civil supplies, passenger buses etc. Besides there was a scandal of trucks carrying wheat. The Food Corporation of India was supplying wheat to the Northeastern states as per the scale of Northern states, though the Northeastern people were rice eaters. It was interesting that 90 per cent of wheat was diverted to the black market at Dimapur itself. Only a small quantity used for milling to wheat flour for the bakeries were actually sent. The rest of the wheat was shown as carried to the hill district capitals using fictitious truck challans and the money for this was claimed from the treasuries in Kohima, Imphal etc. The militants in Manipur found this out and when the Marwari or Meiteis transport contractors cashed these fake bills, they would appear at the treasury and at gun point make the transport contractors sign on the receipt vouchers and take away the money. The militant groups in Manipur had a hand in the supply of rice, sugar, kerosene oil and petrol. When they found the Civil Service officials involved, they interceded and extracted their pound of flesh too. The unfortunate consequence of all this was that the insurgent groups also got corrupted. After this the insurgent groups began to get the accountants of all civil departments to deduct a percentage of the salary of all civil servants and pay to them.

I had gone as Advisor to the Governor of Manipur when Presidents rule was declared in June 2001. I found that the militants of the valley were freely moving in the secretariat and State Government offices in Imphal. CRPF was immediately deployed in all major State Government buildings and all movements in were strictly checked. We also directed that salaries of all State Government employees would be drawn and taken to the 1st Manipur Rifles campus for disbursement. This put a stop to the militants sitting with the cashier and collecting a percentage from each employee at the time of disbursement.

Distribution of POL coming in from Dimapur was a scandal in the State. I found that the POL depot of Assam Oil was manned by clerks from the State Supply department. The staff of the Assam Oil had run away! The silos in the POL depot were empty. Petrol, diesel and kerosene were not decanted into the silos. The tankers that brought petrol, diesel and kerosene went directly to the petrol pumps and kerosene wholesale depots and decanted in their illegal underground tanks. Entries were then made in the ledgers of the depot. I first got the Assam Oil staff to come to Imphal. Then I got a company of CRPF to guard the depot. Then we put one company of Manipur Rifles to escort the convoy of POL tankers from Mao gate at the Manipur- Nagaland border, to the Manipur Rifles campus, where the tankers were parked under guard for the night. The next morning the tankers were to come, ten tankers at a time and decant POL into the silos. For the first time in several months POL was decanted into the silos. After all the tankers had decanted POL into the silos, each wholesale dealer was given one or two tankers of petrol and diesel to be decanted into their underground tanks. The Kerosene oil to the districts was sent under escort to the Deputy Commissioners. In the city the 14 wholesale dealers were allowed to take their tankers and decant into their respective tanks. We also sold 5 litres and later 10 litres to customers at the control rate on their ration cards from each of the depots. Only the balance was then allowed to the retail depots. As the Advisor I used to visit all the 14 depots at random with my escorts to see that the people were getting ten litres on their cards. The result was that there was no more a black market in POL for the period off Presidents rule. There were attempts to demand money from the AOC personnel at the Assam Oil depot, but an alert CRPF foiled all attempts to kidnap the staff. The corrupt politicians and the militants had been short circuited. Given time we could have got this short circuiting done in all development spheres. Unfortunately the Government in Delhi did not release special funds as was normally done during President's rule. We also did not get sufficient troops to open up the interior of Churachandpur and Chandel districts.

I had developed some good sources in Chandel district from the border areas. On a visit I heard from them that a sizeable group of the UNLF was surrounded by the Burmese Army. I heard that the Burmese Army had raised a combined military and Customs group called NASAKA. This group was reported to have surrounded the UNLF party and seized their weapons. Initially their weapons were not returned, but after some negotiations, the weapons were returned to the UNLF. My information was that the Chinese Government had opened some arms manufacturing units in Yunnan and Kunming area of South-western China. I learnt from my contacts that Wa traders' from the tribe of that name in eastern Burma bordering Yunnan was smuggling arms and the UNLF had purchased the arms from the Wa traders. Many years later, I learnt that the Wa arms traders were supplying arms to the Dima Halem Daoga, an insurgent group in the North Cachar Hills through the eastern border of Mizoram, the trijunction of Burma, the Churachandpur district of Manipur and Mizoram.

The operation of clearing Churachandpur district of the UNLF and the PLA was finally done by the Army in 2005-06. The Subdivisions in Churachandpur were opened out without much trouble but the Army had problems in South Chandel, particularly in Sajik Tampak and New Samtal. The area though occupied by the Army, could not be held as no development followed. A network of roads should have been constructed with well defended garrisons for the Army. The PLA and the UNLF retreated into Burma without many casualties. South Chandel district bordering Burma is still a free area for the UNLF and the PLA. So also is part of the eastern border of Chandel district bordering the South Somra tracts of Burma.

One very undesirable feature of the counterinsurgency operations of this period was the way the ragtag band of Kuki militant groups that were raised by the Central Intelligence Agencies was handled. Initially only one groups the Kuki National Organisation with its armed wing the Kuki National Army (KNA) was raised. Two groups spawned out of the KNA, the United Kuki Liberation Front (UKLF) in Chandel and the Kuki Revolutionary Army (KRA) in Saikul area of Senapati district. Both were enticed out by the NSCN IM. All these groups had high sounding names, but they were not worth a candle as a guerrilla group. They were nothing more than brigands extorting money from government and private channels. All these groups were patronised by politicians for protecting their turf during elections. Over the years even more groups were spawned. This disease also hit the once well knit Kangleipak Communist Party (KCP). This insurgent group I believe dissolved into almost ten splinter parties some even working for the Government. I understand that they were even involved in smuggling weapons from Burma for other insurgent groups.

Today the scene in Manipur is abysmal. With the Army and Para Military forces deployed in abundance, the PLA and the UNLF are intact in Burma. They continue to forage in Manipur by extorting money from the Government, its employees and private companies. The camps of the PLA and UNLF in Burma are intact and they continue to operate in Manipur. Corruption in the Government is reported to be worse than ever. Manipur is simply drifting aimlessly and the Central Government is even more helpless than it was before. The PLA formed in 1978 after the visit to China by its leaders maintained its leftist doctrine throughout. It however did not develop any links with the Communist parties in mainland India- the CPI, CPM or the later groups of the CPI ML. The last named split into factions that finally united as the CPI Maoist. It is reliably learnt that the PLA has now developed links with the CPI Maoist. There is also some information that the CPI Maoist in Bihar had some connections with the Maoists in Nepal. It is now learnt that some cadres of an insurgent group in Manipur have been seen in Nepal in a camp. It is possible that there is a final link between the Maoists of Nepal and the PLA in Manipur.

In October 2010, one of my contacts informed me that Rajkumar Meghen, the chief of the UNLF was in Bangladesh. I tried to verify this information. I knew that the UNLF had established a link with the Wa arms traders to get weapons from the Chinese arms factories in Yunnan. Why should the UNLF leader go to Bangladesh, especially after the change of Government there? I could gather from my sources that there were officers from the Defense Forces in Bangladesh who were still loyal to the ISI of Pakistan and could arrange for purchase of weapons from South East Asia and that was why the UNLF leader had taken the risk of going to Bangladesh. Later I heard that the UNLF leader had been picked up by the Bangladesh authorities. I further heard that they wanted to hand him over to the Assam Government authorities as they had handed over several ULFA leaders a few months ago to the Border Security Force on the Bangladesh Assam border. Later I heard that this handing over was not done and that he had been taken to an Indian aircraft that had gone to Dacca to fetch him and that he had been flown to Delhi. This was reported by the BBC correspondent in a dispatch to the BBC London. This information could not be confirmed. The UNLF cadres are reported to be in Chandel district moving across into Burma and coming inside when the Army scouts are not near the borders.

The PLA and UNLF continue to be moving across the border from Burma into Chandel district and vice versa depending on the Army's presence. The Government of India does not appear to have any specific policy to wean the insurgents away from their avowed path of independence.

All the hill districts of Manipur have not been developed in the last 60 years. The Government should take up development schemes in all the hill districts on priority basis, concentrating on developing the village economy. They should first build roads. The roads should be to connect all villages to the nearest towns. The second step would be to have water supply schemes for every single village in the hills. The third stage would be to identify schemes for the villagers to set up poultry and piggery projects in each village. The fourth stage would be to develop orchards in each village. The fifth stage would be to improve the present stage of agriculture in each village. If these are developed the productivity and purchasing power of the villagers will improve.

While these steps are being taken security forces should be garrisoned in the area and see that insurgents do not come to the village to collect money or rations. As development takes place young boys and girls will not take to the gun and join insurgent groups.

All development projects should be continually audited to see that money invested is continually grounded and translated into assets on the ground. The Northeast and particularly Manipur and Nagaland needs to have clean administration desperately.

The Insurgent Groups of Tripura

Geography

Tripura was one of the two princely States of the Northeast. Situated at the southwestern edge of the Northeast, Tripura has five ranges of hills that are roughly north-south with verdant valleys between them. These are from the west, Deotimura, Baramura, Atharimura, Langtrrai, Sakhan and Jampui. The Deotimura has to its west a plain that borders East Bengal. To the north is Sylhet district of East Bengal. In the east, the Jampui hills slope into the Longai valley which is part of the Mizo Hills of Assam, now Mizoram. To the east, wedged between Tripura and Mizoram are the Chittagong Hill Tracts that was erroneously given to Pakistan by Cyril Radcliffe condemning the 98 per centpopulation of Buddhists to a minority existence in East Pakistan and then, later Bangladesh.

History

The population of Tripura consists mainly of Mongoloid people who were part of the great migration from Northwest China who settled in the hills and valleys of Assam. The main tribes of Tripura are the Tripuri, Reang, Jamatia, all anthropologically Tibeto-Burman. There are also a scattering of Chakma, Garo, Mizo tribals in the State. The main tribe, the Tripuris had earlier settled in the Cachar valley and later moved to Tripura. The rule of the Tripuri Manikya dynasty is the longest of all dynasties in Indian History. When the British came into contact, the States' Royal Chronicle had a list of 178 rulers ending with the last sovereign of the State- Bikram Manikya. Tripura traces the beginning of its own historical era to 590 AD, three years earlier than the Bengal kingdom.

The Roots of Insurgency

The roots of insurgency in Tripura were laid when East Bengal on its western border became East Pakistan with the partition of India on 15 August 1947. This set off a wave of migration from the erstwhile East Bengal to Tripura, Assam and West Bengal. It is not that there were no Bengali Hindus and Muslims in Tripura before that. The Tripuri Manikya kings had been inviting Bengali Hindus to migrate and settle in Tripura since long. The figures of tribals to non tribals mainly Bengali Hindus and Muslims were as follows-

1901	-	52.89 %
1921	-	56.37 %
1941	-	50.09 %
1951	-	36.55 %
1961	-	31.53 %
1971	-	28.95 %
1981	-	28.45 %
1991	-	30.95 %

The drop from 50.09 in 1941 to 36.55 in 1951 shows the sharp increase of Bengali Hindus and Muslims who had come in from East Pakistan. It is also clear from this that the tribal percentage had been reduced to 50 per cent even by 1941, when the migration was encouraged by the Tripuri king. By 1951, the tribal percentage was reduced to just 36 per cent. From independence with the high migration of Bengali Hindus into Tripura, the Congress party was seen as siding with the Bengali Hindus and Muslims. The Communist party of India (CPI) and later the Communist Party of India, Marxist (CPIM) however sided with the tribals. The Congress backed the wave of migration from East Pakistan in 1947 as a result of which it got an anti tribal stance. The CPI backed the tribals in forming the *Gana Mukti Parishad* (*GMP*) in 1948. The GMP stood for the civil rights, political power and economic development of the tribals. They organised a rally in August

1948 against the smuggling of rice into East Pakistan. The resultant Police suppression led to the creation of a guerrilla group called the *Shanti Sena*. They attacked Army posts and Khowai Sub Division became a liberated zone for some time. Dasarat Debbarma, the leader became a cult figure in this action. Nripen Chakravarty, the CPI leader and later the legendary Chief Minister of Tripura also joined this struggle. The GMP became the tribal wing of the CPI. The movement created solidarity among all the tribes of Tripura. The CPI became entrenched with the tribals. It highlighted two issues, the socio-economic development of the tribals and their rightful share of political power. After three decades of the GMP movement, the Autonomous District Council had to be set up precisely because of the unwillingness of successive Congress governments to pay serious and sympathetic attention to these basic issues.[1] Demographic imbalance, economic underdevelopment, cultural marginalization gradually intensified the tribal search for a separate identity.

In 1943, the Tripuri king had reserved an area of 1950 square miles for exclusive allotment to the tribals and also prohibiting transfer of this land from tribals to non tribals. The tidal wave of refugees was so much that the Regent Queen transferred 330 square miles to non tribals in 1948. The pressure was so much, that the reduced reserve area also could not be protected. Encroachment and illegal transfer of tribal land continued. This was the primary cause for the alienation of the tribals. The Tripura Land Revenue and Land Reforms Act was passed in 1960. Transfer of tribal land to non tribals was declared illegal. However, the provision for restoration of alienated land was passed only with effect 1 January 1969, thus regularising land alienated even after the Land Reforms Act had been passed nine years ago. The Bengali lobby was still strong.

Insurgency

The first group to take to arms to fight the Government was the *Sengkrak*. It was formed in the foothills of the Jampui range in the late sixties. By this

---

[1] Identity, Autonomy and Development. Satyabrata Chakravarty. Ekusha. Calcutta, 2000.

time the Mizo National Front had gone to East Pakistan and had started the insurgency in the Mizo Hills of Assam. They had set up camps in the Chittagong Hill Tracts (CHT). The Jampui Hills overlooked this tract and the Sengkrak contacted the MNF and were able to get some arms from them. The leaders of the Sengkrak were Ratnasen Reang and Ananta Reang. The Sengkrak tried to evict the Bengali immigrants from the Kanchanpur Dasda areas. Their efforts were not successful and after the two leaders were arrested in late 1969, the organisation petered out.

In 1967 a conference of tribal leaders set up the *Tripura Upa Jati Samiti (TUJS)*. When the TUJS was raised Dasrath Debbarma, CPM and Aghor Debbarma, CPI were present. The CPM however withdrew later and the TUJS established links with the Congress. The TUJS demanded formation of an autonomous District Council under the sixth schedule, restoration of tribal lands and recognition of Kok Barok, the main language of the Tripuri tribals.

In 1979, the Foreigners Agitation was started in Assam. It spread to the other Northeastern States. Tripura was one of the worst affected states as far as migration from Bangladesh was concerned. The TUJS asked for expulsion of all the Bengali Hindus and Muslims who had entered the State after 15 October 1949, when the Princely State had acceded to India. The TUJS developed an armed wing called the Tripura Sena, led by Bijoy Kumar Hrangkhawl. He established links with the Mizo National Front who had camps in the CHT. He renamed the Tripura Sena as the Tripura National Volunteers (TNV). Meanwhile the Left Front pro tribal measures created intransigence among the Bengalis. The Anand Marg, a right wing organisation in Bengal stepped in and formed a group called the *Amra Bengali.* They organised a series of attacks on CPM meetings. Tripura was polarized into two ethnic camps. In Amarpur, 20 TUJS volunteers were beaten to death by an irate Bengali mob. In retaliation 380 Bengalis were butchered by tribals at Mandai on 20 June 1980. Hundreds of Bengalis were killed at Amarpur, Tripura Sadar and Udaipur. In many places the Police sided with the Bengalis against the Tribals. This ethnic riot left a lasting scar on Bengali Tribal relations. In the elections of 1978, the CPM won 58 seats, while the TUJS won the remaining four. Kok Barok was recognised as the second language of the State. The CPM government tried for an Autonomous District Council, but the Congress Government at the Centre refused. The CPM Government then formed the Tripura Tribal Areas Autonomous District Council (TTADC), under the seventh schedule. The TTADC elections were held in 1982. The Congress did not participate. The CPM won 19 seats and the TUJS seven. The support of the Tribals for the CPM was very clear. As a result the TUJS linked up with the Congress, a peculiar case of political pragmatism that led two parties, one siding with the Tribals and the other with the Bengalis coming together.

Bijoy Hrankhawl was arrested in June 1980. He was released in December 1980. This release raised a doubt about his having compromised with a Central Intelligence agency. The suspicion was heightened, when he suddenly dissolved the TNV. Two of his lieutenants, Binanda Jamatiya and Chuni Koloi left the TNV and formed the Army of Tripura Liberation Organisation (ATPLO). The group began extorting money from traders and others. It did not last long, after Binanda Jamatiya surrendered. Meanwhile Hrangkhawl revived the TNV in 1982. After some years he suddenly surrendered in 1988 and signed a tripartite agreement with the Centre and the State. This was an inexplicable decision, since the problem of the tribals had not been solved. This confirmed the suspicion that he had been won over by the Indian Intelligence and the Congress party. Bijoy Hrankhawl's decision led to the creation of the National Liberation Front of Tripura by his lieutenant Dhananjoy Reang in 1989.Two other disgruntled leaders of the TNV, Lalit Debbarma and Ranjit Debbarma formed the All Tripura Tribal Force (ATTF) in 1990. The last group was later rechristened as the All Tripura Tiger Force (ATTF). These two groups established bases in the CHT and in Bangladesh. They were patronised by the Directorate of Forces Intelligence of Bangladesh, who supplied them with weapons and trained them. Both groups after getting weapons and training operated from across the border in hit and run raids. They had camps in the hilly forested portions of the hill ranges that originated in Bangladesh and then traversed Tripura. Their ingress and egress routes were through the forested hill ranges extending between Bangladesh and Tripura. Both groups indulged in extensive extortions from the Bengali Hindu *Mahajans*.

Unfortunately the BSF deployed on the border was under strength, as several battalions were deployed in Kashmir. The border could not be properly sealed. Both the groups' periodically kidnapped leading Mahajans and Tea Garden Managers for ransom. Some of them were taken to Bangladesh. They even kidnapped a group of RSS members and took them to Bangladesh, where they could not cope with the tough terrain and died out of exhaustion and fatigue.

Between April 1998 and April 2000 the NLFT and the ATTF abducted 551 persons. Of these 140 were killed, probably because of nonpayment of ransom. All the kidnapped were taken to Bangladesh. The over ground cadres of these two insurgent groups in Agartala and the other towns were responsible for the negotiations. It is here that there was a clear failure of intelligence. The negotiators should have been arrested and through them the actual kidnappers located. Regrettably there was no intelligence of likely border crossings by the NLFT or the ATTF. Ambushes on the International border were always blind ambushes on the known trails and the results were very poor.

The NLFT and the ATTF carried out spectacular ambushes on the Paramilitary forces. In two ambushes on the Paramilitary forces I had carried out detailed postmortems and found the most abject negligence in movement on tracks and roads, near the international border. One ambush of a Paramilitary force was disgraceful to say the least. A platoon moved in one three ton vehicle up a narrow hill road, thick with vegetation, without a support vehicle and no road opening party. The road was one way. The platoon was ambushed when returning. All the occupants were killed and their weapons taken away. Every rule in the book had been violated.

The NLFT and the ATTF had more than 30 camps in the CHT and in the hills to the north of Kamalpur and Khowai in Bangladesh. Right from the time of Sheikh Hasina's Government, The Government of India kept informing the Bangladesh Government about the location of the camps based on the interrogation reports of captured militants. Sheikh Hasina's writ did not run very far during that Government as the Directorate General of Forces Intelligence (DGFI) of Bangladesh was very close to the Pakistan

ISI. After the Bangladesh National Party formed the Government in 2001 in a coalition with the Jamaat-e-Islami (JEI), things worsened considerably. But, by that time the Counter Insurgency module in Tripura also considerably improved and steadily the Government began to get the better of the insurgents despite the patronage of the Bangladesh DGFI.

The intensity of the Counterinsurgency drive stepped up considerately after a former Police Officer of Assam, G.M.Srivastav, who had good experience of counterinsurgency, took over as the Director General of the Tripura Police. He first tackled the kidnapping for ransom that had almost become endemic in Tripura. These operations were coordinated by cadres who were based in the State. By painstaking intelligence work the cadres were identified and arrested. After they were neutralised, kidnappings petered out. Some confidence returned to the people of the State. The Army meanwhile had managed to carry out some daring intelligence operations across the border into the CHT. These operations demoralised the insurgent groups. Leadership squabbles led to a split in the NLFT. Biswa Mohan Debbarma kept the major group with about 600 cadres, while Nayanbasi Jamatiya led the smaller group with about 100 cadres. The NSCN IM had helped the NLFT in procuring weapons. After the split the NSCM IM continued to help the Biswa Mohan Debbarma group. The ATTF led by Ranjit Debbarma had links with the ULFA, who were also in Bangladesh. The NLFT were openly pro Christian. The animist Reangs and the Hindu Jamatias opposed this. The NLFT banned the worship of Goddess Durga in the Hills. The spiritual head of the Jamatias performed the *puja,* defying the ban.

The movement of Paramilitary forces was considerably tightened and the NLFT and the ATTF could not conduct many ambushes. Gradually the situation improved. Kidnappings had come down to nil. Ambushes were few and far between.

The Insurgent Politics Nexus

The Left Front had controlled the TTADC since its inception. In the elections to the Council in 2000, the NLFT sponsored a new party the Indigenous

Peoples Front of Tripura (IPFT) which campaigned in league with the Congress. The NLFT went on a killing spree after the elections were announced. Their targets were the supporters of the CPM. 78 people were killed by them during the election and 111 after the election results were announced. The IPFT won 18 of the 28 seats. However when the elections to the Assembly came up in 2003, the ATTF linked with the CPM and Left Front. The NLFT supported the Congress and killed the Left Front's supporters. The INPT meanwhile joined the Congress in a coalition. In the Assembly elections this coalition could only get 19 seats. With the improvement in the situation, the Left Front regained the majority in the TTADC by winning the elections in 2005. With concentrated operations the cadres of the NLFT and the ATTF were hard-pressed and by 2004 nearly 600 rebels of both the main insurgent groups surrendered.

There is one underlying fact in the politics of Tripura. The CPM government is the cleanest government in India. This had a very salutary effect on the people of the State, both tribals and Bengali Hindus and Muslims. Development money received from Delhi was very conservatively and economically spent on the ground. Nothing was returned to Delhi by the contractors as is the case with all grants received by all the other Northeastern States. In fact in some of the Northeastern States, 90 to 95 per cent of the money returns to Delhi through the unholy group of contractors called the Delhi Durbar.

With the coming of the Awami League into power in 2009, the situation has further improved as far as the Northeast insurgents were concerned. However as far as Tripura was concerned, effective policing brought the insurgency under control by 2004 itself. Today, under the absolutely clean leadership of the Chief Minister Manik Sarkar, Tripura is free of its insurgency.

The Kashmir Insurgency

Introduction, Geography and History

In any insurgency it is necessary to appreciate the history of the people involved to really understand the causes that led to the people taking to arms. I would therefore briefly recapitulate the history of Kashmir before going into the conditions that prevailed and led to the insurgency. The vale of Kashmir is encircled by mountains all around. To the west is the Shamsabari range that comes in, turns north and later curves east dipping a little and then joining the Himalayan range, which comes in from the north. Between the two is a deep valley called the Gurez valley. Across this valley is another range of the Himalayas. The inhabitants of the Gurez valley are genetically and linguistically different from the Kashmiris. At the point where the Shamsabari comes in from Pakistan another range called the Pir Panjal also comes in parallel to the Shamsabari but turns south and later curves east and joins the Great Himalayan range further south from where the Shamsabari joins it. The vale of Kashmir is thus boxed in by the Shamsabari to the west and north, the Himalayan ranges to the east and the Pir Panjal to the west and south. Roughly between, where the Shamsabari and the Pir Panjal comes in from the west is the Uri gap, through which the main river of the Kashmir valley, the Jhelum flows into Pakistan. To the south a stream emerges from the Pir Panjal at Verinag which flows roughly north through the vale of Kashmir joined by tributeries from the Pir Panjal and the Himalayan range. This is the Jhelum. This river flows north and forms a lake called the Wular in the north of the valley. The river emerges from the Wular, meanders west and flows into Pakistan through the Uri gap. Since the valley is boxed in a rough rectangle by mountain ranges to the north, west, east and south the weather in the valley is distinctly different from the areas outside this valley, particularly to the south. In the 20th century two tunnels were excavated in the south through the Pir Panjal through which the road coming to the Kashmir valley was laid. This was called the Banihal tunnel. Very often when driving upto the Banihal tunnel in heavy rain, one drove out of the tunnel into the Ramban valley to find it bathed in sunlight beyond the Pir Panjal to the south.

There are a number of passes on all the ranges that encircle the Vale of Kashmir. Thus though the valley was encircled by mountains, movement of people was not restricted and the valley very often became a refuge.

The fair handsome people who live in this valley are obviously Aryan. They probably migrated to this valley from the north. This is concluded because they differ drastically from the people who inhabit the area to the west of the Pir Panjal, who are physiologically and linguistically very different from the Kashmiri who settled in the vale of Kashmir. The Kashmiri language is quite different from the language spoken west of the Pir Panjal which is a variation of Punjabi called Pahadi Punjabi.

We do not know what language the Kashmiris who first migrated into this valley spoke, nor what was their religion. We do know that the first recorded religion of these people in history was Hinduism. We do know that Kashmir was part of Ashoka's empire. When he converted to Buddhism Emperor Ashoka sent Buddhist missionaries to Kashmir and many Kashmiris were converted to Buddhism. After he died, the Kushanas conquered Kashmir in the 1st century AD. When the Kushan Empire declined, Kashmir again came under Hindu kings. Avantipur was the capital of a great Hindu kingdom. With the coming of the Muslim kings in the 8th century AD, Islam also moved into Kashmir. The first Muslim king of Kashmir was Syed Shabuddin. He conquered Ladakh, Baltistan and Jammu. One of Shabuddin's successors discriminated against the Hindus and many of them migrated from the valley. However, a later descendent of Shabuddin, Zainul Abedin was a very tolerant king and looked after his Hindu subjects. In fact many Hindus who had left returned to Kashmir during the rule of Zainul Abedin. It was during this time that Persian became the language of the court.

It was in the 12th century that Kashmir saw a religious transformation. A Persian Syed Ali Hamdani, a native of Hamdan in Persia who was travelling east from Persia reached the vale of Kashmir and settled there. He began a gradual conversion of the Kashmiris to Islam. We do not know when the first Sufi saints came to Kashmir after the people were converted to Islam. We only know that many Sufi saints did come to Kashmir. They intermingled with the Hindu Saints and a unique brand of Sufism evolved in the valley. Today there are numerous Sufi shrines all over the valley. In Srinagar city alone there are many Sufi shrines. The more famous Sufi shrines are the Shrine of Nooruddin Wali in Charare Sharief, Dastgir Sahib and Maqdoom Sahib in Srinagar and Baba Rishi on the way to Gulmarg. The majority of Kashmiri Muslims and Hindus worship at these Sufi shrines. When the Mughals began their rule in Delhi, Kashmir came under their control, when Akbar took over the reins of the empire. With this the rule of independent kings in Kashmir ended. After the Mughals, there was an unhappy period when the Afghans took over Kashmir. This ended with the Sikhs under Ranjit Singh conquering Kashmir. The period of Sikh rule was also miserable for the Kashmiri people. It is probably during this period that some ethnic Kashmiris were converted to Sikhism. Though becoming Sikhs, the Kashmiri Sikhs did not forsake their mother tongue Kashmiri, except for a few who learnt Punjabi. It is during this period that the Dogras, who were vassals of Ranjit Singh, became strong. Gulab Singh, the Chief of the Dogras was made a Raja of Jammu by Ranjit Singh. When the British East India Company came into the picture, the Dogra Raja Gulab Singh cleverly remained neutral in the fight against the British. The Sikhs were defeated. The British ceded Jammu and Kashmir taken from the Sikhs to Gulab Singh for the payment of Rupees seventy five lakhs. Gulab Singh's kingdom included Jammu, Kashmir, Ladakh and Baltistan, which his famous general Zorawar Singh had conquered on behalf of the Sikhs. The Kashmiris however continued to be unhappy as they felt that the Dogras considered Jammu as their home. The next stage was the Sepoy Mutiny. In this the Dogras supported the British. British families were also protected in Kashmir. The loyalty of the Dogras was not forgotten by the British. The Kashmiris were not treated well by the Dogra rulers. The Dogra rule was oppressive and the Kashmiri people suffered in silence. They would have rebelled but for the fact that they were afraid that the British would put down their rebellion. Though many British officials who toured reported on the callous rule of the Dogras, the British were consumed by the fear of a Russian advance towards India through the Pamir Mountains. They did not pay heed to the miserable conditions of the Kashmiri people. To the British, Jammu and Kashmir was an ideal buffer State against the Russians and they did not interfere with the Dogra king, leaving the task of a watchdog against the Russians to him. Ranbir Singh the successor of Gulab Singh captured Gilgit and later the British posted an Officer on Special Duty there. Chitral an adjacent principality was obliged to accept suzerainty in 1878 under the Dogras. The Gilgit garrison was manned by 2000 Jammu and Kashmir troops. It was in 1913 that local troops were recruited and trained as the Gilgit Scouts. It was in education that the Kashmiri Muslims suffered. As Government Service was not open to Muslims, they did not send their children to school. The Kashmiri Muslims continued to suffer under Dogra rule. In 1924, when the Kashmiri Muslim silk workers, struck work, their representation revealed that though they were 96 per cent of the population, their literacy was only 0.6 per cent. After Hari Singh became the Maharaja, a campaign against his autocratic rule was orchestrated by a number of Kashmiri Muslims who had graduated from Aligarh Muslim University and had formed a Reading Room Party. These included Muhammad Yusuf Shah, who succeeded his father as the head of a religious order as the Mirwaiz and Sheikh Muhammad Abdullah. Matters came to a head as a Kashmiri Muslim butler who worked under an European made a fiery speech in July 1931 in Srinagar to fight against oppression. When he was arrested, crowds mobbed the jail and police opened fire. Twenty one people died in the firing. Their bodies were carried to the centre of the town. A riot followed and Hindu shops were looted. A reign of terror was unleashed by the Dogra rulers. Sheikh Abdullah and other leaders were arrested and detained in the Srinagar Central jail. Here the arrested leaders' discussed and decided to form a party, the Muslim Conference. After they were released, Sheikh Abdullah became the President of the party. He however took up the cause of both the Muslim and Hindu poorer classes who were being badly treated. Throughout his struggle, his continuing emphasis on secularism led to an internal disagreement. Several Muslim leaders including the Mirwaiz Muhammad Yusuf Shah left the party. At the end of August 1938, the Kashmiri political leaders once again took to the streets, on behalf of the Muslims, Hindus and the Sikhs, to protest against high taxes, unemployment, and lack of medical facilities.

In 1940, the Muslim League adopted its Pakistan Resolution at Lahore which demanded that the areas of the North western and eastern zones of India, where Muslims are predominant should be grouped to constitute independent states. Muhammad Ali Jinnah as President of the Muslim League endorsed the demand. The point of interest for us is of the idea that Jammu and Kashmir a Muslim majority kingdom should be part of the Muslim homeland-Pakistan. In 1941, Ghulam Abbas left Sheikh Abdullah and joined the Mirwaiz Yusuf Shah. They revived the Muslim Conference which eventually came out in support for Pakistan.

Partition of India into India and Pakistan

India and Pakistan were born on 15 August 1947. Hari Singh, the Maharaja dithered about joining India or Pakistan. He did not trust Jawaharlal Nehru's socialist ideals and he of course knew that he would be sacrificed if he opted for Pakistan. He procrastinated. This led to killings of Muslims in the Hindu majority areas of Jammu and killings of Hindus in the Muslim majority areas of Jammu. The Kashmir valley remained peaceful in this respect. In Gilgit, Major Brown the British officer commanding the Gilgit Scouts assembled his troops on the moonlit parade ground kept a Koran on a table and asked his troops to swear on the Koran and join Pakistan. As one by one all his Muslim troops took the oath for Pakistan on the Koran, he had the Dogra Brigadier of Hari Singh arrested. Gilgit thus went to Pakistan. Meanwhile in Pakistan, the Muslim League and the Muslim Conference, when they realised that Hari Singh was going to opt for India and not for independence, joined hands and started organising a revolt. Armed irregulars were constituted and they began to infiltrate into Poonch, Muzaffarabad and Mirpur areas. Pakistan cut off supplies of essential commodities to Kashmir and on 22 October 1947 armed tribesmen and irregular soldiers of the Pakistan army invaded Kashmir.

The Muslim League and the Muslim Conference miscalculated. Instead of buckling under pressure, the Maharaja released Sheikh Abdulla and the National Conference leaders who had been jailed, asked India for military help to ward off the raiders, and then acceded to India. The Muslim group identity in the Punjabi speaking areas of Poonch, Mirpur and Muzaffarabad along with Gilgit and Baltistan became a part of Pakistan and the Kashmiri group identity along with Jammu and Ladakh was retained as part of India. Unfortunately Pakistan's push and Kashmir's accession to India did not settle anything. It only started a war that continues till this day. There are many unanswered questions in this complex story. Is it that the Muslims in Kashmir wanted to be in Pakistan? Are there truly secular Muslims who feel content to be in a secular India? Are the Hindus in Kashmir happy to be in Jammu as part of the state of Jammu and Kashmir? Do the Buddhist Ladhakis want to be part of this State? These are uncomfortable questions that we shall try to answer in the coming pages. The main insurgency in Kashmir broke out in 1989-90. The roots of this insurgency lie in the history of the partition of India in 1947. In fact the war unleashed on India by Pakistan began during the run up to partition and continues till this day. In this context, the main insurgency is only part of this long history. We shall therefore begin with the events that were unleashed by Pakistan when India was divided and it became known that Kashmir was going to be part of India. The trouble was triggered off when Cyril Radcliffe who was detailed by Great Britain to draw the lines dividing India and Pakistan was influenced by the Viceroy Lord Mountbatten to detach three tehsils on the eastern flank of Gurudaspur district when drawing the international boundary. This was done so that India could have access to Jammu and Kashmir as the national highway from Punjab to Jammu ran through these three tehsils. Originally it was decided that Gurudaspur district was to go to Pakistan as it was a Muslim majority district. When Muhammad Ali Jinnah heard of this step he reacted violently as he had decided that Jammu and Kashmir would fall into his hands like a plum once Gurudaspur district was in Pakistan as India would lose its axis to Jammu. He felt cheated of Kashmir and therefore reacted violently. Major General Akbar Khan, the Military Advisor to the

Pakistan Prime Minister was tasked to organise a covert invasion of Jammu and Kashmir. The assault plan envisaged the use of irregulars, former soldiers and a small core of serving personnel armed with 4000 Punjab Police rifles and Army ordnance secretly diverted for use in Jammu and Kashmir.[1]

The First Kashmir War. In October 28 1947, troops of the Muzaffarabad based 4 Jammu and Kashmir Infantry mutinied killing their Commandant. Shortly thereafter, they were joined by Pakistani irregular forces. The invaders were soon in Uri where they brushed off resistance by outnumbered State forces and were in Baramulla by 27 October. Here they dithered as the tribesmen-Mohmand, Afridi, Waziri and Mehsud from the Northwest Frontier and the Federally Administered Tribal Areas indulged in an orgy of destruction, rape and loot.[2] The worst fate was that of Maqbool Sherwani, a National Conference leader who was crucified like Christ, before he was shot after labeling him a traitor. It is generally believed that Britain was sympathetic to Pakistan vis-a-vis India. This is probably due to a belief that Pakistan a Muslim country would be more capable to oppose expansion southwards by communist Russia.[3] The United Nations intervened, but this made no dent in the situation. Several *jihadi* enterprises were to follow. The war of 1947-48 was a crusade initiated as an instrument of State Policy, not an outbreak of religious anger or communal passion.[4] Low level covert activity mirrored Pakistani conventional military responses in India's spring counter offensives of 1948. That year the Jammu and Kashmir Police recovered 643 crude bombs, 666 hand grenades and 83 tins of fuses in raids which led to 22 arrests. The Police claimed that these explosives had been brought from Pakistan. A candid admission has come from Lt. Gen. Gul Hassan Khan, who was the last Commander-in-Chief of the Pakistan Armed Forces that an unnamed older Statesman in Pakistan organised covert supplies of weapons to the rebel State of Hyderabad in 1948, which was

[1] *Raiders in Kashmir,* Akbar Khan. National Book Foundation, Islamabad, 1970.

[2] *Halfway to Freedom*, Margaret Bourke-White. Asia Publishing House Bombay 1950.

[3] *India's Partition and Human Debasement,* Francis Tucker. Akash Deep Publishing House . New Delhi,1988.

[4] *War and Diplomacy in Kashmir, 1947-48,* C.Dasgupta, New Delhi, Sage Publications.

using armed force to resist accession to the Indian Union. Pakistan Intelligence operators trained the first group of saboteurs. They set fire to a Government guest house on the Srinagar Pahalgam road and set fire to bridges at Sagipura, Singhpura and Kangan, all done with the intention of cutting of communications. 14 conspirators were tried of whom 9 were convicted. Quite a good piece of work. These suspects included several Pakistani nationals. Besides this, there were instances of the cease fire line being violated in armed incursions by border Police patrols. It is important to note a significant direction in which Sheikh Abdulla the new Chief Minister was taking Jammu and Kashmir. Sheikh Abdulla's reforms were to implement the land ceiling laws that he had introduced so that the land owning aristocracy, mainly Hindu would be stripped of their disproportionately high holdings without compensation and redistribution of the surplus land among the tenant farmers would be carried out. The peasantry understood that and Abdullah told them that if Kashmir had gone to Pakistan, such reforms could not be thought of in a feudal country. Corruption which was the bane of Kashmiris, however short circuited many of the reforms carried out by Sheikh Abdullah. This was to be the tragedy of Kashmir, for seldom did the people get good governance. Sheikh Abdullah also complicated the situation by once saying that they had joined India for good, and then again talking of the independence option. In 1952, Abdullah finally came to an agreement on Jammu and Kashmir's special status. His pro independence stand meanwhile continued to be expressed and finally Nehru had to listen to his advisors. On 8 August 1953, two of Abdullah's trusted lieutenants Bakshi Gulam Muhammad and Gulam Muhammad Sadiq staged a coup and replaced Abdullah. There was another side to this story. The Intelligence Bureau was steadily getting reports of the Pakistan Intelligence setting up covert warfare cells within Kashmir. Abdullah was not connected to these. One of the aims of these cells was to contest the accession of Jammu and Kashmir to India. Pakistan had learnt one lesson from its first war with India. It was that a military victory against India was not possible without external help. This was not forthcoming. The alternative was to resume covert operations. Major General Akbar Khan was asked to brief the Pakistan President on what he would suggest to renew disturbances in Jammu and Kashmir. Khan laid out a plan for a covert war in which he would use just 500 men well trained in guerrilla warfare and sabotage.[5] Responsibility for the operations was given to a Police officer, Deputy Inspector General Mian Anwar Ali. The relations and close associates of Sheikh Abdullah also took increasingly to underground subversive activities. Pakistani authorities also pumped in arms, ammunition and explosives into Kashmir to such disgruntled elements.[6] These transactions came to be called the Kashmir Conspiracy Case, in which Sheikh Abdulla was an accused. The charges were framed against Mirza Afzal Beg the lieutenant of the Sheikh and five Pakistani Intelligence Bureau personnel. The case was later withdrawn. According to Indian Intelligence, four groups of covert operatives all acting under the command of Khan Muhammad Khan, a Deputy Superintendent of Police in the Pakistan Intelligence Bureau crossed the cease fire line and entered Kashmir. Three operatives, Bagh Ali, Ismail and Rahim were tasked to operate in Jammu, Abdul Rahim and Jamaluddin in Poonch, Two cells were prepared for operations in the valley, one made up of Jahangir Khan, Akbar Mirpuri and Mohibullah Beg, the other under the command of Aziz Parwana.[7] It is interesting to note that the training imparted to these operatives was remarkably similar to the military training given to the Jehadis in 1990 as was reported by the Intelligence Bureau.[8]

Op Gibraltar and the Master Cell. The Indian Army's forward positions in the Rann of Kutch was taken unawares when Pakistan initiated a series of border incursions in the most sensitive of the border posts there in early 1965. The Indian post of Biarbet was overrun. Firing and shelling along the cease fire line in Kashmir also escalated in the first half of 1965. India recorded 1347 cease fire violations in Jammu and Kashmir. India responded in May by opening a new front in Kargil. Op Gibraltar took its name from some of the most valourised battles in the history of Islam. In AD 711, the

---

[5] *Raiders in Kashmir*, Akbar Khan, National Book Foundation Islamabad, 1970.

[6] *India Pakistan and the Secret Jihad*, Praveen Swami, 2006. page 35. Quoting a secret report on Pakistani Organised subversion.

[7] Ibid

[8] Ibid.

Moorish general Tariq Ibn Ziyad launched his invasion of Spain from Jabal Tariq or the Mount of Tariq, now the Rock of Gibraltar. Legend has it that Tariq burnt his boats on landing so that his troops could not retreat. The Pakistani Military columns that invaded Jammu and Kashmir were also named after heroes in battles between Islam and the non-believers. One column was named Salahuddin after the commander who fought against the Crusaders and the other was called Ghaznavi for Muhammad of Ghazni who invaded India 17 times. Surendranath's report on Pakistan Organised Subversion is one of the few detailed accounts of the precise operations and structure of the Pakistani covert groups that spearheaded Operation Gibraltar. The strength of each company, 120 men, was comprised of Razakars and Mujahideen, specially trained volunteers drawn from the Pakistan administered areas of Jammu and Kashmir. The second component was drawn from two Paramilitary components, the Azad Kashmir Rifles and the Northern Light Infantry. The third component was a small group of Special Services Group commandos. The troops who were to be deployed in OP Gibraltar were all trained at four centres-Sinkiari, Mangbajri, Dungi and Sakesar all in Pakistan occupied Jammu and Kashmir. The Azad Kashmir Rifles were also trained at Nikial Kuiratta, Darman, Tarkundi, Bori Mahal, Pir Kalanjar, Hajira, Kotli and Bher. Interestingly many of these locations would be used to train cadres for the 1989 jihad.[9] On 6 August 1965, a force of some 30,000 Pakistani infiltrators was unleashed across the Cease Fire Line. Their objectives were to establish bases, carry out acts of sabotage and create conditions that would be conducive to the intervention of regular Pakistani troops. The first assault column was expected to encourage a local rebellion. Its presence was however betrayed. Though two more groups were sent in by Pakistan, the rebellion which was hoped for never materialised and those who survived the fighting with Indian troops were tracked down by the Kashmir Police with the aid of local people and the whole operation fizzled out. As Operation Gibraltar began to bog down Bhutto did not agree to wind down the operation, and a second operation Grand Slam was commenced on 1 September 1965. Pakistan's attacks in

---

[9] *India Pakistan and the Secret Jihad*, Praveen Swami, 2006 page 61. Quoting from a Secret Report on Pakistani Organised Subversion.

Chamb and Jaurian were checked by Indian Forces. India attacked in a counter offensive along the Ichogil canal. When hostilities ended the Indian XI Corps had captured 362 square kilometres and had yielded only 51 square kilometres. Gen. Malik's core assumption that the presence of irregular troops in Jammu and Kashmir would spark of a rebellion was proved wrong.[10]

A fortnight after OP Gibraltar commenced, posters appeared on the walls of Srinagar calling on the people of the city to overthrow the Government. They were authored by the Revolutionary council a front organisation of a Master Cell, insurgent group of Kashmir, a self proclaimed insurgent group. Within days, a grenade exploded in Regal *Chowk*. The pieces recovered showed Pakistan Ordinance Factory markings. Through September, there were a series of terrorist incidents. On 6 September there was a strike by the Medical College students. As Police was deployed a grenade was thrown that injured two Policemen and several civilians. There were attempts at arson in the city. The Master cell authored several more incidents of arson and grenade attacks in the ensuing days. Abdul Majid and Ahmed Yunus were two Pakistani operatives who had infiltrated and contacted the Master cell and trained local boys how to throw grenades. Another agent Gul Zaman had brought and dumped three rifles, a Sten gun and ammunition in a forest in Harwan.[11]

In the 1960s the Central Government issued a series of orders to reduce the autonomous character of Jammu and Kashmir. The first was an order issued by the President of India. It allowed the Central Government to take charge of the State of Jammu and Kashmir in the event of collapse of the Constitutional machinery. Prior to this order the imposition of emergency powers required the concurrence of the State Legislature. Then in April 1965, the State Legislature approved the renaming of the State's Sadr-i-Riyasat as the Governor. A wide variety of Central legislations on issues ranging from social security to the rights of trade unions was made applicable

---

[10] Ibid.

[11] Ibid. Quoting from a Secret Report on Pakistani Organised Subversion, Sabotage and Infiltration in Jammu and Kashmir. Jammu and Kashmir Criminal Investigation Department, 1966.

to Jammu and Kashmir. Both Sheikh Abdullah and the Mirwaiz saw these steps as an erosion of the State's autonomy. It led to the two joining hands. When war broke out, Maulvi Muhammad Farouq, the Mirwaiz called for-"God to give victory and glory to Islam, give unconcealed political and religious legitimacy to the Pakistani campaign and rid Kashmir of the *zulm* of *zalims*. Make those friends who have come here with hopes successful." A week later on 10 September, by which time it was clear that the Pakistan offensive was being rolled back, the Mirwaiz again invoked God, asking him "to take revenge upon the enemy, make them eat dust, create an earthquake to destroy the enemy." "Pakistan had created some cells that had been working for some years in Kashmir. Peculiarly, people like the Mirwaiz who were openly favouring Pakistan did not extend any significant help to the members of these cells. Religious propaganda however continued after the end of the 1965 war. On 18 October 1965, protesters threw stones on the Police from inside the Hazratbal shrine. On 27 October, protesters dug up the grave of a Sufi shrine at the Ziarrat Rozabal and leaves of the Koran in an adjoining mosque were torn, all done in an effort to provoke Muslim religious fury. The design behind these incidents could not be fully fathomed at the time of their occurrences, but were understood after the Master Cell and its ramifications were unraveled.[12] It was the posturing of the Mirwaiz that led to the unraveling of the cell set up by Pakistan in Kashmir. A source informed the J and K Police that the posters that were appearing in Srinagar were printed at the Mirwaiz Manzil the hereditary home of the Mirwaiz. The tip off led the Police to Sofi Gulam Ahmed, the editor of the *Hurriyat,* the House organ of the Mirwaiz's political organisation, the Awami Action Council. From Sofi Gulam Ahmed, the Police was able to establish that the posters emanated from multiple sources, information that led to the Poster cell, the Students cell, and then to the Master cell.[13]

Investigations and interrogations led to the conclusion that the Master cell planned to assassinate several pro India politicians, including the Chief Minister G.M.Sadiq, his key political associate, Mir Qasim and the Home

---

[12] SECRET. Report on Pakistan Organised Subversion.
[13] Ibid.

Minister D.P.Dhar. Investigations further revealed that the Master cell's war continued and was not dependent on Pakistan's military campaign. Three days after the abortive attempt on Qasim's life a grenade was found concealed just 150 metres from Sadiq's residence presumably for an assassin to pick it up and hurl it at Sadiq as he left his house. The Police investigating the Master cell also believed that six 0.38 revolvers given to the cell during the war were also intended to be used for assassination attempts. The revolvers were brought by two cell members Bashir Ahmed Kitchloo and Muhammad Ali Malik along with several hand grenades and stored with a timber contractor in the Chandji forests. Subsequent investigations revealed that they had the necessary weapons for a prolonged terrorist campaign. A raid on a weapon cache left behind by the Pakistani irregulars for the cell led to the recovery of 40 boxes of plastic explosive and three boxes of ammunition.[14]

Some of the most interesting testimony on this issue came from Sattar Khandey, who along with his covert operatives Shabad Khandey, Samad Wani and Ghulam Nabi had played a key role in enabling one Hayat Mir in operations in Badgam. Shaban Khandey was eventually arrested and led investigators to rifles that had been looted from Badgam but Sattar Khandey made his way back to Pakistan, travelling with a Pakistani column over the Pir Panjal Mountains and then across the Cease Fire Line.

Analysing the sequence of events it is clear that despite trying to remove the defects of the earlier cross border operations, Pakistan's Intelligence and the military campaign failed a second time, the former in destabilising the government of Jammu and Kashmir and the latter in defeating the Indian Army.

Pakistan was not however going to give up so easily. Even as Pakistan talked peace in Tashkent, their Intelligence Service was working on the infrastructure of yet another covert operation. Just before the signing of the Tashkent agreement, Zulfiqar Bhutto had told the United Nations that Pakistan was prepared to wage war with India for a thousand years.[15]

---

[14] Ibid.

Al Fatah

Gulam Rasool Zahgir had worked for the Master Cell and had been detained by the Kashmir Police, but was released in January 1966 as he was not considered dangerous. He was however a committed person and on his release he contacted a group working with the Pakistan High Commission in Delhi and was soon in Kashmir organising another underground group. Zargar and his contact Syed Sarwar of the Students Revolutionary Council opened their account by attacking and stabbing a sentry constable of the Border Security Force who was on duty guarding the Nawakadal Bridge over the Jhelum in Srinagar. The BSF constable died. Zahgir was arrested shortly after this murder under the Defence of India Rules for resuming his anti national activities. His involvement in the attack on the BSF constable did not come to light. The group had by now assumed the name of the Red Kashmir Group. Meanwhile Syed Sarwar and an associate Nazir Ahmed Wani crossed over to Pakistan in September, through the Northern Sector across Bandipora. They were welcomed by the Pakistan Army and trained in small arms and espionage. Zahgir and his associate returned across the International Border opposite Sialkot in November 1967 and soon expanded their group. Three of the new members were sent across to Pakistan. Zahgir was released after some time and he and Wani crossed over to Pakistan together in July 1968.

Two developments put a halt to Pakistan's thinking to continue the secret war in Kashmir. The first was the reaction of the Indian Army when Chinese troops fired on Indian forces working on the Nathu La pass on the Sikkim Tibet border. Indian troops fired back mortar bombs at the Chinese. At this the Chinese also fired mortar bombs on the Indians troops. General Sagat Singh commanding a refurbished 17 Mountain Division retaliated by firing 5.5 inch medium Artillery shells at the Chinese and also ordered his formations to move forward, indicating that he was not to be intimidated. After five days of fighting the Chinese asked for a cease fire. They had

---

[15] Zulfi Bhutto of Pakistan. His life and times. Oxford University Press, New York. 1993.

suffered an estimated 400 dead and wounded. The Indians had 65 killed and 145 injured.

The Nathu La fighting had a clear message for the Pakistan Army. The buildup of the Indian Army after the Chinese debacle of 1962 had clearly tilted the balance in India's favour vis-a-vis Pakistan.

The second development was the rising rebellion in East Pakistan. For years the Government in Pakistan had been exploiting the natural resources of East Pakistan. Jute grown in the rice paddy swamps of East Pakistan was sent to the Jute mills in West Pakistan processed and exported. The leadership in West Pakistan had exploited the natural resources of the eastern part of the country and used it for the development of the western half. This had led to the spawning of left parties in East Pakistan, taking the leadership from her neighbour in West Bengal. Besides the Communist parties, a third leftist party had come up called the Jatiya Samajtantrik Dal or Jashod. They called themselves Socialists but were more leftist than the existing Left parties. As discontent grew in East Pakistan, Pakistan Intelligence unearthed a plot to assassinate President Ayub Khan and establish an independent State in the east. This was the Agartala Conspiracy case in which a number of Bengali Army officers were involved. President Ayub overplayed his hand when he tried to implicate Sheikh Mujibur Rehman in the Agartala conspiracy case. This blew up in his face as the East Pakistan people erupted in strikes and protests that forced the Government to take increasingly stern action. The situation was fast deteriorating.

This affected the next phase of rebellion in Kashmir as the Pakistan Army was preoccupied in the east. When Zahgir returned from Pakistan he brought two new recruits with him Muhammad Aslam Wani and Zahoor Ahmed Shahdad. They planned to rob an armoury of the National Cadet Corps. The attempt failed and in the ensuing melee one of the attackers Gulam Muhammad Baba was arrested. He sang on interrogation and the sequel led to the transaction of the Nawakadal murder and the Red Kashmir Group. This further led to Syed Sarwar who was now working with the officials of the Pakistan High Commission. Sarwar was immediately arrested. Notes maintained by Zahgir gave details of the instructions he had received from the Pakistan Field Intelligence in 1968-69. Zahgir's instructors identified for him three separate planes on which the covert war was to be waged. The most important of these was detailed information on the deployment of the Indian Army, their installations, the details of roads, bridges linking the Army installations. This pointed to the integration of the covert war with the strategic imperatives of the Pakistan Army.[16]

Zahgir's training by his Pakistan handlers is of interest. They had studied several Left Wing insurgencies and the tactics adopted by these Left wing groups were adopted and given a green coating of Islam. Zahgir after his training on methods of subverting the State chose *Al Fatah* as the name of his covert group. It was a name that had acquired fame when a little known Palestinian group had beaten back an attack by the Israeli Army in March 1968. The name could also have been chosen because Al Fatah referred to the day when Muhammad the Prophet entered the *Kaaba* and smashed the idols there in AD 630.

The first major operation of Al Fatah was a dacoity on the Pulwama Education Department office which the group easily carried out as the guards in this office were unarmed. The group of nine persons led by Zahgir raided the office in Pulwama at night and lifted the safe and decamped. They broke open the safe the next day and got Rs 71000/- odd for their efforts. Zahgir spent the major amount of this dacoity on building a head quarters for his group. This he did near Barsoo village near Bijbihara. Zahgir now travelled to Delhi and reported to the Pakistan High Commission in May 1970 about the Pulwama dacoity. He had also collected quite some information about deployment of the Indian Army in Kashmir. The sequel to this visit was the tour of a Pakistani, Mufti Zia ul Haq to Kashmir, obviously to assess the work of Al Fatah. Zahgir had established an unit of Al Fatah in Doda. This unit was able to gather quite some information on the movements of the Indian Army. Indian Intelligence had so far got no clue to the net established by Zahgir. They had also recruited more than three hundred boys from different parts of Kashmir and sent them to Pakistan for

---

[16] Gulam Rasool Zahgir. Fragments of Notes maintained from November 1968 to January 1969.Note 3.

training. All of them had been trained in handling automatic weapons, but strangely the Pakistan Intelligence did not give them weapons when they returned to Kashmir after trainng. Indian Intellignce however maintained that only about two hundred boys were selected of which only twenty five were sent to Pakistan. Zahgir now set about organising a political wing for the AL Fatah. He established a link with Mirza Afzal Beg, the Plebiscite Front leader. He also set up two groups, the Young Men's League and the Students Federation. Meanwhile, Zahgir was planning his next dacoity. He chose the Jammu and Kashmir Bank's Hazratbal branch. He planned it carefully. The success of the plan was based on the ineptness of the bank's officers and other employees. The person chosen to carry out the crime Nazir Ahmed Wani dressed as a Deputy Superintendent of the Kashmir Police walked into the bank and demanded that the Manager and cashier hand over all the cash and record books of the branch, as he was investigating an embezzlement in the Government Treasury that had just taken place. The foolish manager and the cashier handed over the cash and the books of the branch and accompanied Wani and the other members into a waiting car. After driving a short distance, the Manager and the cashier were asked to get down and unceremoniously pushed out of the car. The car then drove off leaving a very foolish manager and cashier on the road. The Kashmir Police was at first nonplussed, but a bank employee recognised one of the boys who had accompanied Nazir Ahmed Wani and this led to the arrest of one Muhammad Yusuf Mir, who cracked under interrogation and revealed the details of Al Fateh. Deputy Inspector General Pir Ghulam Hassan Shah led the raid on the camp at Barsoo. Nazir Ahmed and Farooq Bhat were arrested in the camp. The police seized weapons and explosives from the camp. Further interrogation led to further information and finally Zahgir was arrested. It was only then that the Police learnt about the Pulwama dacoity. They also recovered all the details of the structure of Al Fatah. Pakistan's covert Service had again been disillusioned. The Al Fatah members would watch the progress of the next war from behind bars. Meanwhile Zafar Iqbal Rathore, the Pakistan Intellignce officer, who had handled Al Fatah from the Pakistan High Commission in Delhi was declared Persona Non Grata and asked to leave India. Pir Gulam Hassan

Shah the Police Officer who had broken the back of the Al Fatah, now began a process to win over the misguided young cadres of the Al Fatah as directed by the new Chief Minister Syed Mir Qasim, who was under pressure from the parents of the arrested cadres of the Al Fatah. In 1975, the scheme turned out a success with the majority of the cadres entering the main stream forming the *Inquilabi Mahaz*. Fazl-ul Haq Querishi, Nazir Ahmed Wani, Hamidullah Bhat, Muhammad Shaban Vakil and Farooq Ahmed Bhat rejected the offer. This was a decision that Pir Ghulam Hassan Shah and A.M.Watali, the Police Officers who handled the Al Fatah case were going to regret.

The 1971 War and the Liberation of Bangladesh

Meanwhile in the East, Pakistan was fighting a losing battle with the insurgent groups of the Mukti Bahini who were trained and equipped by India. Pakistan's main blunder was due to their racial arrogance, that the Dravidian East Bengalis had no authority to rule Pakistan. Mujibur Rehman and his Awami League, an East Bengali party won the National elections by a clean majority. He should have been invited with his party to lead the Government of Pakistan. This was something that the West Pakistani leadership could not countenance. Mujib was arrested and the Pakistani Army started a crackdown on the Awami League and on the East Pakistani Bengali people as a whole. In this they were assisted by the Jamaat-e-Islami and Bihari Muslims who had migrated to East Pakistan in 1947. The Jamaat cadres identified Bengali Muslim and Hindu leaders of the Awami League, who were first arrested and later simply massacred. The Pakistani Army led by some fanatical officers and other ranks then began rounding up Bengali men and women, particularly students, both boys and girls and let loose a killing spree. Hundreds of young Bengali Muslim and Hindu girls and women were raped and killed and their bodies disposed by burying in mass graves. Three companies of the East Bengal Regiment of the Pakistan Army revolted after the Pakistan Army massacred more than a company of theirs. The remaining companies retreated into Tripura in India. They were organised into a Guerrilla Force by India's Intelligence agencies and trained and equipped. A large number of civilians, belonging to political parties who opposed Pakistan also crossed over into India. They were organised into guerrilla fighter groups called the *Mukti Bahini* and after training and equipping them, began operating inside East Pakistan cutting off the communications of the Pakistan Army and harassing them, ambushing their columns and attacking them where they were weak. Several Bengali officers who were in the Pakistan Army in the West at the time of the commencement of the pogrom in East Pakistan managed to slip across into India and were escorted by the Border Security Force to the East to lead the Mukti Bahini. Two who were to become famous were Major Abu Taher and Major Ziauddin.

The Indian Army led by General Sam Manekshaw watched and waited till end November and then when the Pakistani forces were beginning to get demoralised advanced across the borders and in a clever move by passed the garrisons of the Pakistan Army in all the sectors and surrounded Dacca. The Pakistan Army was forced to surrender. More than ninety thousand troops surrendered to the Indian Army, were disarmed and transferred to Prisoner of War camps in India along with their weapons. This was a humiliating defeat for Pakistan, one that they were not going to ever forget. As for Kashmir, there was naturally a lull in the Pakistan Army's covert war on India, but this was going to recommence with added vengeance by a Pakistan Army smarting from their humiliation of surrender to the Indian Army. In the elections of 1972, most of the members of the Plebiscite Front were in jail and Sheikh Abdullah was also kept out of the elections. The vacated space was occupied by the rising Jamaat-e-Islami. Similarly in Jammu the right wing Hindu party the Jan Sangh increased its percentage. Jammu and Kashmir was getting polarised on religious lines. In Kashmir, there was a definite trend to right wing Islamism. This was because of the rise of the Jamaat-e-Islami. Here the Government had a role to play that was not known too well. When Sheikh Abdullah had taken over as the Chief Minister after independence; he had started a scheme to encourage the spread of Sufi Islam. He set up a number of units to spread Sufi teaching in the state. Many of these units included schools to be run on the pattern of Madrassas but to spread the message of the Sufi shrines in the Valley.

There were almost a hundred such units spread all over the Vale of Kashmir. Unfortunately when the Sheikh was jailed and had become unpopular with Delhi, his successors neglected these Sufi centres, and the units without patronage started closing down. Regrettably to play down the popularity of the Sheikh, the Government even encouraged the Jamaat-e-Islami to set up their madrassas. This was suicidal. The Jamaat was created in 1941 by Maulana Maudoodi who proclaimed loud and clear that India should not be divided into India and Pakistan. He further stated the reasons for this. According to him and to other Fundamentalist groups in Islam, there were three Caliphates of Islam in the world. The first was of course the Sunni Caliphate in Baghdad. The second was the Shia Caliphate in Isfahan in Persia. The third was the Sunni caliphate of the Mughal Empire in Delhi. Maulana Maudoodi meant that the Caliphate in Delhi should continue to rule. Here was the Government in Delhi allowing the Jamaat to set up their Madrassas in Kashmir. As a result of this step and the coincidental neglect of the Sufi institutions set up by the Sheikh in the Kashmir valley, many of the latter institutions were taken over by the Jamaat and converted to their Madrassas.

In 1975, Mrs. Gandhi, the Indian Prime Minister declared a state of Emergency in the country. Both right wing Islamist and Hindu groups were proscribed. The Jamaat which was proscribed, had by that time more than 125 schools and 500 odd evening schools. These were closed down. Since the teachers would be without jobs, the State offered them alternate jobs, which only meant that the teachers now had a wider platform to spread the cancer of Islamic fundamentalism. Many of the Jamaat schools that closed down opened again as private schools and also continued to spread this cancer among the young children of the valley. There was a temporary reprieve however. After the Emergency when the elections were called, Sheikh Abdullah pulled off a big victory. The Jamaat got just one out of the nineteen seats that it contested. The administration of the Sheikh Abdullah Government was generally peaceful. Pakistan was in trouble internally again as the Baluch started an independence movement. In England the Plebiscite Front had set up a unit in England called the National Liberation Front. At a meeting in London, the Plebiscite Front decided to rename itself as the Jammu and Kashmir Liberation Front (JKLF). Amanullah Khan became the General Secretary. Many Mirpuris from Pakistan Occupied Kashmir had migrated to England and become a prosperous community. They now supported the JKLF. Branches were set up in Pakistan, the United States and several European capitals. Nobody seems to have paid much attention to this development. Another development was significant. Though the Jamaat had fared badly in the elections held after the lifting of the Emergency in 1977, Islamist forces had regrown. Two incidents happened in 1979, both of which gave a big encouragement to Islamist forces in South and South East Asia. One was the revolution of Ayatollah Khomeini in Iran. This spewed off a big wave of Islamism in Africa, the Middle East, South Asia and South East Asia. The second was the *Jihad* against the Russians in Afghanistan which attracted volunteers from North Africa, the Middle East, South Asia and the Islamic countries of South East Asia. It had its impact in Jammu and Kashmir too.

Kashmir after Sheikh Abdullah. Sheikh Abdullah died in September 1982. He had anointed his son Dr. Farooq Abdullah as his heir. This angered the Sheikh's son in law. The first months of Dr. Farooq's rule was flamboyant. Elections were due to the State Assembly in 1983. Mrs. Gandhi now committed a series of blunders. She did not particularly get along with Dr. Farooq. At about this time in far away Andhra Pradesh a new political party had emerged that defeated the Congress for the first time in that State. This was the Telugu Desam led by a former film actor N.T.Rama Rao. This was mainly of a particularly rich and progressive community of Andhra Pradesh called the Kammas. They were as powerful as the ruling Reddy community. Mrs. Gandhi was unhappy with this development and foolishly labeled N.T.Rama Rao as anti national. A regional group had also come up in Assam the All Assam Students Union (AASU) who were fighting for ejecting Bangladeshi Muslims, the vote bank of the Congress party in Assam. N.T.Rama Rao had befriended the AASU leaders. Farooq now joined this group. Mrs. Gandhi promptly called all three anti national. When the elections to the State were announced in Jammu and Kashmir she wanted to have an understanding with Dr. Farooq. By now relations were strained and the National Conference campaigned on its own. Regrettably Mrs.

Gandhi campaigned on communal lines in the Kashmir valley. She was booed in Srinagar when she went dressed in Kashmiri dress to campaign and opened her speech saying she was a daughter of Kashmir. She did not know Kashmiri and when she said this in Hindi, the crowd booed her and she could not make herself heard. The meeting ended in confusion and she never forgave Dr. Farooq for this. Her speeches in Jammu were welcomed. When the results came there was a clear polarisation. The valley voted for the National Conference, while Jammu voted for the Congress. Though the Jamaat did not get a seat, the National Conference had allied with the Mirwaiz, the historic rival of the National Conference. This gave space and legitimacy to the Islamists. This was evidenced by a series of incidents. A bomb was exploded on 15 August during the celebrations of India's Independence Day. A group of Islamists booed the Indian cricket team and waved Pakistani flags in a cricket match in Srinagar. In the next year 1984, there were more such incidents. On 29 May 1984 members of an Islamist procession attacked an Indian Army convoy. Mrs. Gandhi meanwhile had not forgiven Dr, Farooq for the election defeat in 1983. She now befriended Gul Shah, Dr. Farooq's brother in law who was sulking in the sidelines because he was not handed over the *gaddi* by the Sheikh. She called the Governor of Jammu and Kashmir, Mr. B.K.Nehru, and asked him to call Gul Shah and arrange the purchase of some National Conference MLA's and destabilise Dr. Farooq. The Governor refused to do this dirty work and Mrs. Gandhi transferred him to Gujarat. She then brought Jagmohan an officer of the Union Territories cadre, who had earned notoriety in the Turkman Gate incident of forced sterilisation of men during the Emergency as the Governor of Kashmir. Jagmohan won over a number of MLAs and calling them to the Raj Bhavan, did a head count and informed Dr. Farooq that he had lost his majority. Gul Shah was made the Chief Minister with the backing of the Congress. Having entered office through the back door, Gul Shah had no popular support and had to take the help of Islamists and other anti Indian groups. Of his ninety days in office, seventy two days were troubled with curfews and shut downs. The Chief Minister earned the nickname 'Gul-e-Curfew'. In March 1986, Jagmohan dismissed the Ministry and took over the reins himself. Regrettably the new Governor did not or could not understand the ethos of the Kashmiri Muslim and things simply drifted. Mrs. Gandhi was then assassinated by two of her own Sikh guards. The new Prime Minister was her own completely inexperienced son, who had till recently been a pilot in Indian Airlines and knew nothing about piloting a complicated country like India. Instead of calling for fresh elections after the dismissal of the Gul Shah Government, the New Prime Minister under guidance of his advisors reinstalled a National Conference, Congress alliance. A new election was called in 1987. Here Farooq made the mistake of his life when he decided to agree to an alliance with the Congress. The Kashmiri people were aghast. Here was a Chief Minister who had been dismissed without any basis by the Governor at the instance of the Congress Prime Minister in Delhi, now shamelessly agreeing to a coalition with the same party that dismissed him. The Kashmiri people felt that Dr. Farooq Abdulla had no respect for his constituents in Kashmir. The Islamist groups coalesced into a coalition constituted by the Jamaat-e-Islami, Qazi Nissar's, Ummat-e-Islami and Maulvi Abbas Ansari's Shia, Anjuman-e-Ittehad-ul-Mussalmeen. The coalition called itself the Muslim United Front (MUF). It was the clerics and not professional politicians who had the reins of power in this coalition. There was considerable rigging in the elections, but a dispassionate examination of the voting pattern showed that the MUF could never have won the election even if there had been no rigging. The vote share of the JEI rose from 6.6 per cent in 1983 to 31.9 per cent in 1987, while that of the National Conference fell from 59.3 to 49.2 per cent.[17] The rigging done quite blatantly had a distinct fallout as it incensed the Islamist groups. For the first time, Jammu and Kashmir was having a constituency hostile both to the National Conference and to New Delhi. For Pakistan conditions appeared to be more favourable than before to make another attempt for a jihad. Pakistan's covert service was flush with funds for the Afghan Jihad against Russia and they naturally commenced another attempt to destabilise India in her northern frontier. The Jammu and Kashmir Liberation Front (JKLF) was the first to get active. Abdul Hamid Sheikh a JKLF man was the first to cross to Pakistan and get training in small arms. Returning to Kashmir he organised the JKLF along with

---

[17] P.S.Verma. Jammu and Kashmir at the Political Cross roads. New Delhi. Vikas. 1994.

Yasin Malik, Ashfaq Majid Wani and Javed Mir.

Pakistan's Attempt Succeeds

A number of other groups also went to Pakistan for training and getting weapons for a jihad. These included Fazl-ul Haq Querishi, a veteran of the Master Cell and Al Fatah, Abdul Majid Dar who later joined the Hizbul Mujahideen and Ahmed Abdul Waza of the Peoples Conference. At first the objective of these jihadi groups was not to confront the State but to strip it of authority. Of 390 violent incidents in 1988, only six were against the Police and Para Military forces and in 1989, of 2154 attacks, only 49 were on the security forces. Nilkanth Ganjoo, the judge who sentenced Maqbool Bhat to death was killed, The Intelligence Bureau was widely targeted and lost four of their officers, R.N.P.Singh, Kishen Gopal, M.l.Bhan and T.K.Razdan. The organisation was forced to close its offices in the interior. Their officers were accommodated in the Army camps later. The other group targeted was political party workers. The National Conference party men were warned to disassociate themselves from the party. Jihadi groups prohibited voters from voting in the by election to the Parliament in November 1989.

The next development was after the elections of 1989, when V.P.Singh took over as the Prime Minister. He appointed Mufti Muhammad Syed a veteran Congress politician from South Kashmir as the Home Minister of India. In December 1989, the JKLF kidnapped his daughter, Rubaiya Sayeed, a medical student in the Kashmir Medical College. At this point the Government of India committed a serious mistake. Knowing the culture of the Kashmiris, it was absolutely clear that the JKLF would not have dared to touch Rubaiya Sayeed. The JKLF demanded the release of five cadres of theirs held on terrorism charges. The Joint Director of the Intelligence Bureau, an old Kashmir hand advised the Government not to give in. At the last moment a team arrived from Delhi and directed the prisoners to be released. As soon as the prisoners were released, there were thousands of people on the road escorting the prisoners and the Police simply disappeared from the scene. When the Assembly elections of 1987 were held the State had blatantly replaced the ballot boxes and even beaten the candidates and their supporters. This had induced the first wave of young boys leaving for the Line of Control and slipping into Pakistan Occupied Kashmir. By the time the kidnapping of Rubaiya Sayeed had taken place and the arrested JKLF accused were released, the crossing across the LOC had become a flow.

The JKLF had always projected itself as representing all the people of Kashmir, the Hindu Pandits, the Kashmiri Sikhs, and the Kashmiri Muslims. In practice this was far from true. Though broadcasting itself as secular it was far from being so. It was a Muslim party for the Muslims of Kashmir. This answer is provided from the ground practices of the JKLF. The events leading to the exodus of the Hindu Kashmiri Pandits exposes the real picture of the JKLF. The Kashmiri Muslims and the Hindus were of common genealogical descent. The Kashmiri Hindus had been the beneficiaries during the long period of Dogra rule and the consequent resentment built up over the years now found release in the attacks on the Pandit community. From 1989 the community came under threat, with threatening phone calls, letters and then one by one there were targeted killings and then rapes of mothers and daughters of Pandits. Some of the killings were quite brutal. B.K.Ganju was killed when killers entered his house and found him hiding in a drum for storing rice. They pumped bullets into the drum killing him instantly and staining his rice with his blood. Sarla Bhat a nurse working in the Sohra hospital was kidnapped by JKLF militants and repeatedly raped and finally riddled with bullets. The rape was proved in her post mortem. In May 1989, Brij Nath Kaul his wife and sister were kidnapped. The two women were raped in his presence and then he was clubbed to death. By the end of the year some eighty persons had been killed and in early ninety, the fear psychosis was complete and the Pandits realised that the State could not protect them and began to stream out from the valley. By June more than fifty eight thousand were relocated in camps in Jammu and Delhi. Politically the Bharatiya Janata Party espoused the cause of the Pandits, but the Congress and the Janata Dal ignored it. The real culprit was the Government in Delhi headed by V.P.Singh who to shore up its Muslim base ignored the pogrom against the Pandits.[18]

Who were the terrorists of this initial period? A study showed that 42 per cent were engaged in some form of labour for wages, 22 per cent were farmers, 19 per cent were students and 14 per cent were petty traders.[19] The JKLF's Muhammad Yasin Malik was the son of a bus driver, his aide, Javed Mir, a plumber. The Amir of the Hizbul Mujahideen Muhammad Yusuf Shah, later known as Syed Salahuddin was from a family with orchards. As for Pakistan it had been presented on a platter, a jihad that they had been dreaming of organising for decades. Pakistan's Military and covert Services were congratulating themselves. When the news of a large number of people being killed in firing by security forces in Gawkadal was received in Pakistan, their Prime Minister Benazir Bhutto responded by declaring Pakistan's support for the Kashmiris right of self determination. 1998 -89 had seen droves of young people crossing the Line of Control. Pakistan's covert Services welcomed them and set up training camps for this sudden flood. Violence and attacks on Pandits became frequent as 1988 turned to 1989. By December 1989, the State had lost control of the situation. In December 1989, several police men were killed in bomb blasts or shootings. In January of 1990, the Intelligence Bureau lost three of their field officers to militant attacks. Jagmohan was appointed the Governor for the second time. The day he arrived was a bleak cold winter day. The Police had abdicated their responsibility and the senior officers were not on hand to receive the new Governor. On 19 January, the CRPF conducted searches in different parts of downtown Srinagar. The people's reaction to the searches was belligerent and the next day crowds surged forth into the town shouting slogans demanding *Azaadi.* The Police abdicated and virtually abandoned the city to the mobs. That evening the Governor called the 15 Corps Commander and told him to impose curfew and restore order. General Mohammad Ahmed Zaki, the Corps Commander was a professional officer. He informed the Governor that he had been seeing the situation deteriorate. If he had to enforce curfew, his troops would have to fire and there would be many casualties. Would the Governor be able to take this? The Governor told him to restore order and fire if necessary. Throughout the night the

---

[18] Manoj Joshi, *The Lost Rebellion.* Penguin 1999.

[19] Major General Afsar Karim. *Kashmir the Troubled Frontier,* Lancer, New Delhi.

loudspeakers in the mosques were spewing venom. The next day the militants were out asking the crowds to collect and come out in processions. The crowds chanting slogans came marching; the troops confronted them and asked them to disperse as there was a curfew. Probably the crowds did not expect the troops to fire. But they did, when they found the crowds disobeying their orders. There is really no record of how many people died, though officially the number was given as 12. Obviously many more died. As the troops fired again and again, the crowds wilted and then fled till the streets of Srinagar were empty.

For the first time in many months the Government had acted sternly. The next day Srinagar city was in shock. The steam had been taken out of the people and no one wanted to risk challenging the State.

The different Insurgent Groups of Kashmir

The Pakistan Inter Services Intelligence had geared itself to the flood of volunteers coming from Kashmir for training. They set up camps in *Ilaqa Gair* and other places. The JKLF was the first group. In 1989, the group saw its first division when Mushtaq Latrum left with his followers and set up the Al Umar Mujahideen. Then the Peoples League sent a candidate of theirs, Firdaus Ahmed Baba who went across to POK. He along with his followers started a Mujahideen group called the Muslim Janbaz Force. The Peoples Conference of Abdul Gani Lone also got a group called the Al Burq set up by Pakistan. Later this *Tanzeem* catered to Gujjar youth from Bandipore area.

Several such groups came up because of the different political groups in Kashmir. Pakistan also encouraged the setting up of different groups for security reasons. In a like manner, the Jammu and Kashmir Students Liberation Front was converted to the Ikhwan-ul-Mussalmeen.

The other Kashmiri Insurgent group was the Al Jihad. All these Kashmiri groups though belligerent, had poor fighting spirit. This was because they were brought up in the spirit of Sufism, which is a religion of peace unlike the hard Islamic ideology of the Jamaat-e-Islami or the Jamaat-e-Ulemi-

Islam, which was the Pakistan equivalent of the Jamaat-e-Ulema-e Hind founded in India in the 19th century at Deoband in Uttar Pradesh, or the Ahle Hadith, founded in Delhi and whose Pakistan branch produced the ruthless Lashkar-e-Taiba. There were two insurgent groups spawned in Pakistan from the Muslims of Kashmir. These were the Hizbul Mujahideen the *tanzeem* of the Kashmiris who had embraced the Jamaat-e-Islami. The other was the *Allah* Tigers. The Kashmiris who joined this Tanzeem were also cruel and ruthless.

The situation was deteriorating with the State being almost rudderless. One of the key mistakes was the posting of the Director General of Police, J.N. Saxena who was throughout on deputation with the Intelligence Bureau. He may have been a good Intelligence officer, but he had no experience of handling men in uniform. What was required was a tough officer from the cadre who could lead his men on the ground. Saxena was not such a person. The Kashmir Police was rudderless from the beginning of the insurgency and there was no one to put them in the forefront of the Counter Insurgency effort by the Para Military Forces and the Army. The state bureaucracy was in a still worse state with many government servants openly sympathetic with the militants. Strangely, the most affected were the Doctors in the main hospitals of Srinagar. The captain of this team was Dr. Ahad Guru, a leading cardiologist and Professor of the Sohra Institute of Medical Sciences and a member of the Supreme Council of the JKLF.

After the attacks by the Kashmiri insurgent groups like the JKLF, Ikhwan, Al Jihad and the Al Umar, the Hizbul opened their account. Their cadres came and shot dead the Mirwaiz. It is not clear why the ISI decided to kill him. He was absolutely anti India and anti Hindu as could be seen from his utterances in favour of the Pakistanis and totally against the Indians in the 1965 and 1971 wars. When news of his assassination spread, a huge crowd gathered and took his body in a procession to the Idgah. The huge crowd was emotionally charged. Seeing the procession, the JK Police simply abandoned their posts and melted away, leaving the CRPF picquets enroute. One of these picquets, seeing the unruly crowd carrying a dead body opened fire. No one knew how many people died, but the figure could have been at least fifty. The Police recovering from this adverse incident investigated and arrested one Ghulam Muhammad Sofi @Bittacheeni. On interrogation he confessed that the Mirwaiz had been killed on orders of the ISI to a group called the Green Army. This group was later dissolved and formed the Jamiat-ul Mujahideen.

There was almost a mushroom growth of insurgent groups. In order to coordinate their functioning, the ISI called a meeting in April 1991. The first point of this meeting was that the JKLF was left out. This was a clear message. The main decision of the meeting was that all *tanzeems* would work under the guidance of the Tehrik Hurriyat-e-Kashmir (THEK), a political body with a *Muthaida Jihad* Council (United Jihad Council) to unite the militant groups. The THEK was dominated by the JEI. It was headed by one Ashraf Saraf, who was completely controlled by the ISI. The ISI officials controlling these organisations were Brig. Farooq Ahmed and Colonel Shaukat. In all these developments the JKLF was studiously ignored. The ISI was also depriving the JKLF of weapons and money, but they could not reduce their hold in Srinagar. Despite all these attempts at controlling the Tanzeems, they continued to be fractious unruly and ill disciplined. There were a number of rapes by the cadres of different Tanzeems. The victims included Muslim girls too. This gave a bad image to the concerned Tanzeems. The militants also indulged in extortion and kidnappings.

After the initial confusion the State settled into a kind of normalcy with the militants operating, people being killed, encounters taking place between the militants and Security Forces and normal commerce, Government functioning, supplies coming in, handicrafts going out and even tourists coming. This naturally displeased the ISI. To raise the tempo, the *tanzeems* started a series of kidnappings. This was done with a view to get arrested militants released. The Government gave in at the beginning, but when they asked for hard core militants to be released, the Government refused. When the leader of the *Hezbollah* was arrested the militants kidnapped Mr. and Mrs. Wakhloo and demanded the release of their leader in exchange. The Government refused. The Army which had by now been deployed surrounded the area where the Wakhloos had been confined and rescued them.

In the latter half of 1992, the ISI sent the first Afghan militants into Kashmir. They were from the Hizb-e-Islami, a JEI tanzeem, one of the sixteen groups that operated in Afghanistan. This was done to show what a real fighter could do, so that the Kashmiri could try to measure up to them. Akbar Bhai an Afghan and Ibne Masood of Sudan entered Sopore. They were however killed in a fierce encounter with the Army in 1993.

It was at this stage that one of the cardinal mistakes in the context of Hindu Muslim relations was committed. This was the demolition of the Babri Masjid in Uttar Pradesh. The whole story was a disaster from the beginning and happened because the Indian State was weak. The Bharatiya Janata Party held that there was reported to be a temple where the Babri Masjid mosque was constructed. This led to an agitation for quite some time that the Babri Masjid should be demolished and the temple reconstructed.

The facts on the ground were that when the Muslim kings first invaded India in the 8th century AD, they demolished dozens of temples. If the Hindu kings were strong they should have repulsed the Moslem armies. The destruction of temples by the Moslem armies was a fact of history that was reversed when the British came and after that all religions were allowed to practice equally. At the time when the Muslim kings were uppermost, and demolished some Hindu temples, these temples were not rebuilt. If the Hindu kings were strong, they should have driven out the Muslims including the Hindus who had converted to Islam and made India a pure Hindu country. They could not do that because they were not strong. When the BJP government in Uttar Pradesh was agitating to demolish the Babri Masjid, the Congress ruling Central Government in Delhi should have dismissed the BJP Government, declared Presidents rule and deployed Para military forces round the Masjid and ensured that the fanatical BJP were neutralised. Instead they sent Para military forces to Uttar Pradesh, without the State asking for them and they stood by when the crazy hordes under the nose of the Police demolished the Babri Masjid. This left a permanent scar in Hindu Muslim relations in India and particularly in Kashmir.

The first reaction to this was the Bombay blasts of 1993 master minded by the kingpin of the *Hawala* racket in Bombay Dawood Ibrahim. He was also the biggest financier of the Bombay film industry. The *Hawala* was the parallel foreign exchange system between the Gulf countries and India. In Kashmir many level headed Kashmiris who did not believe in the insurgency against India began to reconsider their views.

The Guest Militants

In 1992, the Harkat-ul-Jihad-e-Islami, a *tanzeem* of the *Jamaat-e-Ulema-e- Islam*, the Pakistani equivalent of the *Jamaat-e-Ulema-e-Hind* of Deoband, India, which had begun operating in Afghanistan against the Russians entered Kashmir. They were much more fierce and committed than the *Hizbul Mujahideen* or the Kashmiri *Tanzeems*. They established their presence in Kupwara and Baramulla and engaged the Indian Army in some fierce encounters. Two other groups of this Tanzeem, the Harkat-ul-Mujahideen (HUM) and the Harkat-ul Ansar (HUA) also entered Kashmir. The HUA made its base on the slopes of the Pir Panjal mountain range and operated in South Kashmir. It was at this time that a hard core committed organiser Masood Azhar came to Kashmir, via Bangladesh. The HUA had killed a Major of the Border Roads in South Kashmir and the Army had deployed a number of units to flush out the HUA militants. They found Masood Azhar and picked him up. They also arrested two HUA militants, Sajjad Afghani and Nasrullah Mansoor Langhrial. This was a big catch for the Indian Army. The ISI began a long operation to try and get these three released. They were to succeed much later in 1999.

The next tanzeem to come on the scene was the Lashkar-e-Taiba (LET). This was a tanzeem of the Ahle Hadith, a sect very akin to the Wahabi school of Islam in Saudi Arabia. Its HQs was set up in a very big plot at Muridke near Lahore. The LET was a fanatical tanzeem who generally decapitated or disemboweled their victims after an encounter. The *Lashkar Jehadis* were only recruited from among Pakistanis. The LET has two training modules, the basic Daura-e-Aam and the advanced Daura-e-khas. Once he passes out, an LET cadre adopts a *kuniat* or Arabised nickname like Abu Zubair or similar title. The cadres also stop trimming their beards or cutting their hair. The leaders of the tanzeems probably deliberately did not allow the men under them to trim or shave their beards off. The head of the LET was Hafiz Muhammad Sayeed. He had direct links with the ISI. The construction of the sprawling campus at Muridke was funded by Abdullah Azam and Osama bin Laden and was known as the Markaz-e-Dawa-wal-Irshad. The LET were linked to the Al Qaeda organised by Osama bin Laden.

I had gone to Kashmir as the Inspector General of the Border Security Force in June 1993. At that time the main tanzeems were basically comprised of the people of the Kashmir valley who were mainly Sufis. They were all from local tanzeems-the JKLF, Al Jihad, Ikhwan-ul-Mussalmeen, and Al Umar. I was present in many operations where, when surrounded in a house and asked to surrender, the Pakistani ISI trained Kashmiri militants, who had sheltered there, would throw down their weapons and come out with their hands raised. The only hard tanzeem at that time was the Hizbul Mujahideen, comprising of Kashmiris from the Jamaat-e-Islami. They were mentally tougher. It was the cadres of the HUJI and the HUA who were the really committed militants. When surrounded in a house and asked to surrender after exchange of fire, the reply would come loud and clear- "We will never surrender. We have fought to become *shaheeds"* (martyrs). The odd HUJI or HUA cadres that we arrested were injured militants, who were capable of walking and were sent individually to hospitals for treatment. Such cases were detected by intelligence work. When interrogated, their stock reply to why they did not surrender was that their religious leaders had told them that, if they sacrificed their life as martyrs for the cause of Islam, 72 *houris* (beautiful angels) would be awaiting them. I had visited Israel many years later and when I exchanged notes with my counterparts there, they told me that the Palestinian militants also told them that they were told by their religious leaders that 72 *houris* would be waiting to attend on them if they chose to die as martyrs.

The guest militants or *mehman mujahideen* as the Pakistanis and the Afghans were called came into Kashmir from 1992 onwards. The majority of these Pakistani and Afghan militants were from local madrassas and were committed fighters. By end 1992, nearly 120 militants of Afghan and

Pakistani origin had been martyred in encounters with the Army and BSF. The HUA and the LET were brave fighters but were also cruel and inhuman. They did not fight clean. The HUA had captured a BSF constable from Doda area across the Pir Panjal. They killed this constable Bikash Narzary most brutally gouging his eyes out while he was still alive. In October 1993, an LET group that had infiltrated across the LOC in Kupwara sector overpowered eight Army personnel on a scouting mission. They were betrayed by their informant. All of them were brutally tortured, two were castrated, and finally all were beheaded.

In 1992, the ISI began to target, the Rajouri, Poonch areas and also the Doda Kishtwar and Baderwah areas south of the Pir Panjal. At first the ISI did not have much success in the Rajouri Poonch areas. There were two reasons for this; the first that in 1965, Pakistan was not too successful with the local Muslim population during Op Gibraltar. They were much more successful in Doda Kishtwar area because it was ideal guerrilla country, with steep hills, forested, very few roads and isolated villages. This group later based itself across the Pir Panjal in Kokernag area. The Jamaat-Ulema Islam (JUI) then sent one of their religious leaders to organise the three groups HUJI, HUM and the HUA. The man selected was Masood Azhar, a highly motivated and die hard Islamist. He travelled by plane to Dacca and from there to Delhi and then to Jammu by plane. From here he made it to Srinagar by road and then moved to Kokernag area. Here the HUA made the mistake of killing a Border Roads Engineer. Incensed, the Army took up some sustained operations in this area. They managed to net Nasrullah Manzoor Langryal, the leader of the HUM group operating in the area in one operation and in another picked up Masood Azhar and Sajjad Afghani, who was to take over the HUM. These were good catches and did wonders for the morale of the Army.

The situation in Doda district was not too good. The problem was that the terrain demanded a very large troop deployment. The district sloped down southwards to the Chenab River. There was only one road running parallel to the Chenab River from Doda to Kishtwar to the Dul Hasti project from the Pir Panjal at an altitude of 12000 to 13000 feet. On the road to

Kishtwar from Doda, there was a branch road at Thatri going along a nullah to Gandoh. The hills on either side were forested and high. The villages were isolated and only connected by tracks. This was ideal terrain for insurgents to operate. There were isolated Hindu villages interspersed along the hills. This kind of terrain needed a very large quantum of troops. That was not available. The troops deployed in company strength were thus constantly on the move.

To the north of Kishtwar was a long valley that extended north south to the east of the Himalayan Range. At the northern tip of this valley was a very high narrow pass, the Sonasar Gali. This pass at a height of more than 13000 feet was at the top of a deep gully that came down to Shesh Nag on the track going to Amarnath from Chandanwari. Unfortunately because of the paucity of troops, the Wadwan valley had no deployment. This was where the HUA made its home. From Kokernag south of Anantnag, a road led to a pass, Sinthan on the Himalayan range which came down to a village called Marwah, from where it was a long trek to Kishtwar. BSF had a company post at Marwah. From Kokernag, along the road going to Sinthan pass to the east, another road branched north and curved to reach the foothills of the Himalayan Range to a small village called Matahund. From this village a track led upto a pass called Hathnuk which was about fifteen kilometers north of Sinthan pass. When you traversed the Hathnuk pass you came down to the Wadwan valley to a village called Inshaan. This village was roughly about twenty kilometres north of Marwah post in the Wadwan valley. It was in Inshaan that the HUA found its safest sanctuary.

It is to this remote valley that we must now move for the next part of our story of the insurgency in Kashmir. The Government of India probably did not know that Masood Azhar the HUA theoretician who was sent via Dacca and Delhi to the Kashmir valley was the son of some important person in the Jihadi group in Pakistan. The ISI was very upset about his arrest and they wanted to kidnap some important persons to get this prisoner exchanged. The Intelligence agencies were not aware of the importance of Masood Azhar.

The Pakistan ISI decided to send a team of the HUA with the task of kidnapping some foreign tourists from Kashmir. Though there was militancy in Kashmir and tourists to Srinagar and Gulmarg had virtually stopped, some intrepid foreigners continued to trek in the upper reaches of the Himalayan range from Pahalgam. David Housego, his wife Jenny and son Kim went for a trek to Pahalgam in June 1994. From Pahalgam, the track north splits in a fork, the left goes to Aroo and trekking country beyond, while the right goes to a place called Chandanwari, a camping ground in the first stage of the Amarnath pilgrimage. From Chandanwari, the track climbs up along a narrow stream to a second camping ground called Sheshnag. At Sheshnag, across the stream there is a narrow gully that climbs steeply to about 14,000 feet to a pass called Sonasar Gali that goes down to the Wadwan valley that we have just described.

David Housego his wife Jenny and son Kim trekked for three days beyond Pahalgam on the Aroo axis and were returning when they were accosted by three armed men wearing *salwar* and *kameez*. They were taken towards Aroo, where they met with David Mackie and his wife Cathy. They asked the two women to cover their faces and finally locked David Housego and the two women in the guest house and left with Kim Housego and David Mackie. They left a note behind them demanding the release of Masood Azhar, Langriyal and Sajjad Afghani. The reaction was a surprise for the handlers in Pakistan. The kidnappings were denounced by the All Party Hurriyat Conference in Kashmir, by the local militant groups and even in Pakistan. The strongest denouncement came from Qazi Nissar, a religious leader, head of a moderate group in Anantnag. The British High Commissioner with his officials, obviously of MI-6 reached Srinagar. By this time the Army as well as the BSF had been regularly decoding the wireless signals sent from Pakistan to the guest militants operating in Kashmir. There were three such wireless nets, one for the Hizbul Mujahideen, one for the HUA and the third for the LET operating in Kashmir. The British High Commissioner was informed accordingly that it was the Pakistan based HUA who kidnapped Kim Housego and David Mackie. The matter was taken up by the British authorities with their Government and I came to know that the British Prime Minister placed the evidence of Pakistan's involvement to the Pakistan Government. Shortly thereafter, the two boys were brought and left in Anantnag. There was an unfortunate side issue to this episode. Pakistan took its revenge on Qazi Nissar. The Hizbul Mujahideen called him for a meeting to Bun Dayalgam, a Jamaat stronghold. The Qazi was shot by masked Hizbul gunmen shortly after he met the Hizbul leaders who had called him for a meeting. Thus ended the first kidnapping asking for exchange of Masood Azhar. A year later, in summer the same exercise was repeated.

On I July 1995, John Childs set out for a trek from Pahalgam. He trekked for three days with a Gujjar guide. Tired after the long trek, he was resting in his tent, when his guide called him out and he was confronted by a group of armed men in *salwar* and *kameez*, with four Europeans in custody. They were Keith Mangan and his wife, Julie and Paul Wells and his girl friend Catherine. The armed men left the women behind with a guide and marched the men to Aroo. On the way they ran into another trekker, Donald Hutchings and took him with them to Aroo. The next day after staying in the guest house, the captured group was made to march up into the mountains. News of the kidnapping had reached Srinagar through the militant wireless channels. The next day Gen. Saklani, the Advisor flew in the Governors' helicopter piloted by Group Captain Kahlon, a dare devil pilot. Gen. Saklani had guessed after studying the previous year's kidnapping that the group might be heading for the Wadwan valley through the Sonasar Gali. He asked his pilot to fly towards Sheshnag. After reaching this place Gen. Saklani asked Kahlon to fly into the gully leading up from Sheshnag to Sonasar Gali. Kahlon had to steadily climb between the high walls of the gully. As he climbed struggling to keep the helicopter from being buffeted too much, they noticed a man clinging to the left side of the gully. Seeing the helicopter, the man tried to run up the slope. Gen. Saklani asked the pilot, if he could land the helicopter. Luckily for them Kahlon noticed a small level patch on the slope and cleverly maneuvered the helicopter and landed. Gen Saklani jumped out and shouted to the man who was trying to run up the slope. He stopped on hearing Gen. Saklani and stopped. Gen. Saklani came up to him. The man asked Gen. Saklani if he was in Pakistan. The General asked him if he was one of the trekkers who were kidnapped by militants. If so he need not be afraid and introduced himself and said that he was very much in India. Childs then told him that the rest of the group had gone ahead and his captors told him to come up slowly as he was not well. Gen. Saklani asked Childs to get into the helicopter and then Kahlon took off and descended slowly and when he reached Sheshnag flew back to Srinagar. It is quite likely that the main group with the rest of the kidnapped trekkers had by this time reached Sonasar Gali and gone down into the Wadwan valley.

The All Party Hurriyat Conference again called the kidnapping un-Islamic and demanded their release. The Azad Kashmir Prime Minister, the Hizbul Mujahideen commander Syed Salahuddin all condemned the kidnapping, thus considerably embarrassing the militants and the ISI. On 10 July, the HUA militant gave a press release that they were a group called Al Feran and the Government had a number of arrested people whom they should release if they wanted to get the hostages released. Meanwhile the US ambassador and Intelligence officials had arrived in Kashmir. Like in the previous year, they were shown the militant wireless intercepts showing the conversation between the ISI handlers in Pakistan and the militants. They were told that this kidnapping was done by the Harkut- al- Ansar and that the Al Feran was a mythical organisation. This time, unfortunately like in the previous year, when the intervention by the British Prime Minister to the Pakistan Prime Minister had helped in releasing the kidnapped tourists, no one intervened in Pakistan. At this juncture, the head of the Jamiat-e-Ulema Islam in Pakistan, which is the religious mentor of the HUJI, HUM and the HUA, Fazlur Rehman visited India. He had obviously come for mediation in the kidnapping of the foreign tourists. The Government of India however ignored him. The HUA now banned the Amarnath *Yatra* that was to begin by August. The Government took appropriate measures deploying the Army and Paramilitary forces to see that the *Yatra* would be safely conducted. There were two bomb blasts in Jammu. This only further fortified the Government's determination to conduct the *Yatra*.

On January 26 of that year, when the Governor was taking the salute at the Republic day function in Jammu, a bomb had blasted almost under the dais, injuring a number of security personnel and killing one of them. The security area of the parade had been scanned for improvised explosive devices (IED) well before the parade. Investigation revealed that the IED fuse used was fitted with a delayed action timer device. A few months later a Pakistani, Irfan was arrested when trying to cross the Jammu border. His search revealed that he was carrying several such delayed timer fuses. During the Amarnath Yatra there were three bombs, one on the road from Anantnag to Pahalgam, one in a tent in Chandanwari and one in a tent of the Army at Sheshnag. All three had such delayed timer fuses. Luckily the bomb on the Pahalgam road went off when no bus or vehicle was passing. The bomb at Chandanwari went off when a clerk was sleeping in the tent. He was blown up and died before he hit the ground. The bomb at Sheshnag went off when no one was in the tent. The metal detectors that we had could not detect any explosive beyond a depth of 2 feet. We had missed detecting these three bombs because of this fact. On 13 August, one of the foreigners kidnapped by the HUA was executed. He was decapitated. His body was found near Panzmulla village near Anantnag, with his head lying on his body. The brutal killing was shocking. The Hurriyat and other militant groups condemned it. The APHC called for a bandh. The HUA reacted by pasting posters asking why no strike was observed when Qazi Nissar had been killed? On 23 August, the HUA released a picture of the four hostages looking tired and drawn holding papers with the date 18 August scrawled on the papers. The Government of India remained firm on the demands of the militants. They refused to release any one of the three that the group had demanded. The group suddenly established contact on 9 November, stating that two of the hostages were not well. Then on 17 November they communicated that one of the hostages was very ill and he could die any moment. They blamed the Government of India for this. A message was sent to the HUA that the hostage should be released so that he could be treated. Alternatively a doctor should be allowed to attend to him immediately. The reply came that if the Government was so concerned about the hostage, then they could have exchanged him for Masood Azhar. The days went by in agony for the relations of the hostages and the negotiators in Srinagar. The group was adamant. There was silence for some days. Then on 3 January, a message was received from Javed Ahmed Bhatt @ Sikandar, a

Kashmiri from Anantnag who had joined the HUA that the hostages had been rescued by the Rashtriya Rifles (RR) after an encounter and were being held by them. This was false as there had been no encounter with the RR. Sikandar Bhatt was later killed when an IED that he was preparing exploded on his face. The next year in May 1996, the BSF picked up one Nazir Mahmood Sodzey, a Harkat militant from Pakistan. On interrogation he confessed that the hostages were executed in the Magam area of Kokernag and buried in the forest. Accordingly in June 1996, the Magam forest was combed by a team of about 599 security personnel with tracker dogs brought from abroad. The graves could not be detected. Time went by, till in 1997, two HUA militants were arrested, Nazir Ahmed Chan and Ghulam Nabi Baba. Their account is the most credible story of the execution of the hostages. According to them the hostages were taken to a cave and asked to enter it. As they walked in they were shot from behind. The cave was then sealed.

The Siege of Charar e Sharief

Charare Sharief is a beautiful little town nestled on the slopes of a ridge of the Pir Panjal coming down to the plains of the Kashmir valley. The famous Sufi Saint of Kashmir, Nooruddin Wali is buried in a beautiful wooden shrine by the side of the main road passing through the town leading to Yusmarg and the ridge of the Pir Panjal Range. After militancy started in 1989, some militants of the Hizbul Mujahideen from Anantnag side came to Charare Sharief town in 1993 and sheltered for the winter in the houses of some of the inhabitants of the town. This was probably known to the Army and BSF, but no one conducted any operation for fear of the Shrine of Nooruddin Wali getting burnt if a cordon and search was conducted in the town.

In the winter of 1994-95, two groups of militants, one, of the Hizbul Mujahideen, led by a rather pompous Pakistani called Mast Gul and another, a group from the HUA, both of whom had operated in South Kashmir came to Charare Sharief and settled in the town for the winter. The BSF had a battalion which had its TAC HQs about 2 kilometres outside Charare Sharief town. I was informed about this as and when the two groups came and settled in the town. I discussed this with my officers. The Commandant of the BSF battalion located near Charare Sharief raised two issues. He said that the militants were living in ones and twos in the houses of the people living in the town against the wishes of the people. If we had to do a cordon and search operation, this could be done only after all the civilians were asked to vacate the town. Even if this could be done, there was the issue of the shrine of Nooruddin Wali. It was built of wood. In the exchange of fire it could easily catch fire. We would be blamed for setting fire to a holy shrine of the Kashmiri people. After discussions, we decided that since the responsibility for counter insurgency operations outside Srinagar was with the Army, we would join them in a joint operation if asked by them. Meanwhile the presence of a large group of militants with arms sheltering in Charare Sharief town was raised in the coordination meeting by the Advisor. I replied that we were willing to do the operation. There was however the chance of the shrine of Nooruddin Wali catching fire. We should not be blamed for this. Since the area outside Srinagar was the responsibility of the Army, the subject was referred to them. Shortly thereafter I had a meeting with the General Officer Commanding (GOC) the Division looking after the area. In the discussion it was decided that we should cordon the town and that the responsibility of the southern flank will be that of the BSF. The Army would cordon the northern flank. Since Charar e Sharief was on a ridge sloping down from the Pir Panjal, guarding the north and southern flanks meant securing the reentrants between the spurs on both the northern and southern flanks. In the day time this was not a very difficult task as the hill slopes were sparsely vegetated and visibility was good. The problem was at night. We would have to lay ambushes in relays at night to ensure that the militants did not escape. Also, since the Army was on the northern flank and we were on the southern flank, we had to be doubly careful. If the militants were to escape by the southern flank where we were deployed, BSF would get a bad name. 46 battalion BSF was deployed for this task. The battalion was briefed and after doing a reconnaissance on the ground the Army and we took up our positions. As soon as we occupied the ground, the militants began to fire at our positions. We had one post which was tactically located on a slope just below the level of the town. This overlooked the approach to the main reentrant going down the southern flank. I used to visit this post frequently and since our approach could be seen, the militants who had set up a bunker on the upper slope of the town would fire at us. There was thus a daily exchange of fire between the militants and the BSF. As soon as the Army and the BSF cordoned the town, the civilian inhabitants began to evacuate the town. Within a few days almost all the civilians had evacuated the place. After a week of the siege, the militants made an attempt to slip out though one of the reentrants on the BSF southern flank at night. Our ambush was alert and hearing sounds of movement, they opened fire, killing one militant and injuring another. When daylight came they found the dead body of one militant with his AK rifle and blood stains of another militant who had dragged himself back. After this there were no more attempts to slip out from the southern flank. The siege continued with both the Army and the BSF on continuous alert. After more than three weeks, I had approached from the opposite side driving via Romu and Pakharpur. We stopped short of the Army cordon and met the Commandant of the Infantry battalion. He informed me that they had decided to close the cordon and take on the militants. I accordingly alerted 46 battalion BSF on the southern flank. That night I was informed of firing from Charar e Sharief town. There was no attempt at trying to break through the southern cordon of the BSF. At about 0400 hours, the Advisor telephoned me and informed that the shrine of Nooruddin Wali had been burnt. We left at once for the town. We reached the town and found that six bodies of militants who had been killed were laid out, the leader of the HUA was captured alive. He was reported to have lost his way when trying to escape and been caught. I made enquiries from the Army personnel and was told that the militants had escaped through the *Hapat Nar on* the northern flank. This *nar was* a steep and wide reentrant on the northern flank guarded by the Army. This reentrant ended on the road leading north from Chadoora town which was located below Charar e Sharief. I asked the Commandant of 46 battalion BSF to send a company immediately on this road. The militants had a lead of at least six hours but we could at least get some information about them. The BSF Company immediately left. They started at the point where the Hapat Nar ended and drove up the road. After going a few kilometres, they came to a *nanwai,* (Kashmiri baker) shop. On talking to the baker, they were told that a big group of militants carrying weapons come to their shop shortly after midnight, woke him up and asked him to prepare tea for all of them. They had tea and bread and left. I got this report before we left Charare Sharief and informed the Commander of the Army Division who had also come there about the information I had got. I also alerted the companies of the BSF deployed at Pakharpur and Romu on the southern side of Charare Sharief. The mystery of how the militants could have slipped out of Hapat Nar remained unanswered till a few years later, when the BSF arrested two militants one Pakistani and one Kashmiri from the area north west of Srinagar in two separate operations. A few months after I had taken over as the Director General of the Border Security Force the Inspector General BSF Kashmir informed me one day that two persons had been picked up by one of the BSF units near Chadoora in separate operations. Both of them had mentioned in their interrogations that they were in Charare Sharief the night it was burnt. I went to Srinagar the next day and interrogated both these persons separately. The older militant was Tarique Muhammad, a Kashmiri who was in the Hizbul Mujahideen. He was middle aged had operated for several years and was never captured. He said that he had come to Charare Sharief to spend the winter there in late 1994. At that time Mast Gul and his party also arrived. They also took shelter in the rest house of the Shrine of Nooruddin Wali. When the Army and the BSF surrounded the town, he was there. When the Army started closing the cordon and firing started, Mast Gul told him that he would blow up the shrine if they were attacked by the Army. He told Mast Gul not to blow up the Shrine as the Kashmiris revered the Shrine. To this Mast Gul replied that he was a Jamaat and he did not believe in such Saints. After the Army attacked and closed in he decided to leave and finding no stops in Hapat Nar he went down the Nar and escaped. The second person captured was a young Pakistan boy Khalid Sahni. He had dropped out from school and had joined Mast Gul's gang and had crossed over to Kashmir and had taken part in several encounters with Mast Gul against the Indian Army and BSF. When the Army started to close in and firing started, he saw Mast Gul placing explosives around the Shrine. He followed Mast Gul into Hapat Nar and he heard Mast Gul giving the order to blow up the Shrine to his subordinate on the wireless set. Later in the darkness and confusion he lost sight of Mast Gul and his comrades. He hid in the Hapat Nar the whole of the next day and slipped out only the next night. He was able to meet Mast Gul and crossed over with him to Pakistan. He came back again in 1998. After recording these interesting statements, I met the Inspector General Kashmir Police and told him that we were handing over these two militants and they should be allowed to meet the local Indian and International press and tell their stories. This was required as the people of Kashmir believed that the Army had burnt the Shrine at Charare Sharief. I came back to Delhi and wrote to the Government and also informed the Director General Military Intelligence (DGMI). Two days later the Inspector General BSF rang me up and told me that both the militants had been handed over to the Kashmir Police and both had been eliminated. They were not presented to the press. I immediately informed the Home Ministry and the DGMI about the developments. To me this last action still remains a mystery. Somebody had something to hide.

The Friendly Militant Groups

By 1996, the insurgency was under some measurable degree of control and the government held the elections to Parliament and in 1997, the elections to the Assembly were also held. In 1995, an interesting development had taken place. A number of Kashmiri militants had come out and approached the Army and BSF stating that they would like to surrender and work with the Army and BSF against the Pakistani militant groups. I had also been approached by one such group in 1993. I had made it clear that if they worked with us they would not be allowed to keep weapons and they should not indulge in extortion. To this the group that approached me did not agree. The BSF therefore did not have anything to do with such groups. In the elections the groups however played a significant part in seeing that the elections were held.

The Kargil War and the No Escape Attacks

In April 1999 intrusions across the cease fire line led to a mini war situation in this axis. There were three sub sectors on this axis of the cease fire line beyond the branch of the Himalayan Range that cut south across the Zoji

La pass. These were the Mushko, Dras and Batalik sectors. The people who lived in Kargil and across in Skardu were Shias. There is a small group living in an isolated valley in Kargil considered to be pure Aryan. The Himalayan range extending beyond the Kaobal Gali is steep and virtually impassable except for two passes across which there are old trails, one at Marpo La and the other at Chor Bat La. The road built from Zoji La going through Mushko, Dras and Batalik generally passes through a level plateau, but the terrain from the road to the north consists of tiers of steep ranges that are virtually impassable except for tracks leading to the two passes mentioned above, Marpo La and Chor Bat La. The United Nations Peace Keeping Force that drew the Cease Fire Line in 1949 between India and Pakistan Occupied Kashmir probably knew that there could be very little movement across the stretch from north of Kaobal Gali along Mushko, Dras and Batalik. After the Bangladesh war Gen. Zia ul Haq is reported to have prepared a plan how Pakistan could create problems for India by way of paying India back for the perfidy of supporting East Pakistan in getting liberated as Bangladesh. One of the ideas suggested was to access the Great Himalayan Range across Mushko, Dras and Batalik. This is exactly what was planned by General Musharraf as the Army Chief of Nawaz Hussain, Prime Minister of Pakistan. He probably did not take the Prime Minister into confidence before executing this plan. We do not know when the plans were finalised and when the work started, but it is clear that the work of cutting the tracks up the slopes of the ridges between the plains of Skardu in the Northern Territories and the Great Himalayan Range must have started before the winter of 1998 set in. All we know is that by March, the Pakistan Army had scaled the Great Himalayan Range and had constructed what they called Igloos on the tops of several ridges in Mushko, Dras and Batalik. They had even made Igloos on the tops of two ridges in Dras overlooking the National Highway passing from Mushko to Batalik. One such height was Tuloling. The objective of the Pakistan Army was obviously to cut off the road passing through Mushko, Dras and Batalik to Leh. However in early April, a villager in Dras area went for a hunt towards the first range of mountains in Dras. There he suddenly came across a group of men in black wearing turbans. He managed to escape observation and ran back and informed the nearest Army camp that some mujahideen were sighted by him. A patrol was promptly dispatched who when they went up the axis indicated by the villager ran into the group of Mujahideen. A firefight ensued. Only, they were not Mujahideen but regulars of the Pakistan Northern Light Infantry. That was the beginning of the Kargil war. Alerts went out to all the three sectors and probing patrols from each sector discovered that the Pakistanis had encroached well inside the Line of Control in all three axis.

I was the Director General BSF when this happened and we had one battalion in Dras sector. I was very worried that some intrusion had taken place in the axis of deployment of this battalion and therefore went up to Dras immediately. The 8 battalion BSF deployed in Dras was commanded by C.S.Negi, who was a mountaineer and considered a very good officer. I was confident that he would have been in constant movement along his posts and there would be no intrusion. When I reached Chenigund, the battalion H.Q.s, the Commandant was waiting for me and he briefed me on a map about his posts. He had just gone round the posts before my visit and there had been no attempt at intrusion through his sector. Before reaching Chenigund I had passed though Dras and could hear the Artillery guns booming and the shells screaming across both ways. The next day we visited Batalik and drove upto the base from which the Indian Army had deployed and were preparing to assault the heights where the Pakistanis had made their igloos. Here again I could hear the guns firing from both sides.

The Army, surprised at the discovery of the intrusion decided to move a brigade from the Kashmir Valley deployed on Counter Insurgency duties. Their idea was to replace the void created in the Counterinsurgency grid by getting troops from Peace Areas. This would of course take some time. It was probably what the Pakistanis had anticipated that we would do. They had prepared a plan to move a group of their most hardened Insurgent Group, the Lashkar-e-Taiba into the valley to attack targets left by the Counter Insurgency Brigade moving out to Kargil. It probably took some time for the new LeT groups to move in, for the intrusion across the LOC was discovered and the Indian Army had started retaliatory operations.

About two weeks after the Kargil war started, the LeT started their new operations. Their new plan was to come in a small group of two, three or four men armed with AK rifles and grenades wearing *pherans* (Kashmiri dress like a loose overcoat), surprise a post, as if they were Kashmiris passing by, suddenly veer round, shoot at the sentry and dash into the post and fire indiscriminately causing as many casualties as they could and if possible make a getaway. They were suicide squads. I named such operations as No Escape Attacks. I found later when I discussed this with the Israelis, that they also had Suicide Bombers and No Escape Attacks in Israel by the Hamas.

The first No Escape Attacks was on the BSF, on the campus of the DIG Bandipur, in North Kashmir on 13 July 1999. Two LeT militants entered the campus of the DIG after about 2300 hrs when they noticed that a sentry on the southern side had not come on duty. Having gained access without firing, one of the militants stayed at the perimeter, while the other went in and fired a burst through the window of a family quarter killing the wife of a constable. In the ensuing confusion, a burst from a sentry who was manning a post higher up hit the other militant who was hiding at the perimeter of the camp and injured him badly. He managed to drag himself away as could be seen from the blood marks on the ground. The militant who had entered the campus hid himself on the first floor landing behind some trellis work and managed to shoot and kill the Deputy Inspector General and his Deputy Commandant when they came out and were moving round trying to find out where the firing had come from. The militant remained holed up on the first floor. The building was now surrounded and some desultory exchange of fire continued till morning. The next day a special Commando squad arrived and surrounded the building. At about 1200 hours, the militant realising that he could not escape, suddenly dashed out of the building firing from his AK rifle and died in a hail of bullets, but not before he injured two more personnel who fired at him as he tried to escape.

This initial attack was followed by No Escape Attacks on three Rashtriya Rifles posts at Nutnus, Keegam both in Kupwara district of Kashmir and Beerwah in Badgam district of Kashmir. In all three attacks, the LeT militants achieved surprise, entered the posts and killed 11 personnel. The LeT suffered 10 casualties. None of the attackers could escape. The next attack was on an Intelligence Bureau post in Handwara, North Kashmir. In this attack one BSF constable was killed and another injured. By this time the post was surrounded by the Army and all 3 LeT militants were killed.

I analysed these attacks and wrote and briefed my officers and men in several posts that this kind of attack was a godsend from the enemy. Here he was frontally attacking posts. We only had to be alert 24 hours for this kind of sudden action and fix devices that would alert each sentry to sudden movements towards the post. I emphasized that here was a heaven sent opportunity to oblige the Laskar-e-Taiba in their newly expressed desire to become martyrs. The battalions deployed in Kashmir took this new technique in their stride. We doubled sentries, reduced their shifts to two hours, built special barricades, doubled the lighting around the posts, fitted generators in all posts and fitted electronic devices in all posts. Doubling the sentries reduced manpower from field operations, but this could not be helped. There followed a series of attacks on the Army, Rashtriya Rifles, the Special Operations Group of the Kashmir Police and the Indo Tibetan Border Police camp in Bandipur. In 2000, there were 13 such attacks on different forces camps. Of these attacks, the LeT could not penetrate the BSF post at Kokernag and the CRPF post in Srinagar airfield. In both cases all the attackers were killed.

In 1999, the Pakistan ISI organised a group to hijack an Indian Airlines Airbus A 320 from Kathmandu. The plane was taken to Amritsar and from there to Dubai and finally to Kandahar. Regrettably, the Government capitulated. Hardline officers were not even called for discussions. The hijackers demanded the release of Masood Azhar, for whose exchange we had stood firm and 6 foreigners had been killed by the HUA. They also demanded the release of Omar Sheikh, a British Pakistani, who had been captured in India when he tried to kidnap some foreign tourists to exchange for Masood Azhar and one Zargar, a petty criminal from Kashmir turned militant. The Government gave in and these three militants were taken to

Kandahar and handed over to the local Taliban, who promptly handed them over to the waiting Pakistan ISI.

Masood Azhar on return to Pakistan immediately raised a new *tanzeem* called the *Jaish-e-Muhammad* (JEM). He drew cadres from the two tanzeems that he controlled the Harkat-ul Mujahideen and Harkat-ul-Ansar to create the JEM. Then as if to commemorate the occasion, he organised the next No Escape Attack on the Kashmir Assembly in Srinagar. Four JEM militants hijacked a Sumo vehicle and drove it towards the Assembly building in Srinagar. A little short of the gate, three militants jumped out and firing at the sentries managed to get inside the building. The driver rammed the Sumo on to the gates of the Assembly blowing it up. It took the BSF and the Special Operations Group of the Kashmir Police a few hours to kill the three militants and clear the Assembly. 24 civilians and 9 uniformed personnel died in the operation. The No Escape Attacks continued in Kashmir throughout 2001 and 2002.

On 13 December, 2001, the LeT hit the Parliament at New Delhi. This time they exploited the weakest link in the Parliament security- Access Control. Entry was checked vigorously and strictly for all persons except Members of Parliament, who were allowed to enter on the strength of their vehicle pass. The passengers in the Member of Parliament's vehicle were not being checked. Taking advantage of this the LeT group managed to drive into the Parliament on the strength of a vehicle pass.. As soon as they entered, the suicide squad jumped out and started firing. Luckily the security personnel reacted immediately and all the suicide squad cadres were killed before they could enter the Parliament buildings. The LeT also carried out a raid on the Akshardam temple in Ahmedabad. Two militants who entered the temple managed to kill 21 civilians, 4 policemen and 2 National Security Guard personnel.

Counter Insurgency Operations in Jammu and Kashmir continued till 2003. After the Parliament attack, the Government deployed the Army along the western borders in OP Parakram. This was a step that Pakistan did not accept. In 2004-5, General Musharraf announced a cease fire along the Line of Control between India and Pakistan. I had retired in November

2000. My contacts in Kashmir however continued to keep me informed of intrusions across the Line of Control. After the declaration of a ceasefire by Pakistan, the infiltration gradually came to a stop. General Hamid Gul a former Chief of the ISI of Pakistan once made a public statement that this declaration of ceasefire was a categorical mistake by Gen. Musharraf. It was during this period of ceasefire that the Indian Army extended the barbed wire fencing from the International Border in Jammu to the Line of Control in Jammu and Kashmir.

It was only in 2008 November that the LeT struck again, this time in Bombay. A group of ten LeT cadres after undergoing rigorous training came in a small craft from Karachi, hijacked another Indian fishing boat after killing the four men sailing it and then landed off Bombay city at 2000 hours on 26 November 2008. The ten men, with AK rifles dashed from the boat carrying bags with grenades and ammunition and split into groups. Two men carrying AK rifles went to the Chatrapathi Shivaji rail terminus and opened fire on the commuters in the station. They killed 58 people and injured 104 between 2130 and 2245hrs. Then, they fled from the station and moved towards the Cama Hospital. Enroute, they fired on pedestrians and policemen, killing eight of them. They were intercepted by a police vehicle with three senior police officers. The two LeT militants fired bursts at the police vehicle killing three senior police officers and injuring a constable. The two then proceeded further and seized a passenger car. While they were driving this car, they ran into a police block. In the ensuing firing by the police, one militant was killed and another called Kasab was injured. He was overpowered, disarmed and arrested. His interrogation revealed the details of the plot.

Of the remaining eight LeT cadres, two went to the Leopald café on Colaba causeway. They entered the café and opened fire on the people inside, killng ten persons and injuring many. Two entered Nariman House a Jewish centre in Colaba and held the people hostage inside. The rest entered Trident hotel and the Taj Mahal Palace hotel. The next morning the three places were cordoned by the National Security Guards. They operated till 29/11 morning, rescued a number of persons but more than 300 people were killed during this assault by the ten LeT cadres. Except for Kasab who was captured on the night of 26/11, all the nine were killed in the three buildings that they had occupied.

Confidential information obtained from Hotel sources revealed that some persons had come to the two hotels during the course of an year previous to the assault, had probably worked in at least one of the hotels and possibly kept some stores in the two hotels. Their familiarity in moving inside the hotel gave them away on this point.

In Kashmir, meanwhile with the formation of the Government after the elections in Pakistan and a statement given by the Prime Minister of Pakistan, that their hearts were with the people of Kashmir, infiltration of militants resumed. This was confirmed by my faithful source that fresh crossings took place across the LOC shortly after a Government was formed in Pakistan.

Meanwhile Kashmir saw several incidents of civilian crowds forming and agitating on several issues like firing by the Army or an encounter in the built up areas, alleging high handedness by the security forces. This finally boiled up into continual stone pelting by young people in Srinagar city. This stone pelting spread to other towns like Baramulla, Sopore and Anantnag. Regrettably the Police baton charges were very ineffective. From visuals of the scenes of stone pelting and the ensuing baton charges, it was clear that the Kashmir Police and regrettably the CRPF appeared to have forgotten how to disperse mobs with firm baton charges. Unfortunately a tear gas shell fired at the mobs killed a student and that worsened the situation. A number of young boys were killed and many injured. More than three hundred policemen were also injured in the stone throwing. After some time it was clear that the whole exercise was organised and not spontaneous. The movement was continually encouraged by the All Parties Hurrriyat Conference (APHC) led by the Jamaat-e-Islami head Syed Shah Gilani and supported by the Mirwaiz, Umer Farooq and the JKLF leader Yasin Malik, one of the killers of 4 Air Force Personnel in 1989, who was in jail awaiting trial for that murder, when he was brought out and sent to Srinagar by the Intelligence Bureau in 1995 for starting a peace process.

Conclusion

It will be clear that a careful study of the history of small groups forming in Kashmir and going across to Pakistan for trainng and arms and then indulging in sabotage has been a continual process. The causes for this continual process in Kashmir is understandable in the background of the domination of the Hindus over the Kashmiri Muslims in the history of the valley and the Jammu, Rajouri, Poonch areas. I feel that this will be a continual process and we can do nothing about this but live with it.

As for Pakistan, it will always feel cheated of Kashmir. This feeling that India's Prime Minister designate, Nehru played foul in persuading Lord Mountbatten, the Viceroy, to influence Cyril Radcliffe, who had been designated to draw the borders of India and Pakistan, to take out the three *tehsils* from the eastern border of Gurudaspur district that had been designated to go to Pakistan and giving them to India as a result of which India could get a road to Jammu from Punjab, was the main reason for not securing Kashmir, has been bothering the Pakistan leadership from Jinnah onwards till date. When this is seen in conjunction with the Pakistan Army and the ISI always ready to give a hand to these adventurers, arm them, train them and reinfiltrate them, all we can do is to continually monitor these attempts, detect isolate and then destroy them. This task is best given to the Kashmir Police. India will have to live with this syndrome forever and ever. I do not see Kashmir ever being peaceful.

We must therefore see that Kashmir has good governance, the Kashmir Police is well recruited, trained and kept professionally sound so that it is capable of meeting the challenges that we have identified as continual. We must also see that Kashmir has a very good civil administration, better than all the other states in India. The Army and the Border Security Force also have a task of being continually alert on the border and the LOC and intercepting the Pakistan trained cadres infiltrating. The most difficult task will be in conducting counter insurgency operations in the civil areas of Kashmir. This will have to be done with strict emphasis on human rights. The Border Security Force should be given the counter Insurgency role in

Jammu, Rajouri, Poonch and the Kashmir valley again for the simple reason that they mesh well with the Army, have better weaponry and training.

Rise of Naxalism and Its Implications for the National Security
A Political, Security and Socio-Economic Campaign

If the country does not belong to everyone it will belong to no one.

Tupamaro Manifesto.

I would like to state at the outset that I hold the firm belief that in any insurgency, the first step that the Government should do is to study the economic background to the insurgency, assess the causes and then dovetail the security strategy with the plan of setting right the economic, social and development failures by the Government, so that economic and social injustices are set right as the security operations progress. I believe that handling an insurgency is best left to the professionals. It is absolutely necessary to leave politics out of it. I am basing my paper on two factors only-security and delivering economic and social justice. I feel that when this is done the insurgency will wither away because there will be no cause for any of the people of the affected areas to fight with the government.

I have always held that the best model of a counterinsurgency that succeeded was the campaign conducted by President Magsaysay of the Philippines against the Huk guerrillas. In fact the leftwing extremism or Naxalite insurgency that we are facing in this country strongly resembles the situation in the Philippines when the Huk insurgency erupted before the Second World War and continued after the country was given freedom by the United States. The issue in the Huk insurgency was land. Tenant farmers were being squeezed by big land holders and were getting a raw deal in tenancy rights. Regrettably the Government sided with the landlords and set the Police and the Military against the Huk guerrillas. The Police and the Military were blundering around committing excesses against the tenant farmers for supporting the guerrillas, so much so that when President Magsaysay went touring the affected areas the people told him again and again that they hated his corrupt Police and brutal Army and they hated his corrupt civil servants who sided with the landlords against the poor tenant farmers. Magsyasay went back to his capital, amended the tenancy laws in favour of the tenant farmers, reigned in his Army and ensured that no excesses were allowed to be committed. After a year when he toured the affected areas, the scenario had changed. The people now told him that his soldiers were behaving well, the Police were fair and the civil servants were not sucking the blood of the tenant farmers any more. The Huk insurgency gradually withered away.

In India the obstacles hindering the counter insurgency effort are easily identified. They are bad politics and not just bad politics but rotten politics. One of the major obstacles is something that the Philippines did not have. This is caste and this is at the root of the Naxalite problem. The third problem is a peculiar concept that was introduced into the body politic and administration of India during the emergency and perpetuated thereafter by all political parties without exception.This is the concept of committed bureaucracy to not just the party in power but to the family heading the party in power. When you have a situation of the caste factor being conjoined with the political factor, then you have a stranglehold where on the basis of caste the oppression of the poorer economic communities continue and economic and social justice is continually denied and the concept of committed bureaucracy protects the perpetrators who are oppressing the lower castes. Denied economic and social justice, the oppressed classes are motivated by the Left wing extremist parties and you have an insurgency at your hands.

Let us now examine the incidents of Left Wing Extremism in India briefly, assessing the cause of resorting to violence in each case.

1946 - The Tebhaga movement in undivided Bengal

The demand was for the share of the landlords to be reduced from one half to one third. The movement spread from Rangpur and Dinajpur in the north to 24 Parganas in the south. When their demands were not heard the Kisan Sabhas, dominated by the Communist party, encouraged the peasants to forcibly take two thirds of the harvested crop from the granaries. As a result there were bloody clashes between the peasants and the landlords. The movement petered out when the landlords with the help of the local administration let loose a wave of repression.

1946-51 - The Telengana insurrection

The movement was directed by the Communists from the very beginning. The peasants launched their struggle on economic issues against forced labour, illegal exactions and unauthorised evictions. It soon developed into an uprising against the feudal rule of the Nizam. More than 4000 lives were lost before the Communist party withdrew the struggle. The Telengana insurrection (1946-51) was broad-based and had no parallel in Indian History since the 1857 Sepoy Mutiny.

1967 - Naxalbari

The revolt was in the area of three police stations-Naxalbari, Kharibari and Phansidewa. About 65% of the populations of these three police stations were scheduled castes and tribals. They worked as agricultural labour or in mines, forests and plantations. A small percentage owned small holdings. The majority cultivated on agency basis (*baghchash*). The *baghchashis* were exploited by the *jotedars*. When the land reforms act was passed in 1955, the jotedars started *malafide* transfers of land. Santhals armed with bows and arrows forcibly occupied the lands of the *kulaks*, lifted stocks of hoarded rice and killed an Inspector of police. Thereafter there were a number of such incidents. After this there was a major deployment of police forces by the CPI (M) government and after several operations the movement was squashed. The leadership of the movement was by communist cadres who were following the path set by Mao Tse Tung after the Cultural Revolution. This culminated in the formation of the Communist Party of India Marxist-Leninist (CPI-ML) on 22 April 1969. Not more than a score of people were killed in this uprising, but it left a far reaching impact on the entire agrarian scene throughout India. It was like the throw of a pebble bringing forth a series of ripples in the water.

1968 - Srikakulam

Girijans or tribals comprised about 70% of the population of Srikakulam district living in the agency area of the Eastern Ghats. They were mainly involved in agriculture, while some collected minor forest produce. The British, conscious that they may be harassed by the plainsmen decreed that no land could be transferred from a *girijan* to a plainsman without the permission of the District Collector. The Act was unfortunately observed more in the breach. The traders and money lenders took full advantage of the poverty of the *girijans*. They gave them daily requirements like tobacco, kerosene, salt and cloth on credit and also lent money for purchase of seeds. Those unable to clear their debts were made to part with their land. Thus most of the fertile land was alienated from the girijans and passed into the hands of the plainsmen. The landlords squeezed them to the utmost and paid subsistence wages. Lease holders had to give two-thirds of their produce to the landlord. It was in 1967 that one Vempatapu Satyanarayana started work among the girijans. The movement he led was able to make substantial gains for the poor *girijans*. Wages of farm servants rose, the landlord's share of harvest was reduced from 2/3 to 1/3, 2000 acres of land was wrested from the landlords and more than 5000 acres of wasteland came under the possession of girijans. Then on 31 October 1967 a clash took place between a large group of tribals going for a meeting of the Marxist party and a group of landlords. The landlord group had guns and they shot and killed two tribals. The girijans were incensed and the movement became violent. Vempatapu Satyararayana organized the girijans into guerrilla squads called *dalams*. At this stage, the Srikakulam leadership who had joined the CPI (M) faction of the Communist party broke away from the CPI(M) and joined a group that split from it to form the All India Coordination Committee of Communist Revolutionaries which in due course evolved into the Communist Party of India, Marxist –Leninist CPI (ML). There were a series of raids on houses of landlords and money lenders; their houses were burnt down and cash looted. There were a number of encounters with the police. From December 1968 to January 1969, twenty nine policemen were killed in action by the *dalams*. Charu Mazumdar, the CPI (ML) leader visited Srikakulam and gave a fillip to the movement. During 1969 the Naxalites committed 23 murders and 40 dacoities. Some of the murders were gruesome. For example, on 11 May 1969, a landlord, P. Jammu Naidu of Ethamanuguda was killed and slogans were painted with his blood by the members of the dalam that executed him. He was a notorious man who had grabbed the land of the poor tribals and forcibly taken the daughters of the tribals as his wives. When he was killed he had seven wives, two of whom were little girls he had forcibly taken from tribals. This showed the extent of exploitation of the tribal people by the upper caste landlords. The exploitation of the forest tribals who collected minor forest produce is evidenced by the account of a trial of a *sahukar* by a Peoples Court. The *sahukar* or usurer used to go into the Agency area to collect tamarind from the forest girijans. The list of borrowers which he brought showed that he had lent a sum of Rs. 280/- to peasants of 4 villages. Against this he proposed to collect from them 40 bundles of tamarinds which at the market rate was worth Rs. 1600/-. This meant that the peasants were to pay back nearly six Rupees for every Rupee they had borrowed. The usurer was arrested and tried before a Peoples Court. He repented and promised to behave and not fleece the peasants. He was let off.[1]

1967-71 - West Bengal, Midnapur and Birbhum

The Midnapur district of West Bengal bordering Bihar and Orissa witnessed a well planned and well organized Naxalite movement in the Debra and Gopibhallavpur police stations. The district has a sizeable tribal population of Santhals, Oraons and Lodhas. The majority of them were landless labourers. A small proportion owned small plots of land or cultivated the

---

[1] Liberation. May 1969. Page 83-84.

jotedar's land under the *Barga* system. Gopibhallavpur has a long forested
border with Orissa and Bihar. After the Naxalbari uprising in 1967, a section
of CPI (M) workers in Midnapur started propagating the extremist line.
They supported the *kisans* and *bargadars* and worked for a movement
against the jotedars. Santosh Rana, Ashim Mukherjee, both first class
postgraduates of Calcutta University and a host of students from well to do
upper caste families from Calcutta lived and worked among the tribals,
identifying themselves wholeheartedly with them. From September 1969,
big tribal groups armed with spears, bows and arrows attacked the houses
of jotedars killed some of them, looted cash and burnt all deeds of land. The
State Government alarmed at the spate of killings sent several companies
of CRPF and state police and by March 1970, the area was brought under
control. The Naxalite uprising in Birbhum district was also masterminded
by several students from Calcutta University. The State Government reacted
by deputing CRPF, Sate Armed Police companies and an Army infantry
company for cordoning and searching the area. Nearly 150 CPI (ML) cadres
were arrested and the movement died down.

1968-70 - Bihar and Uttar Pradesh

The Mushahari block of Muzaffarpur district of Bihar covered 12 villages
with a population of about 10,000 people. There were various forms of
oppression by the upper classes on the peasantry. In April 1968, the peasants
of Gangapur harvested the *arahar* crop of the landlord in broad daylight.
Retaliation was quick. Bijli Singh the *zamindar* of Narsingpur organized an
attack on the peasants with 300 men armed with *lathis* swords and firearms
with the landlord leading on an elephant. In the fight that ensued, the landlord
and his hoodlums were routed. The humbling of this powerful landlord by
the *harijan* peasants had a magical effect on the surrounding villages.[2]
Kisan Sangram Samitis were formed and there were incidents of seizing of
land by the peasants. In April 1969, landless peasants forcibly harvested
the crop on 14 acres of land of a landlord. There was a clash in which the
retainer of the landlord was killed. In June 1969, an attack was made in

---

[2] Naxalites in Bihar-Fight for Land, N.K.Singh, *Patriot*, 11 October, 1969.

Paharchat village. The landlord and two associates were killed. Hundreds of peasants gathered after the raid. In their presence all the deeds and documents were burnt and the pawned ornaments returned to the owners. A series of incidents followed. Alarmed, the State sent police forces and after several combing operations, the movement died down. The Mushahari struggle caused ripples to spread into Dharbangha, Champaran and Chota Nagpur. Here in May 1970, 54 *Adivasis* were arrested in the Jaduguda forest during police operations. A British girl Mary Tyler was found among them. Later she wrote poignantly about the movement- "The Naxalites crime was the crime of all those who cannot remain unmoved and inactive in an India where a child crawls in the dust with a begging bowl, where a poor girl can be sold as a rich man's plaything, where an old woman must half starve herself in order to buy social acceptance from the powers that be in her village; where countless people die of sheer neglect, where many are hungry while food is hoarded for profit, where usurers and tricksters extort the fruits of labour from those who do the work, where the honest suffer, while the villainous prosper, where justice is the exception and injustice the rule and where the total physical and mental energy of millions of people is spent on the struggle for mere survival."[3]

The Naxalite violence that erupted in Singhbum and Ranchi had more serious dimensions. Jamshedpur became a mini Calcutta, with instances of attacks on schools and, Government offices and police piquets. Schools were also attacked in Jamshedpur. There were also large scale attacks in Ranchi. In Uttar Pradesh, the Palia area is part of the Lakhimpur district in the Terai region. It was inhabited by Tharu tribals. The state government encouraged poor peasants to go to the Palia area, allotting 10-12 acres of land to each family. In actual fact landlords forcibly occupied big chunks of land, ejecting the poor peasants. This provided the Naxalites with fertile grounds for agitation. Their object was to clear the area of big farmers, thugs, corrupt political leaders and moneylenders.[4] A series of attacks and raids on landlords ensued, in which a number of firearms were also snatched.

---

[3] *My years in an Indian Prison*, Mary Tyler, page 191.

[4] The Naxalite Movement in India, Prakash Singh, page72.

Deployment of the armed police in the area brought the situation under control.

In all these states the Naxalite movements were organized and coordinated by various CPI (ML) groups. Unfortunately the top Marxist-Leninist leaders like Charu Mazumdar in West Bengal, Satyanarain Singh of Bihar, were not tactically sound in their approach. They thought that there would be mass uprisings and they could build up a Peoples Liberation Army from the rag-tag band of peasants who had revolted against the atrocities of landlords and money lenders. Charu Mazumdar succeeded in arousing the students of Calcutta who left their studies and went and lived in the forest villages and shared the tribulations of the tribals. The vital element of building up a guerrilla force training and equipping them to take on the might of the state was lacking. One by one the movements fizzled out as the Central Para-Military forces with the state police were deployed in the interior areas and well planned raids and search operations were carried out. The CPI (ML) leadership lacked the vision to organize the poor peasants against the might of the state, though the cause was just. Also, lumpen elements infiltrated the leftist groups and affected the discipline of the groups.

According to a rough estimate there were about 4000 incidents of Naxalite violence from the middle of 1970 to the middle of 1971, with the break-up as follows-West Bengal-3500, Bihar-220 and Andhra Pradesh-70. The Government of India made a plan for joint operations in West Bengal, Bihar and Orissa with the Army, Paramilitary forces and the State Police. This was undertaken from 1 July to 15 August 1971. This was *OP Steeplechase*. The broad strategy was to surround an area that was a known stronghold with an outer cordon of the Army, an inner cordon of the CRPF, and local police operating inside. The operation disrupted the network of the naxalite cadres and the movement stalled. Meanwhile internal dissensions between the factions of the CPI (ML) also disrupted the movement. A number of top leaders were arrested, including Charu Mazumdar. When he died shortly after, it marked the end of a phase of the Naxalite movement in India. However, it was only a lull. The movement was to surface again, for the Indian Government had not removed the causes of the insurgency. This movement was not going to be finished with cosmetic remedies. The causes were deep rooted in caste, the crucial factor behind the exploitation of the poor and the downtrodden.

1980 - Peoples War Group (PWG) Andhra Pradesh, Madhya Pradesh and Maharashtra

Andhra Pradesh has a radical tradition going back to the Telengana struggle 0f 1946-51. The *Girijan* awakening in Srikakulam had preceded the Naxalite movement. The forces of the state squelched the uprising by 1970. The movement however continued to simmer. After Charu Mazumdar's death, his associates Kondapalli Seetharamiah, KG Satyamurthy and Suniti Kumar Ghosh formed a Central Organising Committee in December 1972, concentrating in organizing and mobilizing the masses. They decided to eschew militancy until such time as the party was strong enough to embark on a course of violence. Kondapalli Seetharamiah encouraged the party workers to commit money actions- an euphemism for dacoity or robbery. He was arrested on 26 April 1977, but jumped bail and thereafter organized underground activities on a large scale. He broke away from the COC CPI (ML) on 20 April 1980 and formed the CPI (ML) Peoples War Group. For the next ten years he moved from strength to strength and the Peoples War Group emerged as the most formidable Naxalite formation in the country.[5]

What led to the resurgence of Naxalism in the Telengana area? The basic reason was the continued economic exploitation of the tribals by the landlords, traders and government officials especially those of the Forest Department. As PS Sundaram wrote- "The tribals owning small pieces of land are expropriated and sharecroppers impoverished. They are all kept under perpetual bondage towards repayment of a small debt supposedly taken generations ago. The forest wealth is freely smuggled out by contractors in connivance with the forest staff. The tribals get neither a remunerative price for their produce nor a fair wage for their labour."[6]

---

[5] Ibid, page130.

[6] Causes of spurt in Naxalite Violence, *Indian Express*, 1 September 1987.

The social dimensions of esploitation were far more revolting. The landlords of the region were commonly known as *dora* (lord). C. Lokeswara Rao has described the high-handedness of the *doras*- "The tyranny of Doras in Telengana is unmatched. Tribal girls working on the Dora's land are forcibly taken in his household and are at the disposal of the master and his guests. She is forced to have abortions when she gets pregnant. She has to subsist on the leftovers passed on by the cook, but has to satisfy the appetite of just about any male in the master's household. Naxalite songs are replete with references to rape by landlords and to girls growing up with the knowledge of the inevitability of rape that awaits them. Only a few such practices have disappeared and the pace of change is slow."[7]

On 20 May 1981, the Naxalites had called for a meeting of tribals at Indraveli in Adilabad district. More than 30,000 tribals had turned up. The administration refused permission for the meeting, apprehending a clash between landlords and tribals. The tribals were determined to have the meeting. There was a *lathi* charge and firing and 13 Gond tribals were killed. The PWG exploited the anger of the tribals and consolidated their hold on the area. Kondapalli Seetharamiah was arrested for the second time on 2 January 1982. He escaped from hospital on 4 January 1984. He now concentrated on organization of the PWG cadres. He constituted Forest Committees for the forest areas and Regional Committees for the plains areas. Armed squads or *dalams* comprising 6 to 10 members were formed. About 50 *dalams* were soon active in Telengana.

The PWG is believed to have redistributed nearly half a million acres across Andhra Pradesh. The modus operandi was to forcibly occupy excess land of big land owners and give them away to the landless or to the labourers working for the landlord. As per the State Government's own admission, counter affidavit 68/82 filed by the state against the Naxalites, the radicals had forcibly redistributed 80,000 acres of agricultural land and 20,000 acres of forest land. I wonder that the court did not react to this. What was the government doing all this time since the land ceiling act came into being? This is the crux of the matter in Andhra Pradesh and in many states of

---

[7] Why Naxalism flourishes in Telengana, *The Times of India*, 1999.

India. The land ceiling act is not enforced. The party activists insisted on a hike in the daily minimum wages from Rs. 15/- to Rs. 25/- and the annual fee for *jeetagadu* (year long labour) from Rs. 2000/- to Rs. 4000/-.[8] The poorer sections were particularly happy at these two measures. They found that what the politicians had been talking about and the Government promising year after year could be translated into a reality only with the intervention of the Naxalites. Gorakala Doras (Lord of the Bushes) is how the Naxalites came to be known in the interior forest areas.

Revolutionary writers helped in furthering the Naxalite ideology. The moving spirit of the *Jana Natya Mandali,* the cultural front of the PWG was Gummadi Vittal Rao, better known as Gaddar. This wandering ministrel's ballads inspired the simple tribal. He became a legend in Andhra Pradesh.

The PWG fought a running battle with the Telugu Desam Government. When the Congress came to power in 1989 they took a soft line with the Naxalites, freeing a number of Naxalite who were under detention and in prison. They however did nothing to control the exploitation of the tribals like enforcing the land ceiling or controlling the moneylenders. The Naxalites began organising, extorting money and running peoples courts, giving the general impression of a parallel government. The Congress resumed the hard line. Soon the PWG had spread to the adjoining areas of Maharashtra, Madhya Pradesh, and Orissa and into some areas of Tamil Nadu and Karnataka. They also acquired 50-60 AK 47 rifles probably from the LTTE. Naxalite violence was gradually stepped up peaking in 1991 with several attacks on railway and electrical installations and police stations and patrols. On 8 May 1992, the PWG was banned and coordinated operations commenced against them by the Central Paramilitary forces and the state police. The results were good with 3500 cadres being arrested and 8500 surrendering. By 1993, the Naxalites surged back with violence again rising.

They now spread to the Bastar district of Madhya Pradesh, which till then was a sleepy forest outpost. The tribals of Bastar were used to a life

---

[8] Madiga Malliah Inherits the Earth, Chidananda Rajghatta, *The Times of India*, 9 December 1990.

of deprivation. The Naxals made the truant teacher to take classes regularly and the absentee doctor to attend to his patients. The tribals began to look at the Naxalite cadres with awe and respect. The Peoples Union of Civil liberties wrote about Bastar-"A lopsided socio-economic development of the district caused by exploitation through cheating and duping was an ideal setting for the Naxalites to take root in the area. With their idealism, free of corruption or other vested interests, they could win the confidence of the tribals. They punished corrupt officials, made the tendu leaf contractors to increase the wages.[9] The movement spread to Balaghat and Rajnandgaon districts.

Gadchiroli district of Maharashtra is largely inhabited by tribals. The jungle is spread through 10,495 square kilometers out of the district area of 15,434 square kilometres. The entire life of the tribals revolves around the forests, yet the tribals were denied access to the forests due to a stupid interpretation of the Forest act and rules. With the coming of the Naxalites, the forest officials abdicated their jurisdiction. The best testimonial of the presence of the Naxalites was given by an innocent tribal who got a lift from the Commissioner of Scheduled castes and tribes during his visit in Gadchiroli district. The Naxalites are called Dadas in Gadchiroli. When asked about the Dadas, the tribal replied- "There is at least one change since the Dadas have come. The government atrocities are over and the police cannot harass us."[10] There were 113 incidents of Naxalite violence in the district in 1990 with 16 deaths. On 12 November 1991, ten SRPF personnel were killed and 13 injured in a landmine explosion under their vehicle. The PWG has attained a high degree of expertise in making and detonating improvised explosive devices (IED).

The New Left in Bihar

The best description of the dismal state of affairs in Bihar is summed up by Arvind N Das- "Bihar's economy has been at a stand still for decades. The

[9] *The Illustrated Weekly of India*, 3 September 1989.
[10] 29th Report of the Commissioner of Scheduled Castes and Tribes. 198789. Page 171.

discriminatory nature of public and private investments, the green revolution bypassing the state, principally on account of non-implementation of land reforms, the willful subversion of whatever social security system existed, all these has pushed the people into poverty, the economy into backwardness, the society into violence."[11] The resentment of the oppressed sections in this environment found an outlet in the emergence of a 'New Left' manifested in the form of three Naxalite groups in the beginning of 1980- The Maoist Communist Centre (MCC), CPI ML (Anti Lin Piao Group) and the CPI ML Party Unity. In May 1982, the Bihar Government reported that 47 out of the 857 blocks were affected by the Naxalite movement. Subsequently the movement has grown enormously in the face of a corrupt, casteist and incompetent administration.[12] When the CPI ML was formed, one Naxalite group Dakshin Desh had remained aloof. Amulya Sen and Kanai Chatterjee were its leaders. They considered mass mobilisation as a precursor to armed action. The group chose Jangal Mahal area of Burdwan, with a sizeable population of scheduled castes and tribals, for its operations. Agricultural land was inadequate, irrigation virtually nonexistent, and the wage rates dismally low, all conditions suitable for a Naxalite uprising. The landlords generally belonged to the upper castes, while the sharecroppers and landless labour were scheduled castes or tribals, the ideal cocktail for the Naxalite to enter. By 1973, the party had 37 militias who organized actions like looting of food grains, killing of class enemies and snatching of arms. In 1975, the group was renamed as the Maoist Communist Centre (MCC). The MCC gradually spread over Central Bihar. Its membership exceeded 10,000 and they had stockpiled about 700 weapons including some AK rifles. There were gruesome slaughters of Rajputs by Yadavs in the MCC. These were more by way of the feuds between the two communities and because of the way the Rajputs had treaed the Yadavs. On 29 May 1987 the Yadav cadres of the MCC slaughtered 42 Rajputs of Baghaura and Dalelchak villages of Aurangabad district. On 12 February 1992, 37 members of the landowning Bumihar caste were hacked to death by the MCC cadres in Bara village of Gaya district.

---

[11] The Republic of Bihar. Arvind N Das. Page 14.

[12] Ibid. Page 107.

Vinod Misra formed the CPI ML anti Lin Piao faction in December 1973. It struck roots in Bhojpur district and spread to Rohtas, Jehanabad, Patna and Nalanda districts. They had 50 underground armed squads and some weapons, mostly country made guns, a few rifles and sten guns. The Indian Peoples Front was the political front of the anti Lin Piao faction.

The CPI (ML) Party Unity was formed in 1982 by the merger of the COC CPI (ML) of Andhra and the Unity Organisation of CPI ML of West Bengal. The Party Unity has about 30,000 members. It has 25 armed squads holding about 150 weapons, including a few sten guns.

The third phase of Naxalite violence commenced with the holding of the 9th Congress of the Peoples War Group in 2001 in which it was decided to give more sophisticated arms to the Peoples Guerrilla Army. This phase has extended the Naxalite war to nine states.

The *Salwa Judum* of Chattisgarh

The case of the exploitation of the *adivasis* of Bastar is a little different from the similar cases in Andhra Pradesh, West Bengal, Bihar and even Maharashtra. The area affected in Madhya Pradesh borders Telengana and Srikakulam and also Koraput in Orissa. The *adivasis* are much simpler than their counterparts in the states mentioned. When Andhra Pradesh organized the Greyhounds a counter insurgency force with the help of a retired Security Service Bureau officer in 1989, the quality of the counterinsurgency operations improved and the leftist guerrillas found themselves at the receiving end. Encounters forced them to retreat into Bastar and Koraput, where they found their brother *adivasis* much more meek and tolerant of the oppression by the caste Hindu landlords and the *banias*. The problem here was less with exploitation on land and much more with sale of forest produce. The hardened guerillas of Andhra found his brother *adivasis* too timid to arouse and join forces with them against the oppressors. At this point they made a mistake and tried to intimidate the *adivasis* of Madhya Pradesh and coerce them to join their groups. This press ganging alienated many of the local *adivasis*. And they began to look for help to the district authorities. It was at this point that some local *adivasi* leaders who were in politics and the local civil bureaucrats and police officers got the idea of resettling the forest dwelling *adivasis* in areas where some control could be exercised over them. This has gravitated into forcing many forest dwellers to leave their huts and come and live in settlements nearer the towns. Sudeep Chakaravarthi traveling in the area was aghast to see the miserable conditions of these forest dwellers living in dirt and squalor in miserable shanties. In many cases the police and civil bureaucracy has forced the forest dwelling families to burn their huts in forest glades and come and live in the settlements.[13]

Madhya Pradesh has meanwhile been divided and Bastar and Dandakarnya forests are now in Chattisgarh. This concept of resettling forest dwelling adivasis is the worst step that a professional fighting an insurgency would take. It is worse than the regrouping of villages done in the Naga Hills and Mizo Hills districts. The Nagas and Mizos have not forgotten the scars of that terrible period. There was one saving grace in that resettlement. Politicians were not involved in it. In the *Salwa Juddum* the lead role is of the politician. Nothing much is left to the imagination as to how much of the funds for the resettlement are reaching the hapless people. The politician and the bureaucrat must be getting at least 70 to 80 per cent and a miserable 20 per cent must be trickling down.

Conclusion

It will be seen that in all the theatres of Naxalite violence, there has been a diagnostic response only in one state-West Bengal. Here the CPM government carried out operation *Barga* under which share croppers were registered and given permanent and inheritable rights on cultivation of their plots covering a total area of 11 lakh acres. Besides 1.37 lakh acres of ceiling surplus and *benami* lands were acquired by the state government and distributed among 25 lakh landless and marginal cultivators. The land reforms have seen the emergence of a new class loosely termed rural rich that weakened the social and political power enjoyed by the landlords in the

---

[13]   Red Sun- Travels in Naxalite Country, Sudeep Chakraavarty. Penguin. 2008.

countryside. This has not even been thought of by Andhra Pradesh, or Bihar where the Land Ceiling Act has not been enforced after more than 50 years of its legislation. And sadly this is not the end of the picture in these two states. The Law enforcing officers say openly that the Naxalites are a band of thugs and criminals and must be wiped out. There is no question of the Land Ceiling being enforced. What they have left unsaid is that it is the right of the upper classes to have hundreds of acres of land and it is the duty of the scheduled classes and tribes to slave on these lands for the benefit of the upper classes. In this regard, the case of land tenancy in Kerala is of interest. The upper classes in Kerala were generally landlords but with medium holdings. The majority of the landlords had tenant farmers on their lands who deposited half of the crop to their landlords. The landlords themselves and their progeny were educated and took up white collar jobs in the metropolises of the country. When the CPI M was elected in the late fifties, they legislated land tenancy laws that transferred ownership of tenant holdings to the tenants who were having tenancy for 12 years. At one stroke hundreds of upper caste landlords lost their holdings and tenant farmers got ownership rights of the lands that they had tilled for long years. This is one reason why the Naxalite movement did not grow roots in Kerala. They had no cause.

The issue in the forest lands of Andhra Pradesh, Maharashtra, Madhya Pradesh, Chattisgarh and Jharkhand is different. Traditionally the forests here have been the home of the tribals for centuries. Here again the root cause is the caste factor. It is the *Vaisya* who trades. It is he who is the moneylender. In thousands of years of Hinduism the roles of the castes have been honed well. You will find that in the forests of all the Naxalite affected states, the bania has had a vice like grip on the tribals. He lends money to them and collects minor forest produce against the loans, taking care to keep the tribal perpetually indebted.

When posted in Hyderabad in 1989, I had chance to discuss the Naxalite problem with the state's Revenue Minister, who asked me how this problem could be solved? When I replied- "You have to enforce the Land Ceiling" the Revenue Minister of the state raised his hands and replied-"But that is impossible." What he did not tell me was that the two major castes of

Andhra, the Reddy and the Kamma, both landlords would never allow the land ceiling to be enforced. And they were the main political force in the state.

Andhra Pradesh has also done something extraordinary about the land that was forcibly taken away from the landlords by the cadres of the Peoples War Group in the nineteen eighties. PWG cadres operating in the interior areas of North and Northeast Andhra Pradesh had managed to forcibly take away from upper caste landlords and redistribute more than 80,000 acres of Revenue land and 20,000 acres of Forest land among the deprived classes. The State Government filed a Counter Affidavit-68 of 82 in Court on this issue and after examining the cases the court directed the State to return this Revenue land and Forest land to the so called owners. What is curious is that the land ceiling laws that had been passed in the Legislature was not even referred to by the Counsel for the State Government. The Court, after a perfunctory examination of some of the crucial witnesses passed a strange order that clearly showed the bias of the Court against the depressed classes. The State Government's counsel reported to the court that the PWG cadres along with the small farmers began aggressively pursuing the land owners and managed to illegally take over more than 80,000 acres of Forest land. Strangely, the court directed that these 80,000 acres of land taken forcibly by the landless peasents from rich landlords be returned to them. Neither the Government who filed the petition in the court, nor the judges referred to the land ceiling laws of the state, which clearly showed that all the landlords from whom the PWG had forcibly taken land were all holding land in violation of the existing land ceiling laws.

It is of interest that China has distributed 90 per cent of arable lands in between 1950 and 1980. More than 90 per cent landless households have received land in China. In India these figures are around 5 per cent and less than 28 per cent respectively.[14]

Here then is the crux of the problem. The same situation exists in Bihar, where the Brahmin, Bumihar and Rajput will have his land holdings in

---

[14] Naxalism Causes and Cure. Dr. P.K.AggarwaL, Manas Publications. 2010.

the names of his pet dogs and cats rather than allow the land ceiling to be enforced.

In the case of the forests, the Adivasis or forest dwellers were pushed into the forests thousands of years ago by the upper caste Hindus and ever since they have been hunter gatherers in the forests. They collect forest produce like tamarinds, collect honey from the wild bees' hives, collect leaves of the *Tendu* trees that are used for rolling the poor mans cigarette, the *beedis*. These are brought to the *haats* at the edge of the forest and sold to the wily *bania* who sits there and enslaves the illiterate Adivasi who unable to read and write believes the fudged record of the transactions of the bania. He is thus perpetually enslaved and continues to pay the bania for the debt advanced to him.

Besides this there is the issue of cutting trees in the forest. Under the provisions of the Forest Act of 1927, it is the Forest Department that controls the forests. Tree cutting is regulated as per the provisions of the Forest Act. After independence, a nexus developed between the Politician, the timber mafia and the Forest officials and widespread cutting of forests took place all over the country. It is only a decade ago that the Supreme Court of India put a stop to this by closing down all timber mills in the vicinity of Reserve Forests. The poor Adivasi living in the forest did not have a part in the unholy nexus between the Politicians, Forest Officials and the timber mafia. The Government of India has now enacted two Acts-the Panchayati Raj Extension to Forest Areas Act (PESA) and the Scheduled Tribes and Other Forest Dwellers Rights Act (STORFA). None of these acts are being enforced.

Much more important than all these is the way the Fifth Schedule of the Constitution has been blatantly overlooked since the Constitution was adopted. The Fifth Schedule states that all Forests in the States are to be administered by the Governor of the States through a Tribal Advisory Council. This Council consists of Tribals who live in the Reserve Forests of that State. If the tribals of that State happen to be MLA's they were to be included in the Tribal Advisory Council. If there were no such Tribal MLA's then tribals of the Forests of that State alone could be made members of the

Advisory Council. The Governor was to be responsible directly to the President of India. Regrettably no Governor of any State in India has ever exercised the powers under the Fifth Schedule of the Constitution. Why has this happened? The fact is that all Governors are abject lackeys of the party in power till date! That is why no Governor has exercised these powers till date.

In the landed areas, the upper castes are the main political factor and he will not allow the lower castes to get their share of land. In the forested lands, it is the *bania*, the *Vaisya*, who is in league with the political class and who bribes the bureaucrat and keeps the poor low castes and the tribals in perpetual subservience. There can be no solution to the problem of the CPI ML leading a proletariat rebellion without solving the basic problem of giving rights to the lower castes and the tribals and putting an end to the exploitation by the upper castes. Measures like the *salwa judum* are clever ploys by the same upper caste political and bureaucrat nexus operating. Above all there can be no military solution to this problem.

The Way Forward

In the landed areas, the first step is to enforce the land ceiling. This has to be done forgetting the political factor of particular political parties wanting to retain power in states like Andhra Pradesh and Bihar. The Central Paramilitary Forces and the state Police which are used in operations against the Naxalites should now be used to enforce the land ceiling evict the landlords from their excessive holdings and ensure that the surplus lands are cultivated by the lowest classes and tribals. They should ensure that the crops grown by the new land holders are secure and they harvest the crop keeping the landlords away. Once this is done the Naxalite cadres will not use landmines on the police forces.

In the forest tracts, laws should be legislated that only forest dwelling tribes and scheduled castes should have access to forest lands. Very strictly, upper castes should be prevented from entering the forests. Cooperatives should be organized of tribals who can be trained and only these tribal cooperatives should be allowed to trade in forest produce. Branches of banks with micro credit loans as operated by the Grameen bank in Bangladesh should be set up with forest cooperatives to sanction loans to the forest tribes. The Para Military forces that were used to hunt the Naxalites should now be used to enforce the new laws for the forests. They should see that the Bania does not enter within 100 kilometers of a forest. They should ensure that all trade is carried out only by the Forest Cooperatives. They should guard the branches of the micro credit Grameen banks.

When this is done the tribal will know that the government is now with him at last and he will befriend the police force and stop putting land mines for them. The Naxalite problem will then wither away.

Today there is a very serious issue hanging fire, concerning the forest dwelling Adivasis. This is the issue of minerals discovered in the forests where the Adivasis are living. The simple issue is –who owns these minerals? The Government, both State and Central and all the political parties, save the CPI Maoist say that the minerals belong to the Government and they have the right to sign a Memorandum of Understanding with any Company, Indian or Foreign to mine the minerals. The CPI Maoist and the Adivasis whom he is organising say that the minerals in a forest in which they have been living for centuries belongs to them and only they can decide to mine the minerals through Mining Companies. Going by the history of exploitation of the Scheduled Castes and Tribes by the upper Castes for thousands of years it is clear that minerals in a forest belong to the Adivasis who were dwelling in that forest for thousands of years. In the United States the Red Indians were pushed into reservations by the White man. Today when oil or minerals are discovered in the Reservation of a particular Red Indian tribe who has been confined; the owners are the Red Indians living in that Reservation. Similarly in Australia, oil and minerals discovered in the Reservations of the Aborigines belong to those Aborigines.

Is it not imperative that we do as the Americans and Australians did in their respective Countries?